MAR - 9 2020

D R Toi
223 Southlake Pl
Newport News, VA 23602

AS A MAN THINKETH
THE COMPLETE
ORIGINAL EDITION;
ALSO INCLUDES THE BONUS
BOOK *MASTERY OF DESTINY*
James Allen.
St. Martin's (pap) 11.99
"As you dream, so shall you become," wrote poet and philosopher James Allen. First published in 1903, his timeless manual laid a foundation for mindfulness practices in the West, and Allen was also one of the first to explore the power of positive thinking, illuminating its effect on character, circumstance, health, and achievement. Sometimes associated with the 19th-century New Thought movement, Allen's book is nonetheless an accessible, undogmatic guide for people of any background. Also here is the 1909 follow-up *Mastery of Destiny*, in which Allen expands on the argument that mankind is progressing in its battle against ignorance and strife.

The
JAMES ALLEN
Collection

As A Man Thinketh

All These Things Added

The Way of Peace

Above Life's Turmoil

The Eight Pillars of Prosperity

The
JAMES ALLEN
Collection

As A Man Thinketh

All These Things Added

The Way of Peace

Above Life's Turmoil

The Eight Pillars of Prosperity

Bottom of the Hill Publishing

www.BottomoftheHillPublishing.com

ISBN: 9781483798585

Contents

AS A MAN THINKETH

Mind is the Master power that moulds and makes,
And Man is Mind, and evermore he takes
The tool of Thought, and, shaping what he wills,
Brings forth a thousand joys, a thousand ills:—
He thinks in secret, and it comes to pass:
Environment is but his looking-glass.

FOREWORD

THIS little volume (the result of meditation and experience) is not intended as an exhaustive treatise on the much-written-upon subject of the power of thought. It is suggestive rather than explanatory, its object being to stimulate men and women to the discovery and perception of the truth that—

"They themselves are makers of themselves."

by virtue of the thoughts, which they choose and encourage; that mind is the master-weaver, both of the inner garment of character and the outer garment of circumstance, and that, as they may have hitherto woven in ignorance and pain they may now weave in enlightenment and happiness.

JAMES ALLEN.

BROAD PARK AVENUE,

ILFRACOMBE,

ENGLAND

THOUGHT AND CHARACTER

THE aphorism, "As a man thinketh in his heart so is he," not only embraces the whole of a man's being, but is so comprehensive as to reach out to every condition and circumstance of his life. A man is literally what he thinks, his character being the complete sum of all his thoughts.

As the plant springs from, and could not be without, the seed, so every act of a man springs from the hidden seeds of thought, and could not have appeared without them. This applies equally to those acts called "spontaneous" and "unpremeditated" as to those, which are deliberately executed.

Act is the blossom of thought, and joy and suffering are its fruits; thus does a man garner in the sweet and bitter fruitage of his own husbandry.

"Thought in the mind hath made us, What we are

By thought was wrought and built. If a man's mind

Hath evil thoughts, pain comes on him as comes

The wheel the ox behind....

..If one endure

In purity of thought, joy follows him

As his own shadow—sure."

Man is a growth by law, and not a creation by artifice, and cause and effect is as absolute and undeviating in the hidden realm of thought as in the world of visible and material things. A noble and Godlike character is not a thing of favour or chance, but is the natural result of continued effort in right thinking, the effect of long-cherished association with Godlike thoughts. An ignoble and bestial character, by the same process, is the result of the continued harbouring of grovelling thoughts.

Man is made or unmade by himself; in the armoury of thought he forges the weapons by which he destroys himself; he also fashions the tools with which he builds for himself heavenly mansions of joy and strength and peace. By the right choice and true application of thought, man ascends to the Divine Perfection; by the abuse and wrong application of thought, he descends below the level of the beast. Between these two extremes are all the grades of character, and man is their maker and master.

Of all the beautiful truths pertaining to the soul which have been restored and brought to light in this age, none is more gladdening or fruitful of divine promise and confidence than this—that man is the master of thought, the moulder of character, and the maker and shaper of condition, environment, and destiny.

As a being of Power, Intelligence, and Love, and the lord of his own thoughts, man holds the key to every situation, and contains within himself that transforming and regenerative agency by which he may make himself what he wills.

Man is always the master, even in his weaker and most abandoned state; but in his weakness and degradation he is the foolish master who misgoverns his "household." When he begins to reflect upon his condition, and to search diligently for the Law upon which his being is established, he then becomes the wise master, directing his energies with intelligence, and fashioning his thoughts to fruitful issues. Such is the conscious master, and man can only thus become by discovering within himself the laws of thought; which discovery is totally a matter of application, self analysis, and experience.

Only by much searching and mining, are gold and diamonds obtained, and man can find every truth connected with his being, if he will dig deep into the mine of his soul; and that he is the maker of his character, the moulder of his life, and the builder of his destiny, he may unerringly prove, if he will watch, control, and alter his thoughts, tracing their effects upon himself, upon others, and upon his life and circumstances, linking cause and effect by patient practice and investigation, and utilizing his every experience, even to the most trivial, everyday occurrence, as a means of obtaining that knowledge of himself which is Understanding, Wisdom, Power. In this direction, as in no other, is the law absolute that "He that seeketh findeth; and to him that knocketh it shall be opened;" for only by patience, practice, and ceaseless importunity can a man enter the Door of the Temple of Knowledge.

EFFECT OF THOUGHT
ON CIRCUMSTANCES

MAN'S mind may be likened to a garden, which may be intelligently cultivated or allowed to run wild; but whether cultivated or neglected, it must, and will, bring forth. If no useful seeds are put into it, then an abundance of useless weed-seeds will fall therein, and will continue to produce their kind.

Just as a gardener cultivates his plot, keeping it free from weeds, and growing the flowers and fruits which he requires, so may a man tend the garden of his mind, weeding out all the wrong, useless, and impure thoughts, and cultivating toward perfection the flowers and fruits of right, useful, and pure thoughts. By pursuing this process, a man sooner or later discovers that he is the master-gardener of his soul, the director of his life. He also reveals, within himself, the laws of thought, and understands, with ever-increasing accuracy, how the thought-forces and mind elements operate in the shaping of his character, circumstances, and destiny.

Thought and character are one and as character can only manifest and discover itself through environment and circumstance, the outer conditions of a person's life will always be found to be harmoniously related to his inner state. This does not mean that a man's circumstances at any given time are an indication of his entire character, but that those circumstances are so intimately connected with some vital thought-element within himself that, for the time being, they are indispensable to his development.

Every man is where he is by the law of his being; the thoughts which he has built into his character have brought him there, and in the arrangement of his life there is no element of chance, but all is the result of a law which cannot err. This is just as true of those who feel "out of harmony" with their surroundings as of those who are contented with them.

As a progressive and evolving being, man is where he is that he may learn that he may grow; and as he learns the spiritual lesson which any circumstance contains for him, it passes away and gives place to other circumstances.

Man is buffeted by circumstances so long as he believes himself to be the creature of outside conditions, but when he realizes that he is a creative power, and that he may command the hidden soil and seeds of his being out of which circumstances grow, he then becomes the rightful master of himself.

That circumstances grow out of thought every man knows who has for any length of time practiced self-control and self-purification, for he will have noticed that the alteration in his circumstances has been in exact ratio with his altered mental condition. So true is this that when a man earnestly applies himself to remedy the defects in his character, and makes swift and marked progress, he passes rapidly through a succession of vicissitudes.

The soul attracts that which it secretly harbours; that which it loves, and also that which it fears; it reaches the height of its cherished aspirations; it falls to the level of its unchastened desires,—and circumstances are the means by which the soul receives its own.

Every thought-seed sown or allowed to fall into the mind, and to take root there, produces its own, blossoming sooner or later into act, and bearing its own fruitage of opportunity and circumstance. Good thoughts bear good fruit, bad thoughts bad fruit.

The outer world of circumstance shapes itself to the inner world of thought, and both pleasant and unpleasant external conditions are factors, which make for the ultimate good of the individual. As the reaper of his own harvest, man learns both by suffering and bliss.

Following the inmost desires, aspirations, thoughts, by which he allows himself to be dominated, (pursuing the will-o'-the-wisps of impure imaginings or steadfastly walking the highway of strong and high endeavour), a man at last arrives at their fruition and fulfillment in the outer conditions of his life. The laws of growth and adjustment everywhere obtains.

A man does not come to the almshouse or the jail by the tyranny of fate or circumstance, but by the pathway of grovelling thoughts and base desires. Nor does a pure-minded man fall suddenly into crime by stress of any mere external force; the criminal thought had long been secretly fostered in the heart, and the hour of opportunity revealed its gathered power. Circumstance does not make the man; it reveals him to himself No such conditions can exist as descending into vice and its attendant sufferings apart from vicious inclinations, or ascending into virtue and its pure happiness without the continued cultivation of virtuous aspirations; and man, therefore, as the lord and master of thought, is the maker of himself the shaper and author of environment. Even at birth the soul comes to its own and through every step of its earthly pilgrimage it attracts those combinations of conditions which reveal itself, which are the reflections of its own purity and, impurity, its strength and weakness.

Men do not attract that which they want, but that which they are. Their whims, fancies, and ambitions are thwarted at every step, but their inmost thoughts and desires are fed with their own food, be it foul or clean. The "divinity that shapes our ends" is in ourselves; it is our very self. Only himself manacles man: thought and action are the gaolers of Fate—they imprison, being base; they are also the angels of Freedom—they liberate, being noble. Not what he wishes and prays for does a man get, but what he justly earns. His wishes and prayers are only gratified and answered when they harmonize with his thoughts and actions.

In the light of this truth, what, then, is the meaning of "fighting against circumstances?" It means that a man is continually revolting against an effect without, while all the time he is nourishing and preserving its cause in his heart. That cause may take the form of a conscious vice or an unconscious weakness; but whatever it is, it stubbornly retards the efforts of its possessor, and thus calls aloud for remedy.

Men are anxious to improve their circumstances, but are unwilling to improve themselves; they therefore remain bound. The man who does not shrink from self-crucifixion can never fail to accomplish the object upon which his heart is set. This is as true of earthly as of heavenly things. Even the man whose sole object is to acquire wealth must be prepared to make great personal sacrifices before he can accomplish his object; and how much more so he who would realize a strong and well-poised life?

Here is a man who is wretchedly poor. He is extremely anxious that his surroundings and home comforts should be improved, yet all the time he shirks his work, and considers he is justified in trying to deceive his employer on the ground of the insufficiency of his wages. Such a man does not understand the simplest rudiments of those principles which are the basis of true prosperity, and is not only totally unfitted to rise out of his wretchedness, but is actually attracting to himself a still deeper wretchedness by dwelling in, and acting out, indolent, deceptive, and unmanly thoughts.

Here is a rich man who is the victim of a painful and persistent disease as the result of gluttony. He is willing to give large sums of money to get rid of it, but he will not sacrifice his gluttonous desires. He wants to gratify his taste for rich and unnatural viands and have his health as well. Such a man is totally unfit to have health, because he has not yet learned the first principles of a healthy life.

Here is an employer of labour who adopts crooked measures to avoid paying the regulation wage, and, in the hope of making larger profits, reduces the wages of his work people. Such a man is altogether unfitted for prosperity, and when he finds himself bankrupt, both as regards reputation and riches, he blames circumstances, not knowing that he is the sole author of his condition.

I have introduced these three cases merely as illustrative of the truth that man is the causer (though nearly always is unconsciously) of his circumstances, and that, whilst aiming at a good end, he is continually frustrating its accomplishment by encouraging thoughts and desires which cannot possibly harmonize with that end. Such cases could be multiplied and varied almost indefinitely, but this is not necessary, as the reader can, if he so resolves, trace the action of the laws of thought in his own mind and life, and until this is done, mere external facts cannot serve as a ground of reasoning.

Circumstances, however, are so complicated, thought is so deeply rooted, and the conditions of happiness vary so, vastly with individuals, that a man's entire soul-condition (although it may be known to himself) cannot be judged by another from the external aspect of his life alone. A man may be honest in certain directions, yet suffer privations; a man may be dishonest in certain directions, yet acquire wealth; but the conclusion usually formed that the one man fails because of his particular honesty, and that the other prospers because of his particular dishonesty, is the result of a superficial judgment, which assumes that the dishonest man is almost totally corrupt, and the honest man almost entirely virtuous. In the light of a deeper knowledge and wider experience such judgment is found to be erroneous. The dishonest man may have some admirable virtues, which the other does, not possess; and the honest man obnoxious vices which are absent in the other. The honest man reaps the good results of his honest thoughts and acts; he also brings upon himself the sufferings, which his vices produce. The dishonest man likewise garners his own suffering and happiness.

It is pleasing to human vanity to believe that one suffers because of one's virtue; but not until a man has extirpated every sickly, bitter, and impure thought from his mind, and washed every sinful stain from his soul, can he be in a position to know and declare that his sufferings are the result of his good, and not of his bad qualities; and on the way to, yet long before he has reached, that supreme perfection, he will have found, working in his mind and life, the Great Law which is absolutely just, and which cannot, therefore, give good for evil, evil for good. Possessed of such knowledge, he will then know, looking back upon his past ignorance and blindness, that his life is, and always was, justly ordered, and that all his past experiences good and bad, were the equitable outworking of his evolving, yet unevolved self.

Good thoughts and actions can never produce bad results; bad thoughts and actions can never, ever produce good results. This is but saying that nothing can come from corn but corn, nothing from nettles but nettles. Men understand this law in the natural world, and work with it; but few understand it in the mental and moral world (though its operation there is just simple and undeviating), and they, therefore, do not co-operate with it.

Suffering is always the effect of wrong thought in some direction. It is an indication that the individual is out of harmony with himself, with the Law of his being. The sole and supreme use of suffering is to purify, to burn out all that is useless and impure. Suffering ceases for him who is pure. There could be no object in burning gold after the dross had been removed, and a perfectly pure and enlightened being could not suffer.

The circumstances, which a man encounters with suffering, are the result of his own mental in harmony. The circumstances, which a man encounters with blessedness, are the result of his own mental harmony. Blessedness, not material possessions, is the measure of right thought; wretchedness, not lack of material possessions, is the measure of wrong thought. A man may be cursed and rich; he may be blessed and poor. Blessedness and riches are only joined together when the riches are rightly and wisely used; and the poor man only descends into wretchedness when he regards his lot as a burden unjustly imposed.

Indigence and indulgence are the two extremes of wretchedness. They are both equally unnatural and the result of mental disorder. A man is not rightly conditioned until he is a happy, healthy, and prosperous being; and happiness, health, and prosperity are the result of a harmonious adjustment of the inner with the outer, of the man with his surroundings.

A man only begins to be a man when he ceases to whine and revile, and commences to search for the hidden justice which regulates his life. And as he adapts his mind to that regulating factor, he ceases to accuse others as the cause of his condition, and builds himself up in strong and noble thoughts; ceases to kick against circumstances, but begins to use them as aids to his more rapid progress, and as a means of discovering the hidden powers and possibilities within himself.

Law, not confusion, is the dominating principle in the universe; justice, not injustice, is the soul and substance of life; and righteousness, not corruption, is the moulding and moving force in the spiritual government of the world. This being so, man has but to right himself to find that the universe is right; and during the process of putting himself right he will find that as he alters his thoughts towards things and other people, things and other people will alter towards him.

The proof of this truth is in every person, and it therefore admits of easy investigation by systematic introspection and self-analysis. Let a man radically alter his thoughts, and he will be astonished at the rapid transformation it will effect in the material conditions of his life. Men imagine that thought can be kept secret, but it cannot; it rapidly crystallizes into habit, and habit solidifies into circumstance. Bestial thoughts crystallize into habits of drunkenness and sensuality, which solidify into circumstances of destitution and disease: impure thoughts of every kind crystallize into enervating and confusing habits, which solidify into distracting and adverse circumstances: thoughts of fear, doubt, and indecision crystallize into weak, unmanly, and irresolute habits, which solidify into circumstances of failure, indigence, and slavish de-

pendence: lazy thoughts crystallize into habits of uncleanliness
and dishonesty, which solidify into circumstances of foulness and
beggary: hateful and condemnatory thoughts crystallize into habits of accusation and violence, which solidify into circumstances
of injury and persecution: selfish thoughts of all kinds crystallize into habits of self-seeking, which solidify into circumstances
more or less distressing. On the other hand, beautiful thoughts
of all kinds crystallize into habits of grace and kindliness, which
solidify into genial and sunny circumstances: pure thoughts crystallize into habits of temperance and self-control, which solidify
into circumstances of repose and peace: thoughts of courage, self-
reliance, and decision crystallize into manly habits, which solidify into circumstances of success, plenty, and freedom: energetic
thoughts crystallize into habits of cleanliness and industry, which
solidify into circumstances of pleasantness: gentle and forgiving
thoughts crystallize into habits of gentleness, which solidify into
protective and preservative circumstances: loving and unselfish
thoughts crystallize into habits of self-forgetfulness for others,
which solidify into circumstances of sure and abiding prosperity
and true riches.

A particular train of thought persisted in, be it good or bad, cannot fail to produce its results on the character and circumstances. A man cannot directly choose his circumstances, but he can
choose his thoughts, and so indirectly, yet surely, shape his circumstances.

Nature helps every man to the gratification of the thoughts, which
he most encourages, and opportunities are presented which will
most speedily bring to the surface both the good and evil thoughts.

Let a man cease from his sinful thoughts, and all the world will
soften towards him, and be ready to help him; let him put away
his weakly and sickly thoughts, and lo, opportunities will spring
up on every hand to aid his strong resolves; let him encourage
good thoughts, and no hard fate shall bind him down to wretchedness and shame. The world is your kaleidoscope, and the varying combinations of colours, which at every succeeding moment
it presents to you, are the exquisitely adjusted pictures of your
ever-moving thoughts.

"So You will be what you will to be;
Let failure find its false content

In that poor word, 'environment,'
But spirit scorns it, and is free.
"It masters time, it conquers space;
It cowes that boastful trickster, Chance,
And bids the tyrant Circumstance
Uncrown, and fill a servant's place.
"The human Will, that force unseen,
The offspring of a deathless Soul,
Can hew a way to any goal,
Though walls of granite intervene.
"Be not impatient in delays
But wait as one who understands;
When spirit rises and commands
The gods are ready to obey."

EFFECT OF THOUGHT
ON HEALTH AND THE BODY

THE body is the servant of the mind. It obeys the operations of the mind, whether they be deliberately chosen or automatically expressed. At the bidding of unlawful thoughts the body sinks rapidly into disease and decay; at the command of glad and beautiful thoughts it becomes clothed with youthfulness and beauty.

Disease and health, like circumstances, are rooted in thought. Sickly thoughts will express themselves through a sickly body. Thoughts of fear have been known to kill a man as speedily as a bullet, and they are continually killing thousands of people just as surely though less rapidly. The people who live in fear of disease are the people who get it. Anxiety quickly demoralizes the whole body, and lays it open to the entrance of disease; while impure thoughts, even if not physically indulged, will soon shatter the nervous system.

Strong, pure, and happy thoughts build up the body in vigour and grace. The body is a delicate and plastic instrument, which responds readily to the thoughts by which it is impressed, and habits of thought will produce their own effects, good or bad, upon it.

Men will continue to have impure and poisoned blood, so long as they propagate unclean thoughts. Out of a clean heart comes a clean life and a clean body. Out of a defiled mind proceeds a defiled life and a corrupt body. Thought is the fount of action, life, and manifestation; make the fountain pure, and all will be pure.

Change of diet will not help a man who will not change his thoughts. When a man makes his thoughts pure, he no longer desires impure food.

Clean thoughts make clean habits. The so-called saint who does not wash his body is not a saint. He who has strengthened and purified his thoughts does not need to consider the malevolent microbe.

If you would protect your body, guard your mind. If you would renew your body, beautify your mind. Thoughts of malice, envy, disappointment, despondency, rob the body of its health and grace. A sour face does not come by chance; it is made by sour thoughts. Wrinkles that mar are drawn by folly, passion, and pride.

I know a woman of ninety-six who has the bright, innocent face of a girl. I know a man well under middle age whose face is drawn into inharmonious contours. The one is the result of a sweet and sunny disposition; the other is the outcome of passion and discontent.

As you cannot have a sweet and wholesome abode unless you admit the air and sunshine freely into your rooms, so a strong body and a bright, happy, or serene countenance can only result from the free admittance into the mind of thoughts of joy and goodwill and serenity.

On the faces of the aged there are wrinkles made by sympathy, others by strong and pure thought, and others are carved by passion: who cannot distinguish them? With those who have lived righteously, age is calm, peaceful, and softly mellowed, like the setting sun. I have recently seen a philosopher on his deathbed. He was not old except in years. He died as sweetly and peacefully as he had lived.

There is no physician like cheerful thought for dissipating the ills of the body; there is no comforter to compare with goodwill for dispersing the shadows of grief and sorrow. To live continually in thoughts of ill will, cynicism, suspicion, and envy, is to be confined in a self made prison-hole. But to think well of all, to be cheerful with all, to patiently learn to find the good in all—such unselfish thoughts are the very portals of heaven; and to dwell day by day in thoughts of peace toward every creature will bring abounding peace to their possessor.

THOUGHT AND PURPOSE

UNTIL thought is linked with purpose there is no intelligent accomplishment. With the majority the bark of thought is allowed to "drift" upon the ocean of life. Aimlessness is a vice, and such drifting must not continue for him who would steer clear of catastrophe and destruction.

They who have no central purpose in their life fall an easy prey to petty worries, fears, troubles, and self-pityings, all of which are indications of weakness, which lead, just as surely as deliberately planned sins (though by a different route), to failure, unhappiness, and loss, for weakness cannot persist in a power evolving universe.

A man should conceive of a legitimate purpose in his heart, and set out to accomplish it. He should make this purpose the centralizing point of his thoughts. It may take the form of a spiritual ideal, or it may be a worldly object, according to his nature at the time being; but whichever it is, he should steadily focus his thought-forces upon the object, which he has set before him. He should make this purpose his supreme duty, and should devote himself to its attainment, not allowing his thoughts to wander away into ephemeral fancies, longings, and imaginings. This is the royal road to self-control and true concentration of thought. Even if he fails again and again to accomplish his purpose (as he necessarily must until weakness is overcome), the strength of character gained will be the measure of his true success, and this will form a new starting-point for future power and triumph.

Those who are not prepared for the apprehension of a great purpose should fix the thoughts upon the faultless performance of their duty, no matter how insignificant their task may appear. Only in this way can the thoughts be gathered and focused, and resolution and energy be developed, which being done, there is nothing which may not be accomplished.

The weakest soul, knowing its own weakness, and believing this truth that strength can only be developed by effort and practice, will, thus believing, at once begin to exert itself, and, adding effort to effort, patience to patience, and strength to strength, will never cease to develop, and will at last grow divinely strong.

As the physically weak man can make himself strong by careful and patient training, so the man of weak thoughts can make them strong by exercising himself in right thinking.

To put away aimlessness and weakness, and to begin to think with purpose, is to enter the ranks of those strong ones who only recognize failure as one of the pathways to attainment; who make all conditions serve them, and who think strongly, attempt fearlessly, and accomplish masterfully.

Having conceived of his purpose, a man should mentally mark out a straight pathway to its achievement, looking neither to the right nor the left. Doubts and fears should be rigorously excluded; they are disintegrating elements, which break up the straight line of effort, rendering it crooked, ineffectual, useless. Thoughts of doubt and fear never accomplished anything, and never can. They always lead to failure. Purpose, energy, power to do, and all strong thoughts cease when doubt and fear creep in.

The will to do springs from the knowledge that we can do. Doubt and fear are the great enemies of knowledge, and he who encourages them, who does not slay them, thwarts himself at every step.

He who has conquered doubt and fear has conquered failure. His every thought is allied with power, and all difficulties are bravely met and wisely overcome. His purposes are seasonably planted, and they bloom and bring forth fruit, which does not fall prematurely to the ground.

Thought allied fearlessly to purpose becomes creative force: he who knows this is ready to become something higher and stronger than a mere bundle of wavering thoughts and fluctuating sensations; he who does this has become the conscious and intelligent wielder of his mental powers.

THE THOUGHT-FACTOR
IN ACHIEVEMENT

ALL that a man achieves and all that he fails to achieve is the direct result of his own thoughts. In a justly ordered universe, where loss of equipoise would mean total destruction, individual responsibility must be absolute. A man's weakness and strength, purity and impurity, are his own, and not another man's; they are brought about by himself, and not by another; and they can only be altered by himself, never by another. His condition is also his own, and not another man's. His suffering and his happiness are evolved from within. As he thinks, so he is; as he continues to think, so he remains.

A strong man cannot help a weaker unless that weaker is willing to be helped, and even then the weak man must become strong of himself; he must, by his own efforts, develop the strength which he admires in another. None but himself can alter his condition.

It has been usual for men to think and to say, "Many men are slaves because one is an oppressor; let us hate the oppressor." Now, however, there is amongst an increasing few a tendency to reverse this judgment, and to say, "One man is an oppressor because many are slaves; let us despise the slaves."

The truth is that oppressor and slave are co-operators in ignorance, and, while seeming to afflict each other, are in reality afflicting themselves. A perfect Knowledge perceives the action of law in the weakness of the oppressed and the misapplied power of the oppressor; a perfect Love, seeing the suffering, which both states entail, condemns neither; a perfect Compassion embraces both oppressor and oppressed.

He who has conquered weakness, and has put away all selfish thoughts, belongs neither to oppressor nor oppressed. He is free.

A man can only rise, conquer, and achieve by lifting up his thoughts. He can only remain weak, and abject, and miserable by refusing to lift up his thoughts.

Before a man can achieve anything, even in worldly things, he must lift his thoughts above slavish animal indulgence. He may not, in order to succeed, give up all animality and selfishness, by any means; but a portion of it must, at least, be sacrificed. A man whose first thought is bestial indulgence could neither think clearly nor plan methodically; he could not find and develop his latent resources, and would fail in any undertaking. Not having commenced to manfully control his thoughts, he is not in a position to control affairs and to adopt serious responsibilities. He is not fit to act independently and stand alone. But he is limited only by the thoughts, which he chooses.

There can be no progress, no achievement without sacrifice, and a man's worldly success will be in the measure that he sacrifices his confused animal thoughts, and fixes his mind on the development of his plans, and the strengthening of his resolution and self-reliance. And the higher he lifts his thoughts, the more manly, upright and righteous he becomes, the greater will be his success, the more blessed and enduring will be his achievements.

The universe does not favour the greedy, the dishonest, the vicious, although on the mere surface it may sometimes appear to do so; it helps the honest, the magnanimous, the virtuous. All the great Teachers of the ages have declared this in varying forms, and to prove and know it a man has but to persist in making himself more and more virtuous by lifting up his thoughts.

Intellectual achievements are the result of thought consecrated to the search for knowledge, or for the beautiful and true in life and nature. Such achievements may be sometimes connected with vanity and ambition, but they are not the outcome of those characteristics; they are the natural outgrowth of long and arduous effort, and of pure and unselfish thoughts.

Spiritual achievements are the consummation of holy aspirations. He who lives constantly in the conception of noble and lofty thoughts, who dwells upon all that is pure and unselfish, will, as surely as the sun reaches its zenith and the moon its full become wise and noble in character, and rise into a position of influence and blessedness.

Achievement, of whatever kind, is the crown of effort, the diadem of thought. By the aid of self-control, resolution, purity, righteousness, and well-directed thought a man ascends; by the aid of animality, indolence, impurity, corruption, and confusion of thought a man descends.

A man may rise to high success in the world, and even to lofty altitudes in the spiritual realm, and again descend into weakness and wretchedness by allowing arrogant, selfish, and corrupt thoughts to take possession of him.

Victories attained by right thought can only be maintained by watchfulness. Many give way when success is assured, and rapidly fall back into failure.

All achievements, whether in the business, intellectual, or spiritual world, are the result of definitely directed thought, are governed by the same law and are of the same method; the only difference lies in the object of attainment.

He who would accomplish little must sacrifice little; he who would achieve much must sacrifice much; he who would attain highly must sacrifice greatly.

VISIONS AND IDEALS

THE dreamers are the saviours of the world. As the visible world is sustained by the invisible, so men, through all their trials and sins and sordid vocations, are nourished by the beautiful visions of their solitary dreamers. Humanity cannot forget its dreamers; it cannot let their ideals fade and die; it lives in them; it knows them as they realities which it shall one day see and know.

Composer, sculptor, painter, poet, prophet, sage, these are the makers of the after-world, the architects of heaven. The world is beautiful because they have lived; without them, labouring humanity would perish.

He who cherishes a beautiful vision, a lofty ideal in his heart, will one day realize it. Columbus cherished a vision of another world, and he discovered it; Copernicus fostered the vision of a multiplicity of worlds and a wider universe, and he revealed it; Buddha beheld the vision of a spiritual world of stainless beauty and perfect peace, and he entered into it.

Cherish your visions; cherish your ideals; cherish the music that stirs in your heart, the beauty that forms in your mind, the loveliness that drapes your purest thoughts, for out of them will grow all delightful conditions, all, heavenly environment; of these, if you but remain true to them, your world will at last be built.

To desire is to obtain; to aspire is to, achieve. Shall man's basest desires receive the fullest measure of gratification, and his purest aspirations starve for lack of sustenance? Such is not the Law: such a condition of things can never obtain: "ask and receive."

Dream lofty dreams, and as you dream, so shall you become. Your Vision is the promise of what you shall one day be; your Ideal is the prophecy of what you shall at last unveil.

The greatest achievement was at first and for a time a dream. The oak sleeps in the acorn; the bird waits in the egg; and in the highest vision of the soul a waking angel stirs. Dreams are the seedlings of realities.

Your circumstances may be uncongenial, but they shall not long remain so if you but perceive an Ideal and strive to reach it. You cannot travel within and stand still without. Here is a youth hard pressed by poverty and labour; confined long hours in an unhealthy workshop; unschooled, and lacking all the arts of refinement. But he dreams of better things; he thinks of intelligence, of refinement, of grace and beauty. He conceives of, mentally builds up, an ideal condition of life; the vision of a wider liberty and a larger scope takes possession of him; unrest urges him to action, and he utilizes all his spare time and means, small though they are, to the development of his latent powers and resources. Very soon so altered has his mind become that the workshop can no longer hold him. It has become so out of harmony with his mentality that it falls out of his life as a garment is cast aside, and, with the growth of opportunities, which fit the scope of his expanding powers, he passes out of it forever. Years later we see this youth as a full-grown man. We find him a master of certain forces of the mind, which he wields with worldwide influence and almost unequalled power. In his hands he holds the cords of gigantic responsibilities; he speaks, and lo, lives are changed; men and women hang upon his words and remould their characters, and sun like, he becomes the fixed and luminous centre round which innumerable destinies revolve. He has realized the Vision of his youth. He has become one with his Ideal.

And you, too, youthful reader, will realize the Vision (not the idle wish) of your heart, be it base or beautiful, or a mixture of both, for you will always gravitate toward that which you, secretly, most love. Into your hands will be placed the exact results of your own thoughts; you will receive that which you earn; no more, no less. Whatever your present environment may be, you will fall, remain, or rise with your thoughts, your Vision, your Ideal. You will become as small as your controlling desire; as great as your dominant aspiration: in the beautiful words of Stanton Kirkham Davis, "You may be keeping accounts, and presently you shall walk out of the door that for so long has seemed to you the barrier of your ideals, and shall find yourself before an audience—the pen still behind your ear, the ink stains on your fingers and then and there shall pour out the torrent of your inspiration. You may be driving sheep, and you shall wander to the city-bucolic and open-mouthed; shall wander under the intrepid guidance of the spirit into the studio of the master, and after a time he shall say, 'I have nothing more to teach you.' And now you have become the master, who did so recently dream of great things while driving sheep. You shall lay down the saw and the plane to take upon yourself the regeneration of the world."

The thoughtless, the ignorant, and the indolent, seeing only the apparent effects of things and not the things themselves, talk of luck, of fortune, and chance. Seeing a man grow rich, they say, "How lucky he is!" Observing another become intellectual, they exclaim, "How highly favoured he is!" And noting the saintly character and wide influence of another, they remark, "How chance aids him at every turn!" They do not see the trials and failures and struggles which these men have voluntarily encountered in order to gain their experience; have no knowledge of the sacrifices they have made, of the undaunted efforts they have put forth, of the faith they have exercised, that they might overcome the apparently insurmountable, and realize the Vision of their heart. They do not know the darkness and the heartaches; they only see the light and joy, and call it "luck". They do not see the long and arduous journey, but only behold the pleasant goal, and call it "good fortune," do not understand the process, but only perceive the result, and call it chance.

In all human affairs there are efforts, and there are results, and the strength of the effort is the measure of the result. Chance is not. Gifts, powers, material, intellectual and spiritual possessions are the fruits of effort; they are thoughts completed, objects accomplished, visions realized.

The Vision that you glorify in your mind, the Ideal that you enthrone in your heart—this you will build your life by, this you will become.

SERENITY

CALMNESS of mind is one of the beautiful jewels of wisdom. It is the result of long and patient effort in self-control. Its presence is an indication of ripened experience, and of a more than ordinary knowledge of the laws and operations of thought.

A man becomes calm in the measure that he understands himself as a thought evolved being, for such knowledge necessitates the understanding of others as the result of thought, and as he develops a right understanding, and sees more and more clearly the internal relations of things by the action of cause and effect he ceases to fuss and fume and worry and grieve, and remains poised, steadfast, serene.

The calm man, having learned how to govern himself, knows how to adapt himself to others; and they, in turn, reverence his spiritual strength, and feel that they can learn of him and rely upon him. The more tranquil a man becomes, the greater is his success, his influence, his power for good. Even the ordinary trader will find his business prosperity increase as he develops a greater self-control and equanimity, for people will always prefer to deal with a man whose demeanor is strongly equable.

The strong, calm man is always loved and revered. He is like a shade-giving tree in a thirsty land, or a sheltering rock in a storm. "Who does not love a tranquil heart, a sweet-tempered, balanced life? It does not matter whether it rains or shines, or what changes come to those possessing these blessings, for they are always sweet, serene, and calm. That exquisite poise of character, which we call serenity, is the last lesson of culture, the fruitage of the soul. It is precious as wisdom, more to be desired than gold—yea, than even fine gold. How insignificant mere money seeking looks in comparison with a serene life—a life that dwells in the ocean of Truth, beneath the waves, beyond the reach of tempests, in the Eternal Calm!

"How many people we know who sour their lives, who ruin all that is sweet and beautiful by explosive tempers, who destroy their poise of character, and make bad blood! It is a question whether the great majority of people, do not ruin their lives and mar their happiness by lack of self-control. How few people we meet in life who are well balanced, who have that exquisite poise which is characteristic of the finished character!

Yes, humanity surges with uncontrolled passion, is tumultuous with ungoverned grief, is blown about by anxiety and doubt only the wise man, only he whose thoughts are controlled and purified, makes the winds and the storms of the soul obey him.

Tempest-tossed souls, wherever ye may be, under whatsoever conditions ye may live, know this in the ocean of life the isles of Blessedness are smiling, and the sunny shore of your ideal awaits your coming. Keep your hand firmly upon the helm of thought. In the bark of your soul reclines the commanding Master; He does but sleep: wake Him. Self-control is strength; Right Thought is mastery; Calmness is power. Say unto your heart, "Peace, be still!"

All These Things Added

Foreword

In seeking for pleasures here and rewards hereafter men have destroyed (in their hearts) the Temple of Righteousness, and have wandered from the Kingdom of Heaven. By ceasing to seek for earthly pleasures and heavenly rewards, the Temple of Righteousness is restored and the Kingdom of Heaven is found. This truth is for those who are ready to receive it; and this book also is for those whose souls have been prepared for the acceptance of its teaching.

James Allen.

Part I: Entering the Kingdom

1. The Soul's Great Need

I sought the world, but Peace was not there;

I courted learning, but Truth was not revealed;

I sojourned with philosophy, but my heart was sore with vanity.

And I cried, Where is Peace to be found!

And where is the hiding place of truth!

  -- Filius Lucis

EVERY HUMAN SOUL IS IN NEED. The expression of that need varies with individuals, but there is not one soul that does not feel it in some degree. It is a spiritual and casual need which takes the form, in souls of a particular development, of a deep and inexpressible hunger which the outward things of life, however abundantly they may be possessed, can never satisfy. Yet the majority, imperfect in knowledge and misled by appearances, seek to satisfy this hunger by striving for material possessions, believing that these will satisfy their need, and bring them peace.

Every soul, consciously or unconsciously, hungers for righteousness, and every soul seeks to gratify that hunger in its own particular way, and in accordance with its own particular state of knowledge. The hunger is one, and the righteousness is one, but the pathways by which righteousness is sought are many.

They who seek consciously are blessed, and shall shortly find that final and permanent satisfaction of soul which righteousness alone can give, for they have come into a knowledge of the true path.

They who seek unconsciously, although for a time they may bathe in a sea of pleasure, are not blessed, for they are carving out for themselves pathways of suffering over which they must walk with torn and wounded feet, and their hunger will increase, and the soul will cry out for its lost heritage—the eternal heritage of righteousness.

Not in any of the three worlds (waking, dream and sleep) can the soul find lasting satisfaction, apart from the realization of righteousness. Bodied or disembodied, it is ceaselessly driven on by the discipline of suffering, until at last, in its extremity, it flies to its only refuge—the refuge of righteousness—and finds that joy, satisfaction, and peace which it had so long and so vainly sought.

The great need of the soul, then, is the need of this permanent principle, called righteousness, on which it may stand securely and restfully amid the tempest of earthly existence, no more bewildered, and whereon it may build the mansion of a beautiful, peaceful, and perfect life.

It is the realization of this principle where the Kingdom of Heaven, the abiding home of the soul, resides, and which is the source and storehouse of every permanent blessing. Finding it, all is found; not finding it, all is lost. It is an attitude of mind, a state of consciousness, an ineffable knowledge, in which the struggle for existence ceases, and the soul finds itself at rest in the midst of plenty, where its great need, yea, its every need, is satisfied, without strife and without fear. Blessed are they who earnestly and intelligently seek, for it is impossible that such should seek in vain.

2. The Competitive Laws and the Law of Love

When I am pure

I shall have solved the mystery of life,

I shall be sure

(When I am free from hatred, lust and strife)

I am in truth, and Truth abides in me.

I shall be safe and sane and wholly free

When I am pure.

IT HAS BEEN SAID that the laws of Nature are cruel; it has likewise been said that they are kind. The one statement is the result of dwelling exclusively upon the fiercely competitive aspect of Nature; the other results from viewing only the protective and kindly aspect. In reality, natural laws are neither cruel or kind; they are absolutely just—are, in fact, the outworking of the indestructible principle of justice itself.

The cruelty, and consequent suffering, which is so prevalent in

Nature, is not inherent in the heart and substance of life; it is a passing phase of evolution, a painful experience, which will ultimately ripen into the fruit of a more perfect knowledge; a dark night of ignorance and unrest, leading to a glorious morning of joy and peace.

When a helpless child is burnt to death, we do not ascribe cruelty to the working of the natural law by virtue of which the child was consumed; we infer ignorance in the child, or carelessness on the part of its guardians. Even so, men and creatures are daily being consumed in the invisible flames of passion, succumbing to the ceaseless interplay of those fiery psychic forces which, in their ignorance, they do not understand, but which they shall at last learn how to control and use to their own protection, and not, as at present, foolishly employ them to their own destruction.

To understand, control and harmoniously adjust the invisible forces of its own soul is the ultimate destiny of every being and creature. Some men and women, in the past, have accomplished this supreme and exalted purpose; some, in the present, have likewise succeeded, and, until this is done, that place of rest wherein one receives all that is necessary for one's well-being and happiness, without striving, and with freedom from pain, cannot be entered.

In an age like the present, when, in all civilized countries, the string of life is strained to its highest pitch, when men and women, striving each with each in every department of life for the vanities and material possessions of this perishable existence, have developed competition to the utmost limit of endurance—in such an age the sublimest heights of knowledge are scaled, the supremest spiritual conquests are achieved; for when the soul is most tired, its need is greatest, and where the need is great, great will be the effort. Where, also, the temptations are powerful, the greater and more enduring will be the victory.

Men love the competitive strife with their fellows, while it promises, and seems to bring them gain and happiness; but when the inevitable reaction comes, and the cold steel of selfish strife which their own hands have forged enters their own hearts, then, and not till then, do they seek a better way.

"Blessed are they that mourn,"—that have come to the end of strife, and have found the pain and sorrow to which it leads; for unto them, and unto them only, can open the door which leads to the Kingdom of Peace.

In searching for this Kingdom, it is necessary to fully understand the nature of that which prevents its realization—namely, the strife of nature, the competitive laws operative in human affairs, and the universal unrest, insecurity and fear which accompany these factors; for without such an understanding there can be no sound comprehension as to what constitutes the true and false in life, and therefore no real spiritual advancement.

Before the true can be apprehended and enjoyed, the false must be unveiled; before the real can be perceived as the real, the illusions which distort it must be dispersed; and before the limitless expanse of Truth can open before us, the limited experience which is confined to the world of visible and superficial effects must be transcended.

Let, therefore, those of my readers who are thoughtful and earnest, and who are diligently seeking, or are willing to seek, for that basis of thought and conduct which shall simplify and harmonize the bewildering complexities and inequalities of life, walk with me step by step as I open up the way to the Kingdom; first descending into Hell (the world of strife and self-seeking) in order that, having comprehended its intricate ways, we may afterwards ascend into Heaven (the world of Peace and Love).

It is the custom in my household, during the hard frosts of winter, to put out food for the birds, and it is a noticeable fact that these creatures, when they are really starving, live together most amicably, huddling together to keep each other warm, and refraining from all strife; and if a small quantity of food be given them they will eat it with comparative freedom from contention; but let a quantity of food which is more than sufficient for all be thrown to them, and fighting over the coveted supply at once ensues.

Occasionally we would put out a whole loaf of bread, and then the contention of the birds became fierce and prolonged, although there was more than they could possibly eat during several days. Some, having gorged themselves until they could eat no more, would stand upon the loaf and hover round it, pecking fiercely at all newcomers, and endeavouring to prevent them from obtaining any of the food. And along with this fierce contention there was noticeably a great fear. With each mouthful of food taken, the birds would look around in nervous terror, apprehensive of losing their food or their lives.

In this simple incident we have an illustration—crude, perhaps, but true—of the basis and outworking of the competitive laws in Nature and in human affairs. It is not scarcity that produces competition, it is abundance; so that the richer and more luxurious a nation becomes, the keener and fiercer becomes the competition for securing the necessaries and luxuries of life.

Let famine overtake a nation, and at once compassion and sympathy take the place of competitive strife; and, in the blessedness of giving and receiving, men enjoy a foretaste of that heavenly bliss which the spiritually wise have found, and which all shall ultimately reach.

The fact that abundance, and not scarcity, creates competition, should be held constantly in mind by the reader during the perusal of this book, as it throws a searching light not only on the statements herein contained, but upon every problem relating to social life and human conduct. Moreover, if it be deeply and earnestly meditated upon, and its lessons applied to individual conduct, it will make plain the Way which leads to the Kingdom.

Let us now search out the cause of this fact, in order that the evils connected with it may be transcended.

Every phenomenon in social and national life (as in Nature) is an effect, and all these effects are embodied by a cause which is not remote and detached, but which is the immediate soul and life of the effect itself. As the seed is contained in the flower, and the flower in the seed, so the relation of cause and effect is intimate and inseparable. An effect also is vivified and propagated, not by any life inherent in itself, but by the life and impulse existing in the cause.

Looking out upon the world, we behold it as an arena of strife in which individuals, communities, and nations are constantly engaged in struggle, striving with each other for superiority, and for the largest share of worldly possessions.

We see, also, that the weaker fall out defeated, and that the strong — those who are equipped to pursue the combat with undiminished ardour — obtain the victory, and enter into possession. And along with this struggle we see the suffering which is inevitably connected with it — men and women, broken down with the weight of their responsibilities, failing in their efforts and losing all; families and communities broken up, and nations subdued and subordinated.

We see seas of tears, telling of unspeakable anguish and grief; we see painful partings and early and unnatural deaths; and we know that this life of strife, when stripped of its surface appearances, is largely a life of sorrow. h that aspect of human life with which we are now dealing; such are the effects as we see them; and they have one common cause which is found in the human heart itself.

As all the multiform varieties of plant life have one common soil from which to draw their sustenance, and by virtue of which they live and thrive, so all the varied activities of human life are rooted in, and draw their vitality from, one common source—the human heart. The cause of all suffering and of all happiness resides, not in the outer activities of human life, but in the inner activities of the heart and mind; and every external agency is sustained by the life which it derives from human conduct.

The organized life-principle in man carves for itself outward channels along which it can pour its pent-up energies, makes for itself vehicles through which it can manifest its potency and reap its experience, and, as a result, we have our religious, social and political organizations.

All the visible manifestations of human life, then, are effects; and as such, although they may possess a reflex action, they can never be causes, but must remain forever what they are—dead effects, galvanized into life by an enduring and profound cause.

It is the custom of men to wander about in this world of effects, and to mistake its illusions for realities, eternally transposing and readjusting these effects in order to arrive at a solution of human problems, instead of reaching down to the underlying cause which is at once the centre of unification and the basis upon which to build a peace-giving solution of human life.

The strife of the world in all its forms, whether it be war, social or political quarrelling, sectarian hatred, private disputes or commercial competition, has its origin in one common cause, namely, individual selfishness. And I employ this term selfishness in a far-reaching sense; in it I include all forms of self-love and egotism— I mean by it the desire to pander to, and preserve at all costs, the personality.

This element of selfishness is the life and soul of competition, and of the competitive laws. Apart from it they have no existence. But in the life of every individual in whose heart selfishness in any form is harboured, these laws are brought into play, and the individual is subject to them.

Innumerable economic systems have failed, and must fail, to exterminate the strife of the world. They are the outcome of the delusion that outward systems of government are the causes of that strife, whereas they are but the visible and transient effect of the inward strife, the channels through which it must necessarily manifest itself. To destroy the channel is, and must ever be ineffectual, as the inward energy will immediately make for itself another, and still another and another.

Strife cannot cease; and the competitive laws must prevail so long as selfishness is fostered in the heart. All reforms fail where this element is ignored or unaccounted for; all reforms will succeed where it is recognized, and steps are taken for its removal.

Selfishness, then, is the root cause of competition, the foundation on which all competitive systems rest, and the sustaining source of the competitive laws. It will thus be seen that all competitive systems, all the visible activities of the struggle of man with man, are as the leaves and branches of a tree which overspreads the whole earth, the root of that tree being individual selfishness, and the ripened fruits of which are pain and sorrow.

This tree cannot be destroyed by merely lopping off its branches; to do this effectively, the root must be destroyed. To introduce measures in the form of changed external conditions is merely lopping off the branches; and as the cutting away of certain branches of a tree gives added vigour to those which remain, even so the very means which are taken to curtail the competitive strife, when those means deal entirely with its outward effects, will but add strength and vigour to the tree whose roots are all the time being fostered and encouraged in the human heart. The most that even legislation can do is to prune the branches, and so prevent the tree from altogether running wild.

Great efforts are now being put forward to found a "Garden City," which shall be a veritable Eden planted in the midst of orchards, and whose inhabitants shall live in comfort and comparative repose. And beautiful and laudable are all such efforts when they are prompted by unselfish love. But such a city cannot exist, or cannot long remain the Eden which it aims to be in its outward form, unless the majority of its inhabitants have subdued and conquered the inward selfishness.

Even one form of selfishness, namely, self-indulgence, if fostered by its inhabitants, will completely undermine that city, levelling its orchards to the ground, converting many of its beautiful dwellings into competitive marts, and obnoxious centres for the personal gratification of appetite, and some of its buildings into institutions for the maintenance of order; and upon its public spaces will rise jails, asylums, and orphanages, for where the spirit of self-indulgence is, the means for its gratification will be immediately adopted, without considering the good of others or of the community (for selfishness is always blind), and the fruits of that gratification will be rapidly reaped.

The building of pleasant houses and the planting of beautiful gardens can never, of itself, constitute a Garden City unless its inhabitants have learned that self-sacrifice is better than self-protection, and have first established in their own hearts the Garden City of unselfish love. And when a sufficient number of men and women have done this, the Garden City will appear, and it will flourish and prosper, and great will be its peace, for "out of the heart are the issues of life."

Having found that selfishness is the root cause of all competition and strife, the question naturally arises as to how this cause shall be dealt with, for it naturally follows that a cause being destroyed, all its effects cease; a cause being propagated, all its effects, however they may be modified from without, must continue.

Every man who has thought at all deeply upon the problem of life, and has brooded sympathetically upon the sufferings of mankind, has seen that selfishness is at the root of all sorrow—in fact, this is one of the truths that is first apprehended by the thoughtful mind. And along with that perception there has been born within him a longing to formulate some methods by which that selfishness might be overcome.

The first impulse of such a man is to endeavour to frame some outward law, or introduce some new social arrangements or regulations, which shall put a check on the selfishness of others.

The second tendency of his mind will be to feel his utter helplessness before the great iron will of selfishness by which he is confronted.

Both these attitudes of mind are the result of an incomplete knowledge of what constitutes selfishness. And this partial knowledge dominates him because, although he has overcome the grosser forms of selfishness in himself, and is so far noble, he is yet selfish in other and more remote and subtle directions.

This feeling of "helplessness" is the prelude to one of two conditions—the man will either give up in despair, and again sink himself in the selfishness of the world, or he will search and meditate until he finds another way out of the difficulty. And that way he will find. Looking deeper and ever deeper into the things of life; reflecting, brooding, examining, and analysing; grappling with every difficulty and problem with intensity of thought, and developing day by day a profounder love of Truth—by these means his heart will grow and his comprehension expand, and at last he will realize that the way to destroy selfishness is not to try to destroy one form of it in other people, but to destroy it utterly, root and branch, in himself.

The perception of this truth constitutes spiritual illumination, and when once it is awakened in the mind, the "straight and narrow way" is revealed, and the Gates of the Kingdom already loom in the distance.

Then does a man apply to himself (not to others) these words—

And why beholdest thou the mote that is in thy brother's eye, but considerest not the beam that is in thy own eye? Or how wilt thou say to thy brother, let me pull out the mote out of thine eye; and, behold, a beam is in thine own eye? Thou hypocrite, first cast out the beam out of thine own eye; and then shall thou see clearly to cast out the mote out of thine brother's eye.

When a man can apply these words to himself and act upon them, judging himself mercilessly, but judging none other, then will he find his way out of the hell of competitive strife, then will he rise above and render of non-effect the laws of competition, and will find the higher Law of Love, subjecting himself to which every evil thing will flee from him, and the joys and blessings which the selfish vainly seek will constantly wait upon him. And not only this, he will, having lifted himself, lift the world. By his example many will see the Way, and will walk it; and the powers of darkness will be weaker for having lived.

It will here be asked, "But will not man who has risen above his selfishness, and therefore above the competitive strife, suffer through the selfishness and competition of those around him? Will he not after all the trouble he has taken to purify himself, suffer at the hands of the impure?"

No, he will not. The equity of the Divine Order is perfect, and cannot be subverted, so that it is impossible for one who has over-come selfishness to be subject to those laws which are brought into operation by the action of selfishness; in other words, each individual suffers by virtue of his own selfishness.

It is true that the selfish all come under the operation of the com-petitive laws, and suffer collectively, each acting, more or less, as the instrument by which the suffering of others is brought about, which makes it appear, on the surface, as though men suffered for the sins of others rather than their own. But the truth is that in a universe the very basis of which is harmony, and which can only be sustained by the perfect adjustment of all its parts, each unit receives its own measure of adjustment, and suffers by and of itself.

Each man comes under the laws of his own being, never un-der those of another. True, he will suffer like another, and even through the instrumentality of another, if he elects to live under the same conditions as that other. But if he chooses to desert those conditions and to live under another and higher set of condi-tions of which that other is ignorant, he will cease to come under, or be affected by, the lower laws.

Let us now go back to the symbol of the tree and carry the anal-ogy a little further. Just as the leaves and branches are sustained by the roots, so the roots derive their nourishment from the soil, groping blindly in the darkness for the sustenance which the tree demands. In like manner, selfishness, the root of the tree of evil and of suffering, derives its nourishment from the dark soil of ig-norance. In this it thrives; upon this it stands and flourishes. By ignorance I mean something vastly different from lack of learning; and the sense in which I use it will be made plain as I proceed.

Selfishness always gropes in the dark. It has no knowledge; by its very nature it is cut off from the source of enlightenment; it is a blind impulse, knowing nothing, obeying no law, for it knows none, and is thereby forcibly bound to those competitive laws by virtue of which suffering is inflicted in order that harmony may be maintained.

We live in a world, a universe, abounding with all good things. So great is the abundance of spiritual, mental and material bless-ings that every man and woman on this globe could not only be provided with every necessary good, but could live in the midst of abounding plenty, and yet have much to spare. Yet, in spite of this, what a spectacle of ignorance do we behold!

We see on the one hand millions of men and women chained to a ceaseless slavery, interminably toiling in order to obtain a poor and scanty meal and a garment to cover their nakedness; and on the other hand we see thousands, who already have more than they require and can well manage, depriving themselves of all the blessings of a true life and of the vast opportunities which their possessions place within their reach, in order to accumulate more of those material things for which they have no legitimate use. Surely men and women have no more wisdom than the beasts which fight over the possession of that which is more than they can all well dispose of, and which they could all enjoy in peace!

Such a condition of things can only occur in a state of ignorance deep and dark; so dark and dense as to be utterly impenetrable save to the unselfish eye of wisdom and truth. And in the midst of all this striving after place and food and raiment, there works unseen, yet potent and unerring, the Overruling Law of Justice, meting out to every individual his own quota of merit and demerit. It is impartial; it bestows no favours; it inflicts no unearned punishments:

It knows not wrath nor pardon; utter-true

It measures mete, its faultless balance weighs;

Times are as nought, tomorrow it will judge,

Or after many days.

The rich and the poor alike suffer for their own selfishness; and none escapes. The rich have their particular sufferings as well as the poor. Moreover, the rich are continually losing their riches; the poor are continually acquiring them. The poor man of today is the rich man of tomorrow, and vice versa.

There is no stability, no security in hell, and only brief and occasional periods of respite from suffering in some form or other. Fear, also, follows men like a great shadow, for the man who obtains and holds by selfish force will always be haunted by a feeling of insecurity, and will continually fear its loss; while the poor man, who is selfishly seeking or coveting material riches, will be harassed by the fear of destitution. And one and all who live in this underworld of strife are overshadowed by one great fear—the fear of death.

Surrounded by the darkness of ignorance, and having no knowledge of those eternal and life-sustaining Principles out of which all things proceed, men labour under the delusion that the most important and essential things in life are food and clothing, and that their first duty is to strive to obtain these, believing that these outward things are the source and cause of all comfort and happiness.

It is the blind animal instinct of self-preservation (the preservation of the body and personality), by virtue of which each man opposes himself to other men in order to "get a living" or "secure a competency," believing that if he does not keep an incessant watch on other men, and constantly renew the struggle, they will ultimately "take the bread out of his mouth."

It is out of this initial delusion that comes all the train of delusions, with their attendant sufferings. Food and clothing are not the essential things of life; not the causes of happiness. They are non-essentials, effects, and, as such, proceed by a process of natural law from the essentials, the underlying cause.

The essential things in life are the enduring elements in character—integrity, faith, righteousness, self-sacrifice, compassion, love; and out of these all good things proceed.

Food and clothing, and money are dead effects; there is in them no life, no power except that which we invest with them. They are without vice and virtue, and can neither bless nor harm. Even the body which men believe to be themselves, to which they pander, and which they long to keep, must very shortly be yielded up to the dust. But the higher elements of character are life itself; and to practice these, to trust them, and to live entirely in them, constitutes the Kingdom of Heaven.

The man who says, "I will first of all earn a competence and secure a good position in life, and will then give my mind to those higher things," does not understand these higher things, does not believe them to be higher, for if he did, it would not be possible for him to neglect them. He believes the material outgrowths of life to be the higher, and therefore he seeks them first. He believes money, clothing and position to be of vast and essential importance, righteousness and truth to be at best secondary; for a man always sacrifices that which he believes to be lesser to that which he believes to be greater.

Immediately after a man realizes that righteousness is of more importance than the getting of food and clothing, he ceases to strive after the latter, and begins to live for the former. It is here where we come to the dividing line between the two Kingdoms— Hell and Heaven.

Once a man perceives the beauty and enduring reality of righteousness, his whole attitude of mind toward himself and others and the things within and around him changes. The love of personal existence gradually loses its hold on him; the instinct of self-preservation begins to die, and the practice of self-renunciation takes its place. For the sacrifice of others, or of the happiness of others, for his own good, he substitutes the sacrifice of self and of his own happiness for the good of others. And thus, rising above self, he rises above the competitive strife which is the outcome of self, and above the competitive laws which operate only in the region of self, and for the regulation of its blind impulses.

He is like the man who has climbed a mountain, and thereby risen above all the disturbing currents in the valleys below him. The clouds pour down their rain, the thunders roll and the lightnings flash, the fogs obscure, and the hurricanes uproot and destroy, but they cannot reach him on the calm heights where he stands, and where he dwells in continual sunshine and peace.

In the life of such a man the lower laws cease to operate, and he now comes under the protection of a higher Law—namely, the Law of Love; and, in accordance with his faithfulness and obedience to this Law, will all that is necessary for his well-being come to him at the time when he requires it.

The idea of gaining a position in the world cannot enter his mind, and the external necessities of life, such as money, food and clothing, he scarcely ever thinks about. But, subjecting himself for the good of others, performing all his duties scrupulously and without thinking of reward, and living day by day in the discipline of righteousness, all other things follow at the right time and in the right order.

Just as suffering and strife inhere in, and spring from, their root cause, selfishness, so blessedness and peace inhere in, and spring from, their root-cause, righteousness. And it is a full and all-embracing blessedness, complete and perfect in every department of life, for that which is morally and spiritually right is physically and materially right.

Such a man is free, for he is freed from all anxiety, worry, fear, despondency, all those mental disturbances which derive their vitality from the elements of self, and he lives in constant joy and peace, and this while living in the very midst of the competitive strife of the world.

Yet, though walking in the midst of Hell, its flames fall back before and around him, so that not one hair of his head can be singed. Though he walks in the midst of the lions of selfish force, for him their jaws are closed and their ferocity is subdued. Though on every hand men are falling around him in the fierce battle of life, he falls not, neither is he dismayed, for no deadly bullet can reach him, no poisoned shaft can pierce the impenetrable armour of his righteousness. Having lost the little, personal, self-seeking life of suffering, anxiety, fear, and want, he has found the illimitable, glorious, self-perfecting life of joy and peace and plenty.

"Therefore take no thought, saying 'What shall we eat?' or, 'What shall we drink?' or, 'Wherewithal shall we be clothed? . . .' For your heavenly Father knoweth ye have need of all these things. But seek ye first the Kingdom of God, and His Righteousness, and all these things shall be added unto you."

3. The Finding of a Principle

Be still, my soul, and know that peace is within

Be steadfast, heart, and know that strength divine

Belongs to thee; cease thy turmoil, mind,

And thou the everlasting rest shall find.

HOW THEN SHALL A MAN reach the Kingdom? By what process shall he find the light which alone can disperse his darkness? And in what way can he overcome the inward selfishness which is strong, and deeply rooted?

A man will reach the Kingdom by purifying himself, and he can only do this by pursuing a process of self-examination and self-analysis. The selfishness must be discovered and understood before it can be removed. It is powerless to remove itself, neither will it pass away of itself.

Darkness ceases only when light is introduced; so ignorance can only be dispersed by Knowledge; selfishness by Love. Seeing that in selfishness there is no security, no stability, no peace, the whole process of seeking the Kingdom resolves itself into a search for a Principle; a divine and permanent Principle on which a man can stand secure, freed from himself—that is, from the personal element, and from the tyranny and slavery which that personal self exacts and demands.

A man must first of all be willing to lose himself (his self-seeking self) before he can find himself (his Divine Self). He must realize that selfishness is not worth clinging to, that it is a master altogether unworthy of his service, and that divine Goodness alone is worthy to be enthroned in his heart as the supreme master of his life.

This means that he must have faith, for without this equipment there can be neither progress nor achievement. He must believe in the desirability of purity, in the supremacy of righteousness, in the sustaining power of integrity; he must ever hold before him the Ideal and Perfect Goodness, and strive for its achievement with ever-renewed effort and unflagging zeal.

This faith must be nurtured and its development encouraged. As a lamp, it must be carefully trimmed and fed and kept burning in the heart, for without its radiating flame no way will be seen in the darkness; he will find no pathway out of self. And as this flame increases and burns with a steadier light, energy, resolution, and self-reliance will come to his aid, and with each step, his progress will be accelerated until at last the Light of Knowledge will begin to take the place of the lamp of faith, and the darkness will commence to disappear before its searching splendour.

Into his spiritual sight will come the Principles of the divine Life, and as he approaches them, their incomparable beauty and majestic symmetry will astonish his vision, and gladden his heart with a gladness hitherto unknown.

Along this pathway of self-control and self-purification (for such it is) every soul must travel on its way to the Kingdom. So narrow is this way, and so overgrown with the weeds of selfishness is its entrance, that it is difficult to find, and, being found, cannot be retained except by daily meditation. Without this the spiritual energies grow weaker, and the man loses the strength necessary to continue. As the body is sustained and invigourated by material food, so the spirit is strengthened and renewed by its own food—namely meditation upon spiritual things.

He, then, who earnestly resolves to find the Kingdom will commence to meditate, and to rigidly examine his heart and mind and life in the light of that Supreme Perfection which is the goal of his attainment.

On his way to that goal, he must pass through three Gateways of Surrender. The first is the Surrender of Desire; the second is the Surrender of Opinion; the third is the Surrender of Self. Entering into meditation, he will commence to examine his desires, tracing them out in his mind, and following up their effects in his life and upon his character; and he will quickly perceive that, without the renunciation of desire, a man remains a slave both to himself and to his surroundings and circumstances. Having discovered this, the first Gate, that of the Surrender of Desire, is entered. Passing through this Gate, he adopts a process of self-discipline which is the first step in the purification of the soul.

Hitherto he has lived as a slavish beast; eating, drinking, sleeping, and pursuing enjoyment at the beck and call of his lower impulses; blindly following and gratifying his inclinations without method, not questioning his conduct, and having no fixed centre from which to regulate his character and life.

Now, however, he begins to live as a man; he curbs his inclinations, controls his passions, and steadies his mind in the practice of virtue. He ceases to pursue enjoyment, but follows the dictates of his reason, and regulates his conduct in accordance with the demands of an ideal. With the introduction of this regulating factor in his life, he at once perceives that certain habits must be abandoned.

He begins to select his food, and to have his meals at stated periods, no longer eating at any time when the sight of food tempts his inclination. He reduces the number of meals per day and also the quantity of food eaten.

He no longer goes to bed, by day or night, to indulge in pleasurable indolence, but to give his body the rest it needs, and he therefore regulates his hours of sleep, rising early, and never encouraging the animal desire to indulge in dreamy indolence after waking.

All those foods and drinks which are particularly associated with gluttony, cruelty, and drunkenness he will dispense with altogether, selecting the mild and refreshing sustenance which Nature provides in such rich profusion.

These preliminary steps will be at once adopted; and as the path

of self-government and self-examination is pursued, a clearer and
ever clearer perception of the nature, meaning, and effects of desire will be developed, until it will be seen that the mere regulation
of one's desires is altogether inadequate and insufficient, and that
the desires themselves must be abandoned, must be allowed to
fall out of the mind and to have no part in the character and life.

It is at this point where the soul of the seeker will enter the dark
Valley of Temptation, for these desires will not die without a struggle, and without many a fierce effort to reassert the power and
authority with which they have hitherto been invested. And here
the lamp of faith must be constantly fed and assiduously trimmed,
for all the light that it can throw out will be required to guide and
encourage the traveller in the dense gloom of this dark Valley.

At first his desires, like so many wild beasts, will clamour loudly
for gratification. Failing in that, they will tempt him to struggle
with them that they may overthrow him. And this last temptation
is greater and more difficult to overcome than the first, for the desires will not be stilled until they are utterly ignored; until they are
left unheeded, unconditionally abandoned, and allowed to perish
for want of food.

In passing through this Valley, the searcher will develop certain
powers which are necessary to his further development, and these
powers are—self-control, self-reliance, fearlessness, and independence of thought.

Here also he will have to pass through ridicule and mockery and
false accusation; so much so, that some of his best friends, yea,
even those whom he most unselfishly loves, will accuse him of
folly and inconsistency, and will do all they can to argue him back
to the life of animal indulgence, self-seeking, and petty personal
strife.

Nearly everybody around him will suddenly discover that they
know his duty better than he knows it himself, and, knowing no
other and higher life than their own of mingled excitement and
suffering, they will take great pains to win him back to it, imagining, in their ignorance, that he is losing so much pleasure and
happiness, and is gaining nothing in return.

At first this attitude of others toward him will arouse in him acute
suffering; but he will rapidly discover that this suffering is caused
by his own vanity and selfishness, and is the result of his own subtle desire to be appreciated, admired, and thought well of; and im-

mediately this knowledge is arrived at, he will rise into a higher state of consciousness, where these things can no longer reach him and inflict pain. It is here where he will begin to stand firm, and to wield with effect the powers of mind already mentioned.

Let him therefore press on courageously, heeding neither the revilings of his friends without nor the clamourings of his enemies within; aspiring, searching, striving; looking ever toward his Ideal with eyes of holy love; day by day ridding his mind of selfish motive, his heart of impure desire; stumbling sometimes, sometimes falling, but ever travelling onward and rising higher; and, recording each night in the silence of his own heart the journey of the day, let him not despair if but each day, in spite of all its failures and falls, record some holy battle fought, though lost, some silent victory attempted, though unachieved. The loss of today will add to the gain of tomorrow for him whose mind is set on the conquest of self.

Passing along the Valley, he will at last come to the Fields of Sorrow and Loneliness. His desires, having received at his hands neither encouragement nor sustenance, have grown weak, and are now falling away and perishing. He is climbing out of the Valley, and the darkness is less dense; but now he realizes for the first time he is alone. He is like a man standing upon the lowest level of a great mountain, and it is night. Above him towers the lofty peak, beyond which shine the everlasting stars; a short distance below him are the glaring lights of the city which he has left, and from it there come up to him the noises of its inhabitants—a confused mingling of shouts, screams, laughter, rumblings of traffic, and the strains of music. He thinks of his friends, all of whom are in the city, pursuing their own particular pleasures, and he is alone upon the mountain.

That city is the City of Desire and Pleasure, the mountain is the Mountain of Renunciation, and the climber now knows that he has left the world, that henceforth for him its excitements and strifes are lifeless things, and can tempt him no more. Resting awhile in this lonely place, he will taste of sorrow and learn its secret; harshness and hatred will pass from him; his heart will grow soft, and the first faint broodings of that divine compassion, which shall afterwards absorb his whole being, will overshadow and inspire him. He will begin to feel with every living thing in its strivings and sufferings, and gradually, as this lesson is learned, his own sorrow and loneliness will be forgotten in his great calm love for others, and will pass away.

Here, also, he will begin to perceive and understand the work-
ings of those hidden laws which govern the destinies of individuals and nations. Having risen above the lower region of strife and
selfishness within himself, he can now look calmly down upon it
in others and in the world, and analyse and comprehend it, and
he will see how selfish striving is at the root of all the world's suffering.

His whole attitude toward others and the world now undergoes a
complete change, and compassion and love begin to take the place
of self-seeking and self-protection in his mind; and as a result of
this, the world alters in its attitude toward him.

At this juncture he perceives the folly of competition, and, ceasing from striving to overtop and get the better of others, he begins
to encourage them, both with unselfish thoughts, and, when necessary, with loving acts; and this he does even to those who selfishly compete with him, no longer defending himself against them.

As a direct result of this, his worldly affairs begin to prosper as
never before; many of his friends who at first mocked him commence to respect, and even to love him, and he suddenly wakes up
to the fact that he is coming in contact with people of a distinctly
unworldly and noble type, of whose existence he had no knowledge while living in his lower selfish nature. From many parts and
from long distances these people will come to him to minister to
him and that he may minister to them, spiritual fellowship and
loving brotherhood will become potent in his life, and so he will
pass beyond the Fields of Sorrow and Loneliness.

The lower competitive laws have now ceased to operate in his
life, and their results, which are failure, disaster, exposure, and
destitution, can no longer enter into and form part of his experience; and this not merely because he has risen above the lower
forms of selfishness in himself, but because also, in so rising, he
has developed certain power of mind by which he is enabled to
direct and govern his affairs with a more powerful and masterly
hand.

He, however, has not yet travelled far, and unless he exercises
constant watchfulness, may at any time fall back into the lower
world of darkness and strife, revivifying its empty pleasures and
galvanizing back to life its dead desires. And especially is there
danger when he reaches the greatest temptation through which

man is called to pass— the temptation of doubt.

Before reaching, or even perceiving, the second Gate, that of Surrender of Opinion, the pilgrim will come upon a great soul-desert, the Desert of Doubt. And here for a time he will wander around, and despondency, indecision, and uncertainty, a melancholy brood, will surround him like a cloud, hiding from his view the way immediately in front of him.

A new and strange fear, too, will possibly overtake him, and he will begin to question the wisdom of the course he is pursuing. Again the allurements of the world will be presented to him, dressed in their most attractive garb, and the drowning din and stimulating excitement of worldly battle will once more assume a desirable aspect.

"After all, am I right? What gain is there in this? Does not life itself consist of pleasure and excitement and battle, and in giving these up am I not giving up all? Am I not sacrificing the very substance of life for a meaningless shadow? May it not be that, after all, I am a poor deluded fool, and that all these around me who live the life of the senses and stand upon its solid, sure, and easily procured enjoyments are wiser than I?"

By such dark doubtings and questionings will he here be tempted and troubled, and these very doubts will drive him to a deeper searching into the intricacies of life, and arouse within him the feeling of necessity for some permanent Principle upon which to stand and take refuge.

He will therefore, while wandering about in this dark Desert, come into contact with the higher and more subtle delusions of his own mind, the delusions of the intellect; and, by contrasting these with his Ideal, will learn to distinguish between the real and the unreal, the shadow and the substance, between effect and cause, between fleeting appearances and permanent Principles.

In the Desert of Doubt a man is confronted with all forms of illusion, not only the illusions of the senses, but also those of abstract thought and religious emotion. It is in the testing of, grappling with, and ultimately destroying, these illusions that he develops still higher powers, those of discrimination, spiritual perception, steadfastness of purpose, and calmness of mind, by the exercise of which he is enabled to unerringly distinguish the true from the false, both in the world of thought and that of material appearances.

Having acquired these powers, and learned how to use them in his holy warfare as weapons against himself, he now emerges from the Desert of Doubt, the mists and mirages of delusion vanish from his pathway, and there looms before him the second Gate, the Gateway of the Surrender of Opinion.

As he approaches this Gate, he sees before him the whole pathway along which he is travelling, and, for a space, obtains a glimpse of the glorious heights of attainment toward which he is moving; he sees the Temple of the Higher Life in all its majesty, and already he feels within him the strength and joy and peace of conquest. With Sir Galahad he can now exclaim:

"I....saw the Grail,

The Holy Grail...

....And one will crown me king

Far in the spiritual city."

for he knows that his ultimate victory is assured.

He now enters upon a process of self-conquest, which is altogether distinct from that which he has hitherto pursued. Up to the present he has been overcoming, transmuting, and simplifying his animal desires; now he commences to transmute and simplify his intellect. He has, so far, been adjusting his feelings to his Ideals; he now begins to adjust his thoughts to that Ideal, which also assumes at this point larger and more beautiful proportions, and for the first time he perceives what really constitutes a permanent and imperishable Principle.

He sees that the righteousness for which he has been searching is fixed and invariable; that it cannot be accommodated to man, but that man must reach up to, and obey it; that it consists of an undeviating line of conduct, apart from all considerations of loss or gain, of reward of punishment; that, in reality, it consists in abandoning self, with all the sins of desire, opinion, and self-interest of which that self is composed, and in living the blameless life of perfect love toward all men and creatures. Such a life is fixed and perfect; it is without turning, change, or qualification, and demands a sinless and perfect conduct. It is, therefore, the direct antithesis of the worldly life of self.

Perceiving this, the seeker sees that, although he has freed himself from the baser passions and desires which enslave mankind, he is still in bondage to the fetters of opinion; that although he has purified himself with a purity to which few aspire, and which the world cannot understand, he is still defiled with a defilement which is difficult to wash away—he loves his own opinions, and has all along been confounding them with Truth, with the Principle for which he is seeking.

He is not yet free from strife, and is still involved in the competitive laws as they occur in the higher realm of thought. He still believes that he (in his opinions) is right, and that others are wrong; and in his egotism, has even fallen so low as to bestow a mock pity on those who hold opinions the reverse of his own. But now, realizing this more subtle form of selfishness with which he is enslaved, and perceiving all the train of sufferings which spring from it, having also acquired the priceless possession of spiritual discernment, he reverently bends his head and passes through the second Gateway toward his final peace.

And now, clothing his soul with the colourless Garment of Humility, he bends all his energies to the uprooting of those opinions which he has hitherto loved and cherished.

He now learns to distinguish between Truth, which is one and unchangeable, and his own and others' opinions about Truth, which are many and changeable.

He sees that his opinions about Goodness, Purity, Compassion, and Love are very distinct from those qualities themselves, and that he must stand upon those divine Principles, and not upon his opinions. Hitherto he has regarded his own opinions as of great value, and the opinions of others as worthless, but now he ceases to so elevate his own opinions and to defend them against those of others, and comes to regard them as utterly worthless.

As a direct result of this attitude of mind, he takes refuge in the practice of pure Goodness, unalloyed with base desire and subtle self-love, and takes his stand upon the divine Principles of Purity, Wisdom, Compassion, and Love, incorporating them into his mind, and manifesting them in his life.

He is now clothed with the Righteousness of Christ (which is incomprehensible to the world) and is rapidly becoming divine. He has not only realized the darkness of desire; he has also perceived the vanity of speculative philosophy, and so rids his mind of all those metaphysical subtleties which have no relation to practical holiness, and which hitherto encumbered his progress and prevented him from seeing the enduring realities in life.

And now he casts from him, one after another, his opinions and speculations, and commences to live the life of perfect love toward all beings. With each opinion overcome and abandoned as a burden, there is an increased lightness of spirit, and he now begins to realize the meaning of being "free."

The divine flowers of Gladness, Joy, and Peace spring up spontaneously in his heart, and his life becomes a blissful song. And as the melody in his heart expands, and grows more and more perfect, his outward life harmonizes itself with the inward music.

All the effort he puts forth being now free from strife, he obtains all that is necessary for his well-being, without pain, anxiety, or fear. He has almost entirely transcended the competitive laws, and the Law of Love is now the governing factor in his life, adjusting all his worldly affairs harmoniously, and without struggle or difficulty on his part.

Indeed, the competitive laws as they occur in the commercial world, have been long left behind, and have ceased to touch him at any point in his material affairs. Here, also, he enters into a wider and more comprehensive consciousness, and viewing the universe and humanity from the higher altitudes of purity and knowledge to which he has ascended, perceives the orderly sequence of law in all human affairs.

The pursuit of this Path brings about the development of still higher powers of mind, and these powers are—divine patience, spiritual equanimity, non-resistance, and prophetic insight. By prophetic insight I do not mean, the foretelling of events, but direct perception of those hidden causes which operate in human life, and, indeed, in all life, and out of which spring the multifarious and universal effects and events.

The man here rises above the competitive laws as they operate in the thought world, so that their results, which are violence, ignominy, grief, humiliation and distress and anxiety in all their forms, no longer occur in his life.

As he proceeds, the imperishable Principles which form the foundation and fabric of the universe loom before him, and assume more and more symmetrical proportions. For him there is no more anguish; no evil can come near his dwelling; and there breaks upon him the dawning of the abiding Peace.

But he is not yet free. He has not yet finished his journey. He may rest here, and that as long as he chooses; but sooner or later he will rouse himself to the last effort, and will reach the final goal of achievement—the selfless state, the divine life.

He is not yet free from self, but still clings, though with less tenacity, to the love of personal existence, and to the idea of exclusive interest in his personal possessions. And when he at last realizes that those selfish elements must also be abandoned, there appears before him the third Gate—the Gateway of Surrender of Self.

It is no dark portal which he now approaches, but one luminous with divine glory, one radiant with a radiance with which no earthly splendour can vie, and he advances toward it with no uncertain step. The clouds of Doubt have long been dispersed; the sounds of the voices of Temptation are lost in the valley below; and with firm gait, erect carriage, and a heart filled with unspeakable joy, he nears the Gate that guards the Kingdom of God.

He has now given up all but self-interest in those things which are his by legal right, but he now perceives that he must hold nothing as his own; and as he pauses at the Gate, he hears the command which cannot be evaded or denied: "Yet lackest thou one thing; sell all that thou hast, and distribute unto the poor, and thou shall have treasure in Heaven."

And passing through the last great Gate, he stands glorious, radiant, free, detached from the tyranny of desire, of opinion, of self; a divine man—harmless, patient, tender, pure; he has found that for which he had been searching—the Kingdom of God and His Righteousness.

The journey to the Kingdom may be a long and tedious one, or it may be short and rapid. It may occupy a minute, or it may take a thousand ages. Everything depends on the faith and belief of the searcher. The majority cannot "enter in because of their unbelief"; for how can men realize righteousness when they do not believe in it nor in the possibility of its accomplishment?

Neither is it necessary to leave the outer world, and one's duties therein. Nay, it can only be found through the unselfish performance of one's duty. Some there are whose faith is so great that, when this truth is presented to them, they can let all the personal elements drop almost immediately out of their minds, and enter into their divine heritage.

But all who believe and aspire to achieve will sooner or later arrive at victory if, amid all their worldly duties, they faint not, nor lose sight of the Ideal Goodness, and continue, with unshaken resolve to "press on to Perfection."

4. At Rest in the Kingdom and All Things Added

THE WHOLE JOURNEY from the Kingdom of Strife to the Kingdom of Love resolves itself into a process which may be summed up in the following words: The regulation and purification of conduct. Such a process must, if assiduously pursued, necessarily lead to perfection. It will also be seen that as the man obtains the mastery over certain forces within himself, he arrives at a knowledge of all the laws which operate in the realm of those forces, and by watching the ceaseless working of cause and effect within himself, until he understands it, he then understands it in its universal adjustments in the body of humanity.

Moreover, seeing that all the laws which govern human affairs are the direct outcome of the necessities of the human heart, he, having reformed and transmuted those necessities, has brought himself under the guidance of other laws which operate in accordance with the altered condition, and that, having mastered and overcome the selfish forces within himself, he can no longer be subject to the laws which exist for their governance.

The process is also one of simplification of the mind, a sifting away of all but the essential gold in character. And as the mind is thus simplified, the apparently unfathomable complexity of the universe assumes simpler and simpler aspects, until the whole is seen to resolve itself into, and rest upon, a few unalterable Principles; and these Principles are ultimately seen to be contained in one, namely LOVE.

The mind thus simplified, the man arrives at peace, and he now really begins to live. Looking back on the personal life which he has forever abandoned, he sees it as a horrible nightmare out of which he has awakened; but looking out and down with the eyes of the spirit, he sees that others continue to live it. He sees men and women struggling, fighting, suffering and perishing for that which is abundantly given to them by the bountiful hand of the Father, if they would only cease from all covetousness, and take it without hurt or hindrance; and compassion fills his heart, and also gladness, for he knows that humanity will wake at last from its long and painful dream.

In the early part of the journey he seemed to be leaving humanity far behind, and he sorrowed in his loneliness. But now, having reached the highest, having attained the goal, he finds himself nearer to humanity than ever before—yea, living in its very heart, sympathizing with all its sorrows, rejoicing in all its joys; for, having no longer any personal considerations to defend, he lives entirely in the heart of humanity.

He lives no longer for himself; he lives for others; and so living, he enjoys the highest bliss, the deepest peace.

For a time he searched for Compassion, Love, Bliss, Truth; but now he has verily become Compassion, Love, Bliss, Truth; and it may literally be said of him that he has ceased to be a personality, for all the personal elements have been extinguished, and there remain only those qualities and principles which are entirely impersonal. And those qualities are now manifested in the man's life, and henceforth the man's character.

And having ceased from the protection of the self, and living constantly in compassion, wisdom and love, he comes under the protection of the highest Law, the Law of Love; and he understands that Law, and consciously co-operates with it; yea, is himself inseparably identified with the Law.

"Forgoing self, the universe grows I": and he whose nature is compassion, wisdom and love cannot possibly need any protection; for those Principles themselves constitute the highest protection, being the real, the divine, the immortal in all men and women, and constituting the indestructible reality in the cosmic order.

Neither does he need to seek enjoyment whose very nature is Bliss, Joy, Peace. As for competing with others, with whom should he compete who has lovingly identified himself with all? With whom should he struggle who has sacrificed himself for all? Whose blind, misguided, and ineffectual competition should he fear who has reached the source of all blessedness, and who receives at the hands of the Father all necessary things?

Having lost himself (his selfish personality), he has found himself (his divine nature, Love); and Love and all the effects of Love now compose his life. He can now joyfully exclaim—

I have made the acquaintance of the Master of Compassion;

I have put on the Garment of the Perfect Law,

I have entered the realm of the Great Reality;

Wandering is ended, for Rest is accomplished;

Pain and sorrow have ceased, for Peace is entered into;

Confusion is dissolved, for Unity is made manifest;

Error is vanquished, for Truth is revealed!

The Harmonizing Principle, Righteousness, or Divine Love, being found, all things are seen as they are, and not through the illusory mediums of selfishness and opinion; the universe is One, and all its manifold operations are the manifestation of one Law.

Hitherto in this work laws have been referred to, and also spoken of as higher and lower, and this distinction was necessary; but now the Kingdom is reached, we see that all the forces operative in human life are the varied manifestations of the One Supreme Law of Love. It is by virtue of this Law that Humanity suffers, that, by the intensity of its sufferings, it shall become purified and wise, and so relinquish the source of suffering, which is selfishness.

The Law and foundation of the universe being Love, it follows that all self-seeking is opposed to that Law, is an effort to overcome or ignore the Law, and as a result, every self-seeking act and thought is followed by an exact quota of suffering which is required to annul its effect, and so maintain the universal harmony. All suffering is, therefore, the restraint which the Law of Love puts upon ignorance and selfishness, and out of such painful restraint Wisdom at last emerges.

There being no strife and no selfishness in the Kingdom, there is therefore no suffering, no restraint; there is perfect harmony, equipoise, rest. Those who have entered it do not follow any animal inclinations (they have none to follow), but live in accordance with the highest Wisdom. Their nature is Love, and they live in love toward all.

They are never troubled about "making a living," as they are Life itself, living in the very Heart of Life; and should any material or other need arise, that need is immediately supplied without any anxiety or struggle on their part.

Should they be called to undertake any work, the money and friends needed to carry out that work are immediately forthcoming. Having ceased to violate their principles, all their needs are supplied through legitimate channels. Any money or help required always comes through the instrumentality of good people who are either living in the Kingdom themselves, or are working for its accomplishment.

Those who live in the Kingdom of Love have all their needs supplied by the Law of Love, with all freedom from unrest, just as those who live in the kingdom of self only meet their needs by much strife and suffering. Having altered the root cause in their heart they have altered all the effects in their inner and outer life. As self is the root cause of all strife and suffering, so Love is the root cause of all peace and bliss.

Those who are at rest in the Kingdom do not look for happiness to any outward possession. They see that all such possessions are mere transient effects that come when they are required, and after their purpose is served, pass away.

They never think of these things (money, clothing, food, etc.) except as mere accessories and effects of the true Life. They are therefore freed from all anxiety and trouble, and resting in Love, they are the embodiment of happiness.

Standing upon the imperishable Principles of Purity, Compassion, Wisdom and Love, they are immortal, and know they are immortal; they are one with God (the Supreme Good), and know they are one with God. Seeing the realities of things, they can find no room anywhere for condemnation. All the operations that occur upon the earth they see as instruments of the Good Law, even those called evil.

All men are essentially divine, though unaware of their divine nature, and all their acts are efforts, even though many of them are dark and impotent, to realize some higher good. All so-called evil is seen to be rooted in ignorance, even those deeds that are called deliberately wicked, so that condemnation ceases, and Love and Compassion become all in all.

But let it not be supposed that the children of the kingdom live in ease and indolence (these two sins are the first that have to be eradicated when the search for the Kingdom is entered upon); they live in a peaceful activity; in fact, they only truly live, for the life of self with its train of worries, griefs, and fears, is not real life.

They perform all their duties with the most scrupulous diligence, apart from thoughts of self, and employ all their means, as well as powers and faculties, which are greatly intensified, in building up the Kingdom of Righteousness in the hearts of others and in the world around them. This is their work—first by example, then by precept.

Having sold all that they have (renounced all self-interest in their possessions), they now give to the poor (give of their rich store of wisdom, love and peace to the needy in spirit, the weary and broken-hearted), and follow the Christ whose name is LOVE.

And they have sorrow no more, but live in perpetual gladness, for though they see suffering in the world, they also see the final Bliss and the Eternal Refuge of Love, to which whosoever is ready may come now, and to which all will come at last.

The children of the Kingdom are known by their life. They manifest the fruits of the Spirit—"love, joy, peace, long-suffering, kindness, goodness, faithfulness, meekness, temperance, self-control"—under all circumstances and vicissitudes. They are entirely free from anger, fear, suspicion, jealousy, caprice, anxiety, and grief. Living in the Righteousness of God, they manifest qualities which are the very reverse of those which occur in the world, and which are regarded by the world as foolishness.

They demand no rights; they do not defend themselves; do not retaliate; do good to those who attempt to injure them; manifest the same gentle spirit toward those who oppose and attack them as toward those who agree with them; do not pass judgement on others; condemn no person and no system, and live at peace with all.

The Kingdom of Heaven is perfect trust, perfect knowledge, perfect peace. All is music, sweetness, and tranquillity. No irritations, no bad tempers, no harsh words, no suspicions, no lust, and no disturbing elements can enter there.

Its children live in perfect sweetness, forgiving and forgiven, ministering to others with kindly thoughts and words, and deeds. And that Kingdom is in the heart of every man and woman; it is their rightful heritage, their own Kingdom; theirs to enter now. But no sin can enter therein; no self-born thought or deed can pass its Golden Gates; no impure desire can defile its radiant robes.

All may enter it who will, but all must pay the price, and that is—the unconditional abandonment of self.

"If thou wilt be perfect, sell all that thou hast"; but at these words the world turns away "sorrowful, for it is very rich"; rich in money which it cannot keep; rich in fears which it cannot let go; rich in selfish loves to which it greedily clings; rich in grievous partings which it would fain escape; rich in seeking enjoyment; rich in pain and sorrow; rich in strife and suffering; rich in excitement and woe; rich in all things which are not riches, but poor in riches themselves which are not to be found outside the Kingdom; rich in all things that pertain to darkness and death, but poor in those things which are Light and Life.

He then, who would realize the Kingdom, let him pay the price and enter. If he have a great and holy faith he can do it now, and, letting fall from him like a garment the self to which he has been clinging, stand free. If he have less faith, he must rise above self more slowly, and find the Kingdom by daily effort and patient work. The Temple of Righteousness is built and its four walls are the four Principles— Purity, Wisdom, Compassion, Love. Peace is its roof; its floor Steadfastness, its entrance-door is Selfless Duty, its atmosphere is Inspiration, and its music is the Joy of the perfect.

It cannot be shaken, and, being eternal and indestructible, there is no more need to seek protection in taking thought for the things of tomorrow. And the Kingdom of Heaven being established in the heart, the obtaining of the material necessities of life is no more considered, for, having found the Highest, all these things are added as effect to cause; the struggle for existence has ceased, and the spiritual, mental, and material needs are daily supplied from the universal abundance.

Long I sought thee, Spirit holy,

Master Spirit, meek and lowly;

Sought thee with a silent sorrow,

  brooding over the woes of men;

Vainly sought thy yoke of meekness

'Neath the weight of woe and weakness;

Finding not, yet in my failing,

  seeking over and over again.

In unrest and doubt and sadness

Dwelt I, yet I knew thy Gladness

Waited somewhere; somewhere

  greeted torn and sorrowing hearts like mine;

Knew that somehow I should find thee,

Leaving sin and woe behind me,

And at last thy Love would bid me
  enter into Rest divine.

Hatred, mockery, and reviling

Scorched my seeking soul defiling

That which should have been thy Temple,
  wherein thou shouldest move and dwell;

Praying, striving, hoping, calling;

Suffering, sorrowing in my falling,

Still I sought thee, groping blindly in the
  gloomy depths of Hell.

And I sought thee till I found thee;

And the dark powers all around me

Fled, and left me silent, peaceful, brooding
  over thy holy themes;

From within me and without me

Fled they when I ceased to doubt thee;

And I found thee in thy Glory, mighty Master
  of my dreams!

Yes, I found thee, Spirit holy,

Beautiful and pure and lowly;

Found thy Joy and Peace and Gladness;
  found thee in thy House of Rest;

Found thy strength in Love and Meekness,

And my pain and woe and weakness left me,

And I walked the Pathway trodden only by the blest.

Part II: The Heavenly Life

1. The Divine Centre

THE secret of life, of abundant life, with its strength, its felicity, and its unbroken peace is to find the Divine Centre within oneself, and to live in and from that, instead of in that outer circumference of disturbances — the clamours, cravings, and argumentations which make up the animal and intellectual man. These selfish elements constitute the mere husks of life, and must be thrown away by him who would penetrate to the Central Heart of things — to Life itself.

Not to know that within you that is changeless, and defiant of time and death, is not to know anything, but is to play vainly with the unsubstantial reflections in the Mirror of Time. Not to find within you those passionless Principles which are not moved by the strifes and shows and vanities of the world, is to find nothing but illusions which vanish as they are grasped.

He who resolves that he will not rest satisfied with appearances, shadows, illusions shall, by the piercing light of that resolve, disperse every fleeting phantasy, and shall enter into the substance and reality of life. He shall learn how to live, and he shall live. He shall be the slave of no passion, the servant of no opinion, the votary of no fond error. Finding the Divine Centre within his own heart, he will be pure and calm and strong and wise, and will ceaselessly radiate the Heavenly Life in which he lives — which is himself.

Having betaken himself to the Divine Refuge within, and remaining there, a man is free from sin. All his yesterdays are as the tide-washed and untrodden sands; no sin shall rise up against him to torment and accuse him and destroy his sacred peace; the fires of remorse cannot scorch him, nor can the storms of regret devastate his dwelling-place. His to-morrows are as seeds which shall germinate, bursting into beauty and potency of life, and no doubt shall shake his trust, no uncertainty rob him of repose. The Present is his, only in the immortal Present does he live, and it is as the eternal vault of blue above which looks down silently and calmly, yet radiant with purity and light, upon the upturned and tear-stained faces of the centuries.

Men love their desires, for gratification seems sweet to them, but its end is pain and vacuity; they love the argumentations of the intellect, for egotism seems most desirable to them, but the fruits thereof are humiliation and sorrow. When the soul has reached the end of gratification and reaped the bitter fruits of egotism, it is ready to receive the Divine Wisdom and to enter into the Divine Life. Only the crucified can be transfigured; only by the death of self can the Lord of the heart rise again into the Immortal Life, and stand radiant upon the Olivet of Wisdom.

Thou hast thy trials? Every outward trial is the replica of an inward imperfection. Thou shalt grow wise by knowing this, and shalt thereby transmute trial into active joy, finding the Kingdom where trial cannot come. When wilt thou learn thy lessons, O child of earth! All thy sorrows cry out against thee; every pain is thy just accuser, and thy griefs are but the shadows of thy unworthy and perishable self. The Kingdom of Heaven is thine; how long wilt thou reject it, preferring the lurid atmosphere of Hell — the hell of thy self-seeking self?

Where self is not there is the Garden of the Heavenly Life, and

"There spring the healing streams

Quenching all thirst! there bloom the immortal flowers

Carpeting all the way with joy! there throng Swiftest and sweetest hours !"

The redeemed sons of God, the glorified in body and spirit, are"bought with a price," and that price is the crucifixion of the personality, the death of self; and having put away that within which is the source of all discord, they have found the universal Music, the abiding Joy.

Life is more than motion, it is Music; more than rest, it is Peace; more than work, it is Duty; more than labour, it is Love; more than enjoyment, it is Blessedness; more than acquiring money and position and reputation, it is Knowledge, Purpose, strong and high Resolve.

Let the impure turn to Purity, and they shall be pure; let the weak resort to Strength, and they shall be strong; let the ignorant fly to Knowledge, and they shall be wise. All things are man's, and

he chooses that which he will have. To-day he chooses in ignorance, to-morrow he shall choose in Wisdom. He shall "work out
his own salvation" whether he believe it or not, for he cannot escape himself, nor transfer to another the eternal responsibility of
his own soul. By no theological subterfuge shall he trick the Law
of his being, which shall shatter all his selfish makeshifts and ex-
cuses for right thinking and right doing. Nor shall God do for him
that which it is destined his soul shall accomplish for itself. What
would you say of a man who, wanting to possess a mansion in
which to dwell peacefully, purchased the site and then knelt down
and asked God to build the house for him? Would you not say that
such a man was foolish? And of another man who, having purchased the land, set the architects and builders and carpenters
at work to erect the edifice, would you not say that he was wise?
And as it is in the building of a material house, even so it is in the
building of a spiritual mansion. Brick by brick, pure thought upon
pure thought, good deed upon good deed, must the habitation of
a blameless life rise from its sure foundation until at last it stands
out in all the majesty of its faultless proportions. Not by caprice,
nor gift, nor favour does a man obtain the spiritual realities, but
by diligence, watchfulness, energy, and effort.

"Strong is the soul, and wise and beautiful;

The seeds of God-like power are in us still;

Gods are we, bards, saints, heroes, if we will."

The spiritual Heart of man is the Heart of the universe, and, finding that Heart, man finds the strength to accomplish all things.
He finds there also the Wisdom to see things as they are. He finds
there the Peace that is divine. At the centre of man's being is the
Music which orders the stars — the Eternal Harmony. He who
would find Blessedness, let him find himself; let him abandon every discordant desire, every inharmonious thought, every unlovely
habit and deed, and he will find that Grace and Beauty and Harmony which form the indestructible essence of his own being.

Men fly from creed to creed, and find — unrest; they travel in
many lands, and discover — disappointment; they build themselves beautiful mansions, and plant pleasant gardens, and reap
— ennui and discomfort. Not until a man falls back upon the
Truth within himself does he find rest and satisfaction; not until
he builds the inward Mansion of Faultless Conduct does he find

the endless and incorruptible Joy, and, having obtained that, he will infuse it into all his outward doings and possessions.

If a man would have peace, let him exercise the spirit of Peace; if he would find love, let him dwell in the spirit of Love; if he would escape suffering, let him cease to inflict it; if he would do noble things for humanity, let him cease to do ignoble things for himself. If he will but quarry the mine of his own soul, he shall find there all the materials for building whatsoever he will, and he shall find there also the central Rock on which to build in safety.

Howsoever a man works to right the world, it will never be righted until he has put himself right. This may be written upon the heart as a mathematical axiom. It is not enough to preach Purity, men must cease from lust; to exhort to love, they must abandon hatred; to extol self-sacrifice, they must yield up self; to adorn with mere words the Perfect Life, they must be perfect.

When a man can no longer carry the weight of his many sins, let him fly to the Christ, whose throne is the centre of his own heart, and he shall become light-hearted, entering the glad company of the Immortals.

When he can no longer bear the burden of his accumulated learning, let a man leave his books, his science, his philosophy, and come back to himself, and he shall find within, that which he outwardly sought and found not — his own divinity.

He ceases to argue about God who has found God within. Relying upon that calm strength which is not the strength of self, he lives God, manifesting in his daily life the Highest Goodness, which is Eternal Life.

2. The Eternal Now

NOW is thy reality in which time is contained. It is more and greater than time; it is an ever-present reality. It knows neither past nor future, and is eternally potent and substantial. Every minute, every day, every year is a dream as soon as it has passed, and exists only as an imperfect and unsubstantial picture in the memory, if it be not entirely obliterated.

Past and future are dreams; now is a reality. All things are now; all power, all possibility, all action is now. Not to act and accomplish now is not to act and accomplish at all. To live in thoughts of what you might have done, or in dreams of what you mean to do, this is folly: but to put away regret, to anchor anticipation, and to do and to work now, this is wisdom.

Whilst a man is dwelling upon the past or future he is missing the present; he is forgetting to live now. All things are possible now, and only now. Without wisdom to guide him, and mistaking the unreal for the real, a man says, "If I had done so and so last week, last month, or last year, it would have been better with me to-day"; or, "I know what is best to be done, and I will do it to-morrow." The selfish cannot comprehend the vast importance and value of the present, and fail to see it as the substantial reality of which past and future are the empty reflections. It may truly be said that past and future do not exist except as negative shadows, and to live in them — that is, in the regretful and selfish contemplation of them— is to miss the reality in life.

"The Present, the Present is all thou hast

For thy sure possessing;

Like the patriarch's angel, hold it fast,

Till it gives its blessing.

"All which is real now remaineth,

And fadeth never:

The hand which upholds it now sustaineth

The soul for ever.

"Then of what is to be, and of what is done,

Why queriest thou?

The past and the time to be are one,

And both are NOW !"

Man has all power now; but not knowing this, he says, "I will be perfect next year, or in so many years, or in so many lives." The dwellers in the Kingdom of God, who live only in the now, say, "I am perfect now," and refraining from all sin now, and ceaselessly guarding the portals of the mind, not looking to the past nor to the future, nor turning to the left or right, they remain eternally holy and blessed." Now is the accepted time; now is the day of salvation."

Say to yourself, "I will live in my Ideal now; I will manifest my Ideal now; I will be my Ideal now; and all that tempts me away from my Ideal I will not listen to; I will listen only to the voice of my Ideal." Thus resolving, and thus doing, you shall not de-part from the Highest, and shall eternally manifest the True.

"Afoot and light-hearted, I take to the open road.

Henceforth I ask not good fortune: I myself am good fortune.

Henceforth I whimper no more, postpone no more, need nothing;

Done with indoor complaints, libraries, querulous criticisms.

Strong and content, I take to the open road."

Cease to tread every byway of dependence, every winding side-way that tempts thy soul into the shadow-land of the past and the future, and manifest thy native and divine strength now. Come out into "the open road." That which you would be, and hope to be you may be now. Non-accomplishment resides in your perpetual postponement, and, having the power to postpone, you also have the power to accomplish — to perpetually accomplish: realize this truth, and you shall be to-day, and every day, the ideal man of whom you dreamed.

Virtue consists in fighting sin day after day. but holiness consists in leaving sin, Unnoticed and ignored, to die by the wayside; and this is done, can only be done, in the living now. Say not unto thy soul, "Thou shall be purer to-morrow"; but rather say, "Thou shalt be pure now." To-morrow is too late for anything, and he who sees his help and salvation in to-morrow shall continually fail and fall to-day.

Thou didst fall yesterday? Didst sin grievously? Having realized this, leave it instantly and forever, and watch that thou sinnest not now. The while thou art bewailing the past, every gate of thy soul remains unguarded against the entrance of sin now. Thou shalt not rise by grieving over the irremediable past, but by remedying the present.

The foolish man, loving the boggy side-path of procrastination rather than the firm Highway of Present Effort, says, "I will rise early to-morrow; I will get out of debt to-morrow; I will carry out my intentions to-morrow." But the wise man, realizing the momentous import of the Eternal Now, rises early to-day; keeps out of debt to-day; carries out his intentions to-day; and so never departs from strength and peace and ripe accomplishment.

That which is done now remains; that which is to be done to-

morrow does not appear. It is wisdom to leave that which has not
arrived, and to attend to that which is; and to attend to it with
such a consecration of soul and concentration of effort as shall
leave no possible loophole for regret to creep in.

A man's spiritual comprehension being clouded by the illusions
of self, he says, "I was born on such a day, so many years ago, and
shall die at my allotted time." But he was not born, neither will
he die, for how can that which is immortal, which eternally is, be
subject to birth and death? Let a man throw off his illusions, and
then he will see that the birth and death of the body are the mere
incidents of a journey, and not its beginning and end.

Looking back to happy beginnings, and forward to mournful
endings, a man's eyes are blinded, so that he beholds not his own
immortality; his ears are closed, so that he hears not the ever-
present harmonies of Joy; and his heart is hardened, so that it
pulsates not to the rhythmic sounds of Peace.

The universe, with all that it contains, is now. Put out thy hand,
O man, and receive the fruits of Wisdom! Cease from thy greedy
striving, thy selfish sorrowing, thy foolish regretting, and he content to live.

Act now, and, lo! all things are done; live now, and, behold! thou
art in the midst of Plenty; be now, and know that thou art perfect.

3. The "Original Simplicity"

LIFE is simple. Being is simple. The universe is simple. Complexity arises in ignorance and self-delusion. The "Original Simplicity"
of Lao-tze is a term expressive of the universe as it is, and not as it
appears. Looking through the woven network of his own illusions,
man sees interminable complication and unfathomable mystery,
and so loses himself in the labyrinths of his own making. Let a
man put away egotism, and he will see the universe in all the
beauty of its pristine simplicity. Let him annihilate the delusion of
the personal "I," and he will destroy all the illusions which spring
from that "I." He will thus "re-become a little child," and will "revert
to Original Simplicity."

When a man succeeds in entirely forgetting (annihilating) his
personal self, he be-comes a mirror in which the universal Reality
is faultlessly reflected. He is awakened, and henceforward he lives,
not in dreams, but realities.

Pythagoras saw the universe in the ten numbers, but even this simplicity may be further reduced, and the universe ultimately be found to be contained in the number ONE, for all the numerals and all their infinite complications are but additions of the One.

Let life cease to be lived as a fragmentary thing, and let it be lived as a perfect Whole; the simplicity of the Perfect will then be revealed. How shall the fragment comprehend the Whole? Yet how simple that the Whole should comprehend the fragment. How shall sin perceive Holiness? Yet how plain that Holiness should understand sin. He who would become the Greater let him abandon the lesser. In no form is the circle contained, but in the circle all forms are contained. In no colour is the radiant light imprisoned, but in the radiant light all colours are embodied, Let a man destroy all the forms of self, and he shall apprehend the Circle of Perfection; let him submerge, in the silent depths of his being, the varying colours of his thoughts and desires, and he shall be illuminated with the White Light of Divine Knowledge. In the perfect chord of music the single note, though forgotten, is indispensably contained, and the drop of water becomes of supreme usefulness by losing itself in the ocean. Sink thyself compassionately in the heart of humanity, and thou shalt reproduce the harmonies of Heaven; lose thyself in unlimited love toward all, and thou shalt work enduring works and shalt become one with the eternal Ocean of Bliss.

Man evolves outward to the periphery of complexity, and then involves backward to the Central Simplicity. When a man discovers that it is mathematically impossible for him to know the universe before knowing himself, he then starts upon the Way which leads to the Original Simplicity. He begins to unfold from within, and as he Unfolds himself, he enfolds the universe.

Cease to speculate about God, and find the all-embracing Good within thee, then shalt thou see the emptiness and vanity of speculation, knowing thyself one with God.

He who will not give up his secret lust, his covetousness, his anger, his opinion about this or that, can see nor know nothing; he will remain a dullard in the school of Wisdom, though he be accounted learned in the colleges.

If a man would find the Key of Knowledge, let him find himself. Thy sins are not thyself; they are not any part of thyself; they are diseases which thou hast come to love. Cease to cling to them, and they will no longer cling to thee. Let them fall away, and thy self shall stand revealed. Thou shalt then know thyself as Comprehensive Vision, Invincible Principle, Immortal Life, and Eternal Good.

The impure man believes impurity to be his rightful condition, but the pure man knows himself as pure being; he also, penetrating the Veils, sees all others as pure being. Purity is extremely simple, and needs no argument to support it; impurity is interminably complex, and is ever involved in defensive argument. Truth lives itself. A blameless life is the only witness of Truth. Men cannot see, and will not accept the witness until they find it within themselves; and having found it, a man becomes silent before his fellows. Truth is so simple that it cannot be found in the region of argument and advertisement, and so silent that it is only manifested in actions.

So extremely simple is Original Simplicity, that a man must let go his hold of everything before he can perceive it. The great arch is strong by virtue of the hollowness underneath, and a wise man becomes strong and invincible by emptying himself.

Meekness, Patience, Love, Compassion, and Wisdom — these are the dominant qualities of Original Simplicity; therefore the imperfect cannot understand it. Wisdom only can apprehend Wisdom, therefore the fool says, "No man is wise." The imperfect man says, "No man can be perfect," and he therefore remains where he is. Though he live with a perfect man all his life, he shall not behold his perfection. Meekness he will call cowardice; Patience, Love, and Compassion he will see as weakness; and Wisdom will appear to him as folly. Faultless discrimination belongs to the Perfect Whole, and resides not in any part, therefore men are exhorted to refrain from judgement until they have themselves manifested the Perfect Life.

Arriving at Original Simplicity, opacity disappears, and the universal transparency becomes apparent. He who has found the indwelling Reality of his own being has found the original and universal Reality. Knowing the Divine Heart within, all hearts are known, and the thoughts of all men become his who has become the master of his own thoughts; therefore the good man does not defend himself, but moulds the minds of others to his own likeness.

As the problematical transcends crudity, so Pure Goodness transcends the problematical. All problems vanish when Pure Goodness is reached; therefore the good man is called "The slayer of illusions." What problem can vex where sin is not? O thou who strivest loudly and restest not! retire into the holy silence of thine own being, and live therefrom. So shalt thou, finding Pure Goodness, rend in twain the Veil of the Temple of Illusion, and shalt enter into the Patience, Peace, and transcendent Glory of the Perfect, for Pure Goodness and Original Simplicity are one.

4. The Unfailing Wisdom

A MAN should be superior to his possessions, his body, his circumstances and surroundings, and the opinions of others, and their attitude towards him. Until he is this, he is not strong and steadfast. He should also rise superior to his own desires and opinions; and until he is this, he is not wise.

The man who identifies himself with his possessions will feel that all is lost when these are lost; he who regards himself as the outcome and the tool of circumstances will weakly fluctuate with every change in his outward condition; and great will be his unrest and pain who seeks to stand upon the approbation of others.

To detach oneself from every outward thing, and to rest securely upon the inward Virtue, this is the Unfailing Wisdom. Having this Wisdom, a man will be the same whether in riches or poverty. The one cannot add to his strength, nor the other rob him of his serenity. Neither can riches defile him who has washed away all the inward defilement, nor the lack of them degrade him who has ceased to degrade the temple of his soul.

To refuse to be enslaved by any outward thing or happening, regarding all such things and happenings as for your use, for your education, this is Wisdom. To the wise all occurrences are good, and, having no eye for evil, they grow wiser every day. They utilize all things, and thus put all things under their feet. They see all their mistakes as soon as made, and accept them as lessons of intrinsic value, knowing that are no mistakes in the Divine Order. They thus rapidly approach the Divine Perfection. They are moved by none, yet learn from all. They crave love from none, yet give love to all. To learn, and not to be shaken; to love where one is not Loved : herein lies the strength which shall never fail a man. The man who says in his heart, "I will teach all men, and learn from none," will neither teach nor learn whilst he is in that frame of mind, but will remain in his folly.

All strength and wisdom and power and knowledge a man will

find within himself, but. he will not find it in egotism; he will only find it in obedience, submission, and willingness to learn. He must obey the Higher, and not glorify himself in the lower. He who stands upon egotism, rejecting reproof, instruction, and the lessons of experience, will surely fall; yea, he is already fallen. Said a great Teacher to his disciples, "Those who shall be a lamp unto them-selves, relying upon themselves only, and not relying upon any external help, but holding fast to the Truth as their lamp, and, seeking their salvation in the Truth alone, shall not look for assistance to any besides themselves, it is they among my disciples who shall reach the very topmost height! But they must be willing to learn." The wise man is always anxious to learn, but never anxious to teach, for he knows that the true Teacher is in the heart of every man, and must ultimately be found there by all. The foolish man, being governed largely by vanity, is very anxious to teach, but unwilling to learn, not having found the Holy Teacher within who speaks wisdom to the humbly listening soul. Be self-reliant, but let thy self-reliance be saintly and not selfish.

Folly and wisdom, weakness and strength are within a man, and not in any external thing, neither do they spring from any external cause. A man cannot be strong for another, he can only be strong for himself; he cannot overcome for another, he can only overcome of himself. You may learn of another, but you must accomplish for yourself. Put away all external props, and rely upon thy Truth within you. A creed will not bear a man up in the hour of temptation; he must possess the inward Knowledge which slays temptation. A speculative philosophy will prove a shadowy thing in the time of calamity; a man must have the inward Wisdom which puts an end to grief.

Goodness, which is the aim of all religions, is distinct from religions themselves. Wisdom, which is the aim of every philosophy, is distinct from all philosophies. The Unfailing Wisdom is found only by constant practice in pure thinking and well-doing; by harmonizing one's mind and heart to those things which are beautiful, lovable, and true.

In whatever condition a man finds himself, he can always find the True; and he can find it only by so utilizing his present condition as to become strong and wise. The effeminate hankering after rewards, and the craven fear of punishment, let them be put away forever, and let a man joyfully bend himself to the faithful performance of all his duties, forgetting himself and his worthless pleasures, and living strong and pure and self-contained; so shall he surely find the Unfailing Wisdom, the God-like Patience and strength. "The situation that has not its Duty, its Ideal, was never yet occupied by man. . . . Here or nowhere is thy Ideal. Work it out therefrom, and, working, believe, live, be free. The Ideal is in thyself, the impediment, too, is in thyself: thy condition is but the stuff thou art to shape that same Ideal out of. What matters whether such stuff be of this sort or that, so the form thou give it be heroic, be poetic? Oh, thou that pinest in the imprisonment of the Actual, and criest bitterly to the gods for a kingdom wherein to rule and create, know this of a truth: the thing thou seekest is already within thee, here and now, couldest thou only see!"

All that is beautiful and blessed is in thyself, not in thy neighbour's wealth. Thou art poor? Thou art poor indeed if thou art not stronger than thy poverty! Thou hast suffered calamities? Well, wilt thou cure calamity by adding anxiety to it? Canst thou mend a broken vase by weeping over it or restore a lost delight by thy lamentations? There is no evil but will vanish if thou wilt wisely meet it. The God-like soul does not grieve over that which has been, is, or will be, hut perpetually rinds the Divine Good, and gains wisdom by every occurrence.

Fear is the shadow of selfishness, and cannot live where loving Wisdom is. Doubt, anxiety, and worry are unsubstantial shades in the underworld of self, and shall no more trouble him who will climb the serene altitudes of his soul. Grief, also, will be for ever dispelled by him who will comprehend the Law of his being. He who so comprehends shall find the Supreme Law of Life, and he shall find that it is Love, that it is imperishable Love. He shall become one with that Love, and loving all, with mind freed from all hatred and folly, he shall receive the invincible protection which Love affords. Claiming nothing, he shall suffer no loss; seeking no pleasure, he shall find no grief; and employing all his powers as instruments of service, he shall evermore live in the highest state of blessedness and bliss.

Know this: — thou makest and unmakest thyself; thou standest and fallest by what thou art. Thou art a slave if thou prefer-rest to be; thou art a master if thou wilt make thyself one. Build upon thy animal desires and intellectual opinions, and thou buildest upon the sand; build upon Virtue and Holiness, and no wind nor tide shall shake thy strong abode. So shall the Unfailing Wisdom uphold thee in every emergency, and the Everlasting Arms gather thee to thy peace.

"Lay up each year Thy harvest of well-doing, wealth that kings

Nor thieves can take away. When all the things

Thou callest thine, goods, pleasures, honours fall,

Thou in thy virtue shalt survive them all."

5. The Might Of Meekness

THE mountain bends not to the fiercest storm, but it shields the fledgling and the lamb; and though all men tread upon it, yet it protects them, and bears them up upon its deathless bosom. Even so is it with the meek man who, though shaken and disturbed by none, yet compassionately bends to shield the lowliest creature, and, though he may be despised, lifts all men up, and lovingly protects them.

As glorious as the mountain in its silent is the divine man in his silent Meekness; like its form, his loving comparison is expansive and sublime. Truly his body, like the mountain's base, is fixed in the valleys and the mists; but the summit of his being is eternally bathed in cloudless glory, and lives with the Silences.

He who has found Meekness has found divinity; he has realized the divine consciousness, and knows himself as divine. He also knows all others as divine, though they know it not themselves, being asleep and dreaming. Meekness is a divine quality, and as such is all powerful. The meek man overcomes by not resisting, and by allowing himself to be defeated he attains to the Supreme Conquest.

The man who conquers another by force is strong; the man who conquers himself by Meekness is mighty. He who conquers another by force will himself likewise be conquered; he who conquers himself by Meekness will never be overthrown, for the human cannot overcome the divine. The meek man is triumphant in defeat. Socrates lives the more by being put to death; in the crucified Jesus the risen Christ is revealed, and Stephen in receiving his stoning defies the hurting power of stones. That which is real cannot be destroyed, but only that which is unreal. When a man finds that within him which is real, which is constant, abiding, changeless, and eternal, he enters into that Reality, and becomes meek. All the powers of darkness will come against him. but they will do him no hurt, and will at last, depart from him.

The meek man is found in the time of trial; when other men fall he stands. His patience is not destroyed by the foolish passions of others, and when they come against him he does not "strive nor cry," He knows the utter powerlessness of all evil, having overcome it in himself, and lives in the changeless strength and power of divine Good.

Meekness is one aspect of the operation of that changeless Love which is at the Heart of all things, and is therefore an imperishable quality. He who lives in it is without fear, knowing the Highest, and having the lowest under his feet.

The meek man shines in darkness, and flourishes in obscurity. Meekness cannot boast, nor advertise itself, nor thrive on popularity. It is practised, and is seen or not seen; being a spiritual quality it is perceived only by the eye of the spirit. Those who are not spiritually awakened see it not, nor do they love it, being enamoured of, and blinded by, worldly shows and appearances. Nor does history take note of the meek man. Its glory is that of strife and self-aggrandizement; his is the glory of peace and gentleness. History chronicles the earthly, not the heavenly acts. Yet though he lives in obscurity he cannot be hidden (how can light be hid?); he continues to shine after he has withdrawn himself from the world, and is worshipped by the world which knew him not.

That the meek man should be neglected, abused, or misunderstood is reckoned by him as of no account, and therefore not to be considered, much less resisted. He knows that all such weapons are the flimsiest and most ineffectual of shadows. To them, therefore, who give him evil he gives good. He resists none, and thereby conquers all.

He who imagines he can be injured by others, and who seeks to justify and defend himself against them, does not understand Meekness, does not comprehend the essence and meaning of life. "He abused me, he beat me, he defeated me, he robbed me.— In those who harbour such thoughts hatred will never cease . . . for hatred ceases not by hatred at any time; hatred ceases by love." What sayest thou, thy neighbour has spoken thee falsely? Well, what of that? Can a falsity hurt thee? That which is false is false, and there is an end of it. It is without life, and without power to hurt any but him who seeks to hurt by it. It is nothing to thee that thy neighbour should speak falsely of thee, but it is much to thee that thou shouldst resist him, and seek to justify thyself, for, by so doing, thou givest life and vitality to thy neighbour's falseness, so that thou art injured and distressed. Take all evil out of thine own heart, then shalt thou see the folly of resisting it in another. Thou wilt be trodden on? Thou art trodden on already if thou thinkest thus. The injury that thou seest as coming from another comes only from thyself. The wrong thought, or word, or act of another has no power to hurt thee unless thou galvanize it into life by thy passionate resistance, and so receivest it into thyself. If any man slander me, that is his concern, not mine. I have to do with my own soul, not with my neighbour's. Though all the world misjudge me, it is no business of mine; but that I should possess my soul in Purity and Love, that is all my business. There shall be no end to strife until men cease to justify themselves. He who would have wars cease let him cease to defend any party — let him cease to defend himself. Not by strife can peace come, but by ceasing from strife. The glory of Cæsar resides in the resistance of his enemies. They resist and fall. Give to Cæsar that which Cæsar demands, and Cæsar's glory and power are gone. Thus, by submission does the meek man conquer the strong man : but it is not that outward show of submission which is slavery, it is that inward and spiritual submission which is freedom.

Claiming no rights, the meek man is not troubled with self-defence and self-justification; he lives in love, and therefore comes under the immediate and vital protection of the Great Love which is the Eternal Law of the universe. He neither claims nor seeks his own; thus do all things come to him, and all the universe shields and protects him.

He who says, "I have tried Meekness, and it has failed," has not tried Meekness. It cannot be tried as an experiment. It is only arrived at by unreserved self-sacrifice. Meekness does not consist merely in non-resistance in action; it consists pre-eminently in non-resistance in thought, in ceasing to hold or to have any selfish, condemnatory, or retaliatory thoughts. The meek man, therefore, cannot "take offence" or have his "feelings hurt," living above hatred, folly, and vanity. Meekness can never fail.

O thou who searchest for the Heavenly Life! Strive after Meekness; increase thy patience and forbearance day by day; bid thy tongue cease from all harsh words; withdraw thy mind from selfish arguments, and refuse to brood upon thy wrongs: so living, thou shalt carefully tend and cultivate the pure and delicate flower of Meekness in thy heart, until at last, its divine sweetness and purity and beauteous perfection shall be revealed to thee, and thou shalt become gentle, joyful, and strong. Repine not that thou art surrounded by irritable and selfish people; but rather rejoice that thou art so favoured as to have thine own imperfections revealed to thee, and that thou art so placed as to necessitate within thee a constant struggle for self-mastery and the attainment, of perfection. The more there is of harshness and selfishness around thee the greater is the need of thy Meekness and love. If others seek to wrong thee, all the more is it needful that thou shouldst cease from all wrong, and live in love; if others preach Meekness, humility, and love, and do not practice these, trouble not. nor be annoyed; but do thou, in the silence of thy heart, and in thy contact with others, practice these things, and they shall preach themselves. And though thou utter no declamatory word, and stand before no gathered audience, thou shalt teach the whole world. As thou becomest meek, thou shalt learn the deepest secrets of the universe. Nothing is hidden from him who overcomes himself. Into the cause of causes shalt thou penetrate, and lifting, one after another, every veil of illusion, shalt reach at last the inmost Heart of Being. Thus becoming one with Life, thou shalt know till life, and, seeing into causes, and knowing realities, thou shalt be no more anxious about thyself, and others, and the world, but shalt see that all things that are, are engines of the Great Law. Canopied with gentleness, thou shalt bless where others curse; love where others hate; forgive where others condemn; yield where others strive; give up where others grasp: lose where others gain, And in their strength they shall be weak ; and in thy weakness thou shalt be strong; yea, thou shalt mightily prevail. He that hath not unbroken gentleness hath not Truth:

"Therefore when Heaven would save a man, it enfolds him with gentleness."

6. The Righteous Man

THE righteous man is invincible. No enemy can possibly overcome or confound him; and he needs no other protection than that of his own integrity and holiness.

As it is impossible for evil to overcome Good, so the righteous man can never be brought low by the unrighteous. Slander, envy, hatred, malice can never reach him, nor cause him any suffering, and those who try to injure him only succeed ultimately in bringing ignominy upon themselves.

The righteous man, having nothing to hide, committing no acts which require stealth, and harbouring no thoughts and desires which he would not like others to know, is fearless and unashamed. His step is firm, his body upright, and his speech direct and without ambiguity. He looks everybody in the face. How can he fear any who wrongs none? How can he be ashamed before any who deceives none? And ceasing from all wrong he can never be wronged; ceasing from all deceit he can never be deceived.

The righteous man, performing all his duties with scrupulous diligence, and living above sin, is invulnerable at every point. He who has slain the inward enemies of virtue can never be brought low by any outward enemy; neither does he need to seek any protection against them, righteousness being an all-sufficient protection.

The unrighteous man is vulnerable at almost every point; living in his passions, the slave of prejudices, impulses, and ill-formed opinions, he is continually suffering (as he imagines) at the hands of others. The slanders, attacks, and accusations of others cause him great suffering because they have a basis of truth in himself; and not having the protection of righteousness, he endeavours to justify and protect himself by resorting to retaliation and specious argument, and even to subterfuge and deceit.

The partially righteous man is vulnerable at all those points where he falls short of righteousness, and should the righteous man fall from his righteousness, and give way to one sin, his invincibility is gone, for he has thereby placed himself where attack and accusation can justly reach and injure him, because he has first injured himself.

If a man suffers or is injured through the instrumentality of others, let him look to himself, and, putting aside self-pity and self-defence, he will find in his own heart the source of all his woe.

No evil can happen to the righteous man who has cut off the source of evil in himself; living in the All-Good, and abstaining from sin in thought, word and deed, whatever happens to him is good; neither can any person, event, or circumstance cause him suffering, for the tyranny of circumstance is utterly destroyed for him who has broken the bonds of sin.

The suffering, the sorrowing, the weary, and broken-hearted ever seek a sorrowless refuge, a haven of perpetual peace. Let such fly to the refuge of the righteous life; let them come now and enter the haven of the sinless state, for sorrow cannot overtake the righteous; suffering cannot reach him who does not waste in self-seeking his spiritual substance; and he cannot be afflicted by weariness and unrest whose heart is at peace with all.

7. Perfect Love

THE Children of Light, who abide in the Kingdom of Heaven, see the universe, and all that it contains, as the manifestation of one Law — the Law of Love. They see Love as the moulding, sustaining, protecting, and perfecting Power immanent in all things animate and inanimate. To them Love is not merely and only a rule of life, it is the Law of Life, it is Life itself. Knowing this, they order their whole life in accordance with Love, not regarding their own personality. By thus practising obedience to the Highest, to divine Love, they become conscious partakers of the power of Love, and so arrive at perfect Freedom as Masters of Destiny.

The universe is preserved because Love is at the Heart of it. Love is the only preservative power. Whilst there is hatred in the heart of man, he imagines the Law to be cruel, but when his heart is mellowed by Compassion and Love, he perceives that the Law is Infinite Kindness. So kind is the Law that it protects man against his own ignorance, Man, in his puny efforts to subvert the Law by attaching undue importance to his own little personality, brings upon himself such trains of suffering that he is at last compelled, in the depth of his afflictions, to seek for Wisdom; and finding Wisdom, he finds Love, and knows it as the Law of his being, the Law of the universe. Love does not punish; man punishes himself by his own hatred; by striving to preserve evil which has no life by which to preserve itself, and by trying to subvert Love, which can neither be overcome nor destroyed, being of the substance of Life. When a man burns himself, does he accuse the fire? Therefore, when a man suffers, let him look for some ignorance or disobedience within himself.

Love is Perfect Harmony, pure Bliss, and contains, therefore, no element of suffering. Let a man think no thought and do no act which is not in accordance with pure Love, and suffering shall no more trouble him. If a man would know Love, and partake of its undying bliss, he must practice it in his heart; he must become Love.

He who always acts from the spirit of Love is never deserted, is never left in a dilemma or difficulty, for Love (impersonal Love) is both Knowledge and Power. He who has learned how to Love has learned how to master every difficulty, how to transmute every failure into success, how to clothe every event and condition in garments of blessedness and beauty.

The way to Love is by self-mastery, and, travelling that way, a man builds himself up in Knowledge as he proceeds. Arriving at Love, he enters into full possession of body and mind, by right of the divine Power which he has earned.

"Perfect Love casteth out fear." To know Love is to know that there is no harmful power in the whole Universe. Even sin itself, which the worldly and unbelieving imagine is so unconquerable, is known as a very weak and perishable thing, that shrinks away and disappears before the compelling power of Good. Perfect Love is perfect Harmlessness. And he who has destroyed, in himself, all thoughts of harm, and all desire to harm, receives the universal protection, and knows himself to be invincible.

Perfect Love is perfect Patience. Anger and irritability cannot dwell with it nor come near it. It sweetens every bitter occasion with the perfume of holiness, and transmutes trial into divine strength. Complaint, is foreign to it. He who loves bewails nothing, but accepts all things and conditions as heavenly guests; he is therefore constantly blessed, and sorrow does not overtake him.

Perfect Love is perfect Trust. He who has destroyed the desire to grasp can never be troubled with the fear of loss. Loss and gain are alike foreign to him. Steadfastly maintaining a loving attitude of mind toward all, and pursuing, in the performance of his duties, a constant and loving activity, Love protects him and evermore supplies him in fullest measure with all that he needs.

Perfect Love is perfect Power. The wisely loving heart commands without exercising any authority. All things and all men obey him who obeys the Highest. He thinks, and lo! he has already accomplished! He speaks, and behold! a world hangs upon his simple utterances! He has harmonized his thoughts with the Imperishable and Unconquerable Forces, and for him weakness and uncertainty are no more. His every thought is a purpose; his every act an accomplishment; he moves with the Great Law, not setting his puny personal will against it, and he thus becomes a channel through which the Divine Power can flow in unimpeded and beneficent expression. He has thus become Power itself.

Perfect Love is perfect Wisdom. The man who loves all is the man who knows all. Having thoroughly learned the lessons of his own heart, he knows the tasks and trials of other hearts, and adapts himself to them gently and without ostentation. Love illuminates the intellect; without it the intellect is blind and cold and lifeless. Love succeeds where the intellect fails; sees where the intellect is blind ; knows where the intellect is ignorant, Reason is only completed in Love, and is ultimately absorbed in it. Love is the Supreme Reality in the universe, and as such it contains all Truth. Infinite Tenderness enfolds and cherishes the universe; therefore is the wise man gentle and childlike and tender-hearted. He sees that the one thing which all creatures need is Love, and he gives unstintingly. He knows that all occasions require the adjusting power of Love, and he ceases from harshness.

To the eye of Love all things are revealed, not as an infinity of complex effects, but in the light of Eternal Principles, out of which spring all causes and effects, and back into which they return. "God is Love;" therefore than Love there is nothing more perfect. He who would find pure Knowledge let him find pure Love.

Perfect Love is perfect Peace. He who dwells with it has completed his pilgrimage in the underworld of sorrow. With mind calm and heart at rest, he has banished the shadows of grief, and knows the deathless Life.

If thou wouldst perfect thyself in Knowledge, perfect thyself in Love. If thou wouldst reach the Highest, ceaselessly cultivate a loving and compassionate heart.

8. Perfect Freedom

THERE is no bondage in the Heavenly Life. There is Perfect Freedom. This is its great glory. This Supreme Freedom is gained only by obedience. He who obeys the Highest cooperates with the Highest, and so masters every force within himself and every condition without. A man may choose the lower and neglect the Higher, but the Higher is never overcome by the lower: herein lies the revelation of Freedom. Let a man choose the Higher and abandon the lower; he shall then establish himself as an Overcomer, and shall realize Perfect Freedom.

To give the reins to inclination is the only slavery; to conquer oneself is the only freedom. The slave to self loves his chains, and will not have one of them broken for fear he would be depriving himself of some cherished delight. He clings to his gratifications and vanities, regarding freedom from them as an empty and undesirable condition. He thus defeats and enslaves himself.

By self-enlightenment is Perfect Freedom found. Whilst a man remains ignorant of himself, of his desires, of his emotions and thoughts, and of the inward causes which mould his life and destiny, having neither control nor understanding of himself, he will remain in bondage to passion, sorrow, suffering, and fluctuating fortune. The Land of Perfect Freedom lies through the Gate of Knowledge.

All outward oppression is but the shadow and effect of the real oppression within. For ages the oppressed have cried for liberty, and a thousand man-made statutes have failed to give it to them. They can give it only to themselves; they shall find it only in obedience to the Divine Statutes which are inscribed upon their hearts. Let them resort to the inward Freedom, and the shadow of oppression shall no more darken the earth. Let men cease to oppress themselves, and no man shall oppress his brother.

Men legislate for an outward freedom, yet continue to render such freedom impossible of achievement by fostering an inward condition of enslavement. They thus pursue a shadow without, and ignore the substance within. Man will be free when he is freed from self. All outward forms of bondage and oppression will cease to be when man ceases to be the willing bond-slave of passion, error, and ignorance. Freedom is to the free.

Whilst men cling to weakness they cannot have strength; whilst they love darkness they can receive no light; and so long as they prefer bondage they can enjoy no liberty. Strength, light, and freedom are ready now, and can be had by all who love them, who aspire to them. Freedom does not reside in coöperative aggression, for this will always produce, reactively, coöperative defence — warfare, hatred, party strife, and the destruction of liberty. Freedom resides in individual self-conquest. The emancipation of Humanity is frustrated and withheld by the self-enslavement of the unit. Thou who criest to man and God for liberty, liberate thyself!

The Heavenly Freedom is freedom from passion, from cravings, from opinions, from the tyranny of the flesh, and the tyranny of the intellect — this first, and then all outward freedom, as effect to cause. The Freedom that begins within, and extends outwardly until it embraces the whole man, is an emancipation so complete, all-embracing, and perfect as to leave no galling fetter unbroken. Free thy soul from all sin, and thou shalt walk a freed and fearless man in the midst of a world of fearful slaves; and, seeing thee, many slaves shall take heart and shall join thee in thy glorious freedom.

He who says, "My worldly duties are irksome to me: I will leave them and go into solitude, where I shall be as free as the air," and thinks to gain freedom thus, will find only a harder slavery. The tree of Freedom is rooted in Duty, and he who would pluck its sweet fruits must discover joy in Duty.

Glad-hearted, calm, and ready for all tasks is he who is freed from self. Irksomeness and weariness cannot enter his heart, and his divine strength lightens every burden so that its weight is not felt. He does not run away from Duty with his chains about him, but breaks them and stands free.

Make thyself pure; make thyself proof against weakness, temptation, and sin; for only in thine own heart and mind shalt thou find that Perfect Freedom for which the whole world sighs and seeks in vain.

9. Greatness And Goodness

GOODNESS, simplicity, greatness — these three are one, and this trinity of perfection cannot be separated. All greatness springs from goodness, and all goodness is profoundly simple, Without goodness there is no greatness. Some men pass through the world as destructive forces, like the tornado or the avalanche, but they are not great; they are to greatness as the avalanche is to the mountain. The work of greatness is enduring and preservative, and not violent and destructive. The greatest souls are the most gentle.

Greatness is never obtrusive. It works in silence, seeking no recognition. This is why it is not easily perceived and recognized. Like the mountain, it towers up in its vastness, so that those in its immediate vicinity, who receive its shelter and shade, do not see it. Its sublime grandeur is only beheld as they recede from it. The great man is not seen by his contemporaries; the majesty of his form is only outlined by its recession in time. This is the awe and enchantment of distance. Men occupy themselves with the small things; their houses, trees, lands. Few contemplate the mountain at whose base they live, and fewer still essay to explore it. But in the distance these small thing disappear, and then the solitary beauty of the mountain is perceived. Popularity, noisy obtrusiveness, and shallow show, these superficialities rapidly disappear, and leave behind no enduring mark: whereas greatness slowly emerges from obscurity, and endures for ever.

Jewish Rabbi and rabble alike saw not the divine beauty of Jesus; they saw only an unlettered carpenter. To his acquaintances, Homer was only a blind beggar, but the centuries reveal him as Homer the immortal poet. Two hundred years after the farmer of Stratford (and all that is known of him) has disappeared, the real Shakespeare is discerned. All true genius is impersonal. It belongs not to the man through whom it is manifested; it belongs to all. It is a diffusion of pure Truth: the Light of Heaven descending on all mankind.

Every work of genius, in whatsoever department of art, is a symbolic manifestation of impersonal Truth. It is universal, and finds a response in every heart in every age and race. Anything short of this is not genius, is not greatness. That work which defends a religion perishes; it is religion that lives. Theories about immortality fade away; immortal man endures; commentaries upon Truth come to the dust; Truth alone remains. That only is true in art which represents the True; that only is great in life which is universally and eternally true. And the True is the Good; the Good is the True.

Every immortal work springs from the Eternal Goodness in the human heart, and it is clothed with the sweet and unaffected simplicity of goodness. The greatest art is, like nature, artless. It knows no trick, no pose, no studied effort. There are no stage-tricks in Shakespeare; and he is the greatest of dramatists because he is the simplest. The critics, not understanding the wise simplicity of greatness, always condemn the loftiest work. They cannot discriminate between the childish and the childlike. The True, the Beautiful, the Great, is always childlike, and is perennially fresh and young.

The great man is always the good man; he is always simple. He draws from, nay, lives in, the inexhaustible fountain of divine Goodness within; he inhabits the Heavenly Places; communes with the vanished great ones; lives with the Invisible: he is inspired, and breathes the airs of Heaven.

He who would be great let him learn to be good. He will therefore become great by not seeking greatness. Aiming at greatness a man arrives at nothingness; aiming at nothingness he arrives at greatness. The desire to be great is an indication of littleness, of personal vanity and obtrusiveness. The willingness to disappear from gaze, the utter absence of self-aggrandizement is the witness of greatness.

Littleness seeks and loves authority. Greatness is never authoritative, and it thereby becomes the authority to which the after ages appeal. He who seeks, loses; he who is willing to lose, wins all men. Be thy simple self, thy better self, thy impersonal self, and lo! thou art great! He who selfishly seeks authority shall succeed only in becoming a trembling apologist courting protection behind the back of acknowledged greatness. He who will become the servant of all men, desiring no personal authority, shall live as a man, and shall be called great. "Abide in the simple and noble regions of thy life, obey thy heart, and thou shalt reproduce the foreworld again." Forget thine own little self, and fall back upon the Universal self, and thou shalt reproduce, in living and enduring forms, a thousand beautiful experiences; thou shalt find within thyself that simple goodness which is greatness.

"It is as easy to be great as to be small," says Emerson; and he utters a profound truth. Forgetfulness of self is the whole of greatness, as it is the whole of goodness and happiness. In a fleeting moment of self-forgetfulness the smallest soul becomes great; extend that moment indefinitely, and there is a great soul, a great life. Cast away thy personality (thy petty cravings, vanities, and ambitions) as a worthless garment, and dwell in the loving, compassionate, selfless regions of thy soul, and thou art no longer small—thou art great.

Claiming personal authority, a man descends into littleness; practising goodness, a man ascends into greatness. The presumptuousness of the small may, for a time, obscure the humility of the great, but it is at last swallowed up by it, as the noisy river is lost in the calm ocean.

The vulgarity of ignorance and the pride of learning must disappear. Their worthlessness is equal. They have no part in the Soul of Goodness. If thou wouldst do, thou must be. Thou shalt not mistake information for Knowledge; thou must know thyself as pure Knowledge. Thou shalt not confuse learning with Wisdom; thou must apprehend thyself as undefiled Wisdom.

Wouldst thou write a living book? Thou must first live; thou shalt draw around thee the mystic garment of a manifold experience, and shalt learn, in enjoyment and suffering, gladness and sorrow, conquest and defeat, that which no book and no teacher can teach thee. Thou shalt learn of life, of thy soul; thou shalt tread the Lonely Road, and shalt become; thou shalt be. Thou shalt then write thy book, and it shall live; it shall be more than a book. Let thy book first live in thee, then shalt thou live in thy book.

Wouldst thou carve a statue that shall captivate the ages, or paint a picture that shall endure? Thou shalt acquaint thyself with the divine Beauty within thee. Thou shalt comprehend and adore the Invisible Beauty ; thou shalt know the Principles which are the soul of Form; thou shalt perceive the matchless symmetry and faultless proportions of Life, of Being, of the Universe; thus knowing the eternally True thou shalt carve or paint the indescribably Beautiful.

Wouldst thou produce an imperishable poem? Thou shalt first live thy poem; thou shalt think and act rhythmically; thou shalt find the never-failing source of inspiration in the loving places of thy heart. Then shall immortal lines flow from thee without effort, and, as the flowers of wood and field spontaneously spring, so shall beautiful thoughts grow up in thine heart and, enshrined in words as moulds to their beauty, shall subdue the hearts of men.

Wouldst thou compose such music as shall gladden and uplift the world? Thou shalt adjust thy soul to the Heavenly Harmonies. Thou shalt know that thyself, that life and the universe is Music. Thou shalt touch the chords of Life. Thou shalt know that Music is everywhere; that it is the Heart of Being; then shalt thou hear with thy spiritual ear the Deathless Symphonies.

Wouldst thou preach the living word? Thou shalt forego thyself, and become that Word. Thou shalt know one thing—that the human heart is good, is divine; thou shalt live on one thing—Love. Thou shalt love all, seeing no evil, thinking no evil, believing no evil; then, though thou speak but little, thy every act shall be a power, thy every word a precept. By thy pure thought, thy selfless deed, though it appear hidden, thou shalt preach, down the ages, to untold multitudes of aspiring souls.

To him who chooses Goodness, sacrificing all, is given that which is more than and includes all. He becomes the possessor of the Best, communes with the Highest, and enters the company of the Great.

The greatness that is flawless, rounded, and complete is above and beyond all art. It is Perfect Goodness in manifestation; therefore the greatest souls are always Teachers.

10. Heaven In The Heart

THE toil of life ceases when the heart is pure. When the mind is harmonized with the Divine Law the wheel of drudgery ceases to turn, and all work is transmuted into joyful activity. The pure-hearted are as the lilies of the field, which toil not, yet are fed and clothed from the abundant storehouse of the All-Good. But the lily is not lethargic; it is ceaselessly active, drawing nourishment from earth and air and sun. By the Divine Power immanent within it, it builds itself up, cell by cell, opening itself to the light, growing and expanding towards the perfect flower. So is it with those who, having yielded up self-will, have learned to coöperate with the Divine Will. They grow in grace, goodness, and beauty, freed from anxiety, and without friction and toil. And they never work in vain; there is no waste action. Every thought, act, and thing done subserves the Divine Purpose, and adds to the sum-total of the world's happiness.

Heaven is in the heart. They will look for it in vain who look elsewhere. In no outward place will the soul find Heaven until it finds it within itself; for, wherever the soul goes, its thoughts and desires will go with it; and, howsoever beautiful may be its outward dwelling-place, if there is sin within, there will be darkness and gloom without, for sin always casts a dark shadow over the pathway of the soul—the shadow of sorrow.

This world is beautiful, transcendently and wonderfully beautiful. Its beauties and inspiring wonders cannot be numbered; yet, to the sin-sodden mind, it appears as a dark and joyless place. Where passion and self are, there is hell, and there are all the pains of hell; where Holiness and Love are, there is Heaven, and there are all the joys of Heaven.

Heaven is here. It is also everywhere. It is wherever there is a pure heart. The whole universe is abounding with joy, but the sin-bound heart can neither see, hear, nor partake of it. No one is, or can be, arbitrarily shut out from Heaven; each shuts himself out. Its Golden Gates are eternally ajar, but the selfish cannot find them; they mourn, yet see not; they cry, but hear not. Only to those who turn their eyes to heavenly things, their ears to heavenly sounds, are the happy Portals of the Kingdom revealed, and they enter and are glad.

All life is gladness when the heart is right, when it is attuned to the sweet chords of holy Love. Life is Religion, Religion is life and all is Joy and Gladness. The jarring notes of creeds and parties, the black shadows of sin, let them pass away for ever; they cannot enter the Door of Life; they form no part of Religion. Joy, Music, Beauty—these belong to the True Order of things; they are of the texture of the universe; of these is the divine Garment of Life woven. Pure Religion is glad, not gloomy. It is Light without darkness or shadow.

Despondency, disappointment, grief — these are the reflex aspects of pleasurable excitement, self-seeking, and desire. Give up the latter, and the former will for ever disappear; then there remains the perfect Bliss of Heaven.

Abounding and unalloyed Happiness is man's true life; perfect Blessedness is his rightful portion ; and when he loses his false life and finds the true he enters into the full possession of his Kingdom. The Kingdom of Heaven is man's Home; and it is here and now, it is in his own heart, and he is not left without Guides, if he wills to find it. All man's sorrows and sufferings are the result of his own self-elected estrangement from the Divine Source, the All-Good, the Father, the Heart of Love. Let him return to his Home; his peace awaits him.

The Heavenly-hearted are without sorrow and suffering, because they are without sin. What the worldly-minded call troubles they regard as pleasant tasks of Love and Wisdom. Troubles belong to hell; they do not enter Heaven. This is so simple it should not appear strange. If you have a trouble it is in your own mind, and nowhere else; you make it, it is not made for you; it is not in your task; it is not in that outward thing. You are its creator, and it derives its life from you only. Look upon all your difficulties as lessons to be learned, as' aids to spiritual growth, and lo! they are difficulties no longer! This is one of the Pathways up to Heaven.

To transmute everything into Happiness and Joy, this is supremely the work and duty of the Heavenly-minded man. To reduce everything to wretchedness and deprivation is the process which the worldly-minded unconsciously pursue. To live in Love is to work in Joy. Love is the magic that transforms all things into power and beauty. It brings plenty out of poverty, power out of weakness, loveliness out of deformity, sweetness out of bitterness, light out of darkness, and produces all blissful conditions out of its own substantial but indefinable essence.

He who loves can never want. The universe belongs to Goodness, and it therefore belongs to the good man. It can be possessed by all without stint or shrinking, for Goodness, and the abundance of Goodness (material, mental, and spiritual abundance), is inexhaustible. Think lovingly, speak lovingly, act lovingly, and your every need shall be supplied; you shall not walk in desert places, and no danger shall overtake you.

Love sees with faultless vision, judges true judgement, acts in wisdom. Look through the eyes of Love, and you shall see everywhere the Beautiful and True; judge with the mind of Love, and you shall err not, shall wake no wail of sorrow; act in the spirit of Love, and you shall strike undying harmonies upon the Harp of Life.

Make no compromise with self. Cease not to strive until your whole being is swallowed up in Love. To love all and always—this is the Heaven of heavens. "Let there be nothing within thee that is not very beautiful and very gentle, and then will there be nothing without thee that is not beautified and softened by the spell of thy presence." All that you do, let it be done in calm wisdom, and not from desire, impulse, or opinion; this is the Heavenly way of action.

Purify your thought-world until no stain is left, and you will ascend into Heaven while living in the body. You will then see the things of the outward world clothed in all beautiful forms. Having found the Divine Beauty within ourselves, it springs to life in every outward thing. To the beautified soul the world is beautiful.

Undeveloped souls are merely unopened flowers. The perfect Beauty lies concealed within, and will one day reveal itself to the full-orbed light of Heaven. Seeing men thus, we stand where evil is not, and where the eye beholds only good. Herein lies the peace and patience and beauty of Love—it sees no evil. He who loves thus becomes the protector of all men. Though in their ignorance they should hate him, he shields and loves them.

What gardener is so foolish as to condemn his flowers because they do not develop in a day? Learn to love, and you shall see in all souls, even those called "degraded," the Divine Beauty, and shall know that it will not fail to come forth in its own season. This is one of the Heavenly Visions; it is out of this that Gladness comes.

Sin, sorrow, suffering — these are the dark gropings of the un-opened soul for Light. Open the petals of your soul and let the glorious Light stream in.

Every sinful soul is an unresolved harmony. It shall at last strike the Perfect Chord, and swell the joyful melodies of Heaven.

Hell is the preparation for Heaven; and out of the debris of its ruined hovels are built pleasant mansions wherein the perfected soul may dwell.

Night is only a fleeting shadow which the world casts, and sorrow is but a transient shade cast by the self. "Come out into the Sunlight." Know this, O reader! that you are divine. You are not cut off from the Divine except in your own unbelief. Rise up, O Son of God! and shake off the nightmare of sin which binds you; accept your heritage—the Kingdom of Heaven! Drug your soul no longer with the poisons of false beliefs. You are not "a worm of the dust" unless you choose to make yourself one. You are a divine, immortal, God-born being, and this you may know if you will to seek and find. Cling no longer to your impure and grovelling thoughts, and you shall know that you are a radiant and celestial spirit, filled with all pure and lovable thoughts. Wretchedness and sin and sorrow are not your portion here unless you accept them as such; and if you do this, they will be your portion hereafter, for these things are not apart from your soul-condition: they will go wherever you go; they are only within you.

Heaven, not hell, is your portion here and always. It only requires you to take that which belongs to you. You are the master, and you choose whom you will serve. You are the maker of your state, and your choice determines your condition. What you pray and ask for (with your mind and heart, not with your lips merely), this you receive. You are served as you serve. You are conditioned as you condition. You garner in your own.

Heaven is yours; you have but to enter in and take possession; and Heaven means Supreme Happiness, Perfect Blessedness; it leaves nothing to be desired; nothing to be grieved over. It is complete satisfaction now and in this world. It is within you ; and if you do not know this, it is because you persist in turning the back of your soul upon it. Turn round and you shall behold it.

Come and live in the sunshine of your being. Come out of the shadows and the dark places. You are framed for Happiness. You are a child of Heaven. Purity, Wisdom, Love, Plenty, Joy, and

Peace—these are the eternal Realities of the Kingdom, and they are yours, but you cannot possess them in sin; they have no part in the Realm of Darkness. They belong to "the Light which lighteth every man that cometh into the world," the Light of spotless Love. They are the heritage of the holy Christ-Child who shall come to birth in your soul when you are ready to divest yourself of all your impurities. They are your real self.

But he whose soul has been safely delivered of the Wonderful Joy-Child does not forget the travail of the world.

THE WAY OF PEACE

THE POWER OF MEDITATION

Spiritual meditation is the pathway to Divinity. It is the mystic ladder which reaches from earth to heaven, from error to Truth, from pain to peace. Every saint has climbed it; every sinner must sooner or later come to it, and every weary pilgrim that turns his back upon self and the world, and sets his face resolutely toward the Father's Home, must plant his feet upon its golden rounds. Without its aid you cannot grow into the divine state, the divine likeness, the divine peace, and the fadeless glories and unpolluting joys of Truth will remain hidden from you.

Meditation is the intense dwelling, in thought, upon an idea or theme, with the object of thoroughly comprehending it, and whatsoever you constantly meditate upon you will not only come to understand, but will grow more and more into its likeness, for it will become incorporated into your very being, will become, in fact, your very self. If, therefore, you constantly dwell upon that which is selfish and debasing, you will ultimately become selfish and debased; if you ceaselessly think upon that which is pure and unselfish you will surely become pure and unselfish.

Tell me what that is upon which you most frequently and intensely think, that to which, in your silent hours, your soul most naturally turns, and I will tell you to what place of pain or peace you are traveling, and whether you are growing into the likeness of the divine or the bestial.

There is an unavoidable tendency to become literally the embodiment of that quality upon which one most constantly thinks. Let, therefore, the object of your meditation be above and not below, so that every time you revert to it in thought you will be lifted up; let it be pure and unmixed with any selfish element; so shall your heart become purified and drawn nearer to Truth, and not defiled and dragged more hopelessly into error.

Meditation, in the spiritual sense in which I am now using it, is the secret of all growth in spiritual life and knowledge. Every prophet, sage, and savior became such by the power of meditation. Buddha meditated upon the Truth until he could say, "I am the Truth." Jesus brooded upon the Divine immanence until at last he could declare, "I and my Father are One."

Meditation centered upon divine realities is the very essence and soul of prayer. It is the silent reaching of the soul toward the Eternal. Mere petitionary prayer without meditation is a body without a soul, and is powerless to lift the mind and heart above sin and affliction. If you are daily praying for wisdom, for peace, for loftier purity and a fuller realization of Truth, and that for which you pray is still far from you, it means that you are praying for one thing while living out in thought and act another. If you will cease from such waywardness, taking your mind off those things the selfish clinging to which debars you from the possession of the stainless realities for which you pray: if you will no longer ask God to grant you that which you do not deserve, or to bestow upon you that love and compassion which you refuse to bestow upon others, but will commence to think and act in the spirit of Truth, you will day by day be growing into those realities, so that ultimately you will become one with them.

He who would secure any worldly advantage must be willing to work vigorously for it, and he would be foolish indeed who, waiting with folded hands, expected it to come to him for the mere asking. Do not then vainly imagine that you can obtain the heavenly possessions without making an effort. Only when you commence to work earnestly in the Kingdom of Truth will you be allowed to partake of the Bread of Life, and when you have, by patient and uncomplaining effort, earned the spiritual wages for which you ask, they will not be withheld from you.

If you really seek Truth, and not merely your own gratification; if you love it above all worldly pleasures and gains; more, even, than happiness itself, you will be willing to make the effort necessary for its achievement.

If you would be freed from sin and sorrow; if you would taste of that spotless purity for which you sigh and pray; if you would realize wisdom and knowledge, and would enter into the possession of profound and abiding peace, come now and enter the path of meditation, and let the supreme object of your meditation be Truth.

At the outset, meditation must be distinguished from idle reverie. There is nothing dreamy and unpractical about it. It is a process of searching and uncompromising thought which allows nothing to remain but the simple and naked truth. Thus meditating you will no longer strive to build yourself up in your prejudices, but, forgetting self, you will remember only that you are seeking the Truth. And so you will remove, one by one, the errors which you have built around yourself in the past, and will patiently wait for the revelation of Truth which will come when your errors have been sufficiently removed. In the silent humility of your heart you will realize that

"There is an inmost centre in us all

Where Truth abides in fullness; and around,

Wall upon wall, the gross flesh hems it in;

This perfect, clear perception, which is Truth,

A baffling and perverting carnal mesh

Blinds it, and makes all error; and to know,

Rather consists in opening out a way

Whence the imprisoned splendour may escape,

Than in effecting entry for a light

Supposed to be without."

Select some portion of the day in which to meditate, and keep that period sacred to your purpose. The best time is the very early morning when the spirit of repose is upon everything. All natural conditions will then be in your favor; the passions, after the long bodily fast of the night, will be subdued, the excitements and worries of the previous day will have died away, and the mind, strong and yet restful, will be receptive to spiritual instruction. Indeed, one of the first efforts you will be called upon to make will be to shake off lethargy and indulgence, and if you refuse you will be unable to advance, for the demands of the spirit are imperative.

To be spiritually awakened is also to be mentally and physically awakened. The sluggard and the self-indulgent can have no knowledge of Truth. He who, possessed of health and strength, wastes the calm, precious hours of the silent morning in drowsy indulgence is totally unfit to climb the heavenly heights.

He whose awakening consciousness has become alive to its lofty possibilities, who is beginning to shake off the darkness of ignorance in which the world is enveloped, rises before the stars have ceased their vigil, and, grappling with the darkness within his soul, strives, by holy aspiration, to perceive the light of Truth while the unawakened world dreams on.

"The heights by great men reached and kept,

Were not attained by sudden flight,

But they, while their companions slept,

Were toiling upward in the night."

No saint, no holy man, no teacher of Truth ever lived who did not rise early in the morning. Jesus habitually rose early, and climbed the solitary mountains to engage in Holy Communion. Buddha always rose an hour before sunrise and engaged in meditation, and all his disciples were enjoined to do the same.

If you have to commence your daily duties at a very early hour, and are thus debarred from giving the early morning to systematic meditation, try to give an hour at night, and should this, by the length and laboriousness of your daily task be denied you, you need not despair, for you may turn your thoughts upward in holy meditation in the intervals of your work, or in those few idle minutes which you now waste in aimlessness; and should your work be of that kind which becomes by practice automatic, you may meditate while engaged upon it. That eminent Christian saint and philosopher Jacob Boehme, realized his vast knowledge of divine things whilst, working long hours as a shoemaker. In every life there is time to think, and the busiest, the most laborious is not shut out from aspiration and meditation.

Spiritual meditation and self-discipline are inseparable; you will, therefore, commence to meditate upon yourself so as to try and understand yourself, for, remember, the great object you will have in view will be the complete removal of all your errors in order that you may realize Truth. You will begin to question your motives, thoughts, and acts, comparing them with your ideal, and endeavoring to look upon them with a calm and impartial eye. In this manner you will be continually gaining more of that mental and spiritual equilibrium without which men are but helpless straws upon the ocean of life. If you are given to hatred or anger you will meditate upon gentleness and forgiveness, so as to become acutely alive to a sense of your harsh and foolish conduct. You will then begin to dwell in thoughts of love, of gentleness, of abounding forgiveness; and as you overcome the lower by the higher, there will gradually, silently steal into your heart a knowledge of the divine Law of Love with an understanding of its bearing upon all the intricacies of life and conduct. And in applying this knowledge to your every thought, word, and act, you will grow more and more gentle, more and more loving, more and more divine. And thus with every error, every selfish desire, every human weakness; by the power of meditation is it overcome, and as each sin, each error is thrust out, a fuller and clearer measure of the Light of Truth illumines the pilgrim soul.

Thus meditating, you will be ceaselessly fortifying yourself against your only real enemy, your selfish, perishable self, and will be establishing yourself more and more firmly in the divine and imperishable self that is inseparable from Truth. The direct outcome of your meditations will be a calm, spiritual strength which will be your stay and resting-place in the struggle of life. Great is the overcoming power of holy thought, and the strength and knowledge gained in the hour of silent meditation will enrich the soul with saving remembrance in the hour of strife, of sorrow, or of temptation.

As, by the power of meditation, you grow in wisdom, you will relinquish, more and more, your selfish desires which are fickle, impermanent, and productive of sorrow and pain; and will take your stand, with increasing steadfastness and trust, upon unchangeable principles, and will realize heavenly rest.

The use of meditation is the acquirement of a knowledge of eternal principles, and the power which results from meditation is the ability to rest upon and trust those principles, and so become one with the Eternal. The end of meditation is, therefore, direct knowledge of Truth, God, and the realization of divine and profound peace.

Let your meditations take their rise from the ethical ground which you now occupy. Remember that you are to grow into Truth by steady perseverance. If you are an orthodox Christian, meditate ceaselessly upon the spotless purity and divine excellence of the character of Jesus, and apply his every precept to your inner life and outward conduct, so as to approximate more and more toward his perfection. Do not be as those religious ones, who, refusing to meditate upon the Law of Truth, and to put into practice the precepts given to them by their Master, are content to formally worship, to cling to their particular creeds, and to continue in the ceaseless round of sin and suffering. Strive to rise, by the power of meditation, above all selfish clinging to partial gods or party creeds; above dead formalities and lifeless ignorance. Thus walking the high way of wisdom, with mind fixed upon the spotless Truth, you shall know no halting-place short of the realization of Truth.

He who earnestly meditates first perceives a truth, as it were, afar off, and then realizes it by daily practice. It is only the doer of the Word of Truth that can know of the doctrine of Truth, for though by pure thought the Truth is perceived, it is only actualized by practice.

Said the divine Gautama, the Buddha, "He who gives himself up to vanity, and does not give himself up to meditation, forgetting the real aim of life and grasping at pleasure, will in time envy him who has exerted himself in meditation," and he instructed his disciples in the following "Five Great Meditations":

"The first meditation is the meditation of love, in which you so adjust your heart that you long for the weal and welfare of all beings, including the happiness of your enemies.

"The second meditation is the meditation of pity, in which you think of all beings in distress, vividly representing in your imagination their sorrows and anxieties so as to arouse a deep compassion for them in your soul.

"The third meditation is the meditation of joy, in which you think of the prosperity of others, and rejoice with their rejoicings.

"The fourth meditation is the meditation of impurity, in which you consider the evil consequences of corruption, the effects of sin and diseases. How trivial often the pleasure of the moment, and how fatal its consequences.

"The fifth meditation is the meditation on serenity, in which you rise above love and hate, tyranny and oppression, wealth and want, and regard your own fate with impartial calmness and perfect tranquility."

By engaging in these meditations the disciples of the Buddha arrived at a knowledge of the Truth. But whether you engage in these particular meditations or not matters little so long as your object is Truth, so long as you hunger and thirst for that righteousness which is a holy heart and a blameless life. In your meditations, therefore, let your heart grow and expand with ever-broadening love, until, freed from all hatred, and passion, and condemnation, it embraces the whole universe with thoughtful tenderness. As the flower opens its petals to receive the morning light, so open your soul more and more to the glorious light of Truth. Soar upward upon the wings of aspiration; be fearless, and believe in the loftiest possibilities. Believe that a life of absolute meekness is possible; believe that a life of stainless purity is possible; believe that a life of perfect holiness is possible; believe that the realization of the highest truth is possible. He who so believes climbs rapidly the heavenly hills, whilst the unbelievers continue to grope darkly and painfully in the fog-bound valleys.

So believing, so aspiring, so meditating, divinely sweet and beautiful will be your spiritual experiences, and glorious the revelations that will enrapture your inward vision. As you realize the divine Love, the divine Justice, the divine Purity, the Perfect Law of Good, or God, great will be your bliss and deep your peace. Old things will pass away, and all things will become new. The veil of the material universe, so dense and impenetrable to the eye of error, so thin and gauzy to the eye of Truth, will be lifted and the spiritual universe will be revealed. Time will cease, and you will live only in Eternity. Change and mortality will no more cause you anxiety and sorrow, for you will become established in the unchangeable, and will dwell in the very heart of immortality.

STAR OF WISDOM

Star that of the birth of Vishnu,

Birth of Krishna, Buddha, Jesus,

Told the wise ones, Heavenward looking,

Waiting, watching for thy gleaming

In the darkness of the night-time,

In the starless gloom of midnight;

Shining Herald of the coming

Of the kingdom of the righteous;

Teller of the Mystic story

Of the lowly birth of Godhead

In the stable of the passions,

In the manger of the mind-soul;

Silent singer of the secret

Of compassion deep and holy

To the heart with sorrow burdened,
To the soul with waiting weary:--
Star of all-surpassing brightness,
Thou again dost deck the midnight;
Thou again dost cheer the wise ones
Watching in the creedal darkness,
Weary of the endless battle
With the grinding blades of error;
Tired of lifeless, useless idols,
Of the dead forms of religions;
Spent with watching for thy shining;
Thou hast ended their despairing;
Thou hast lighted up their pathway;
Thou hast brought again the old Truths
To the hearts of all thy Watchers;
To the souls of them that love thee
Thou dost speak of Joy and Gladness,
Of the peace that comes of Sorrow.
Blessed are they that can see thee,
Weary wanderers in the Night-time;
Blessed they who feel the throbbing,
In their bosoms feel the pulsing
Of a deep Love stirred within them
By the great power of thy shining.
Let us learn thy lesson truly;
Learn it faithfully and humbly;
Learn it meekly, wisely, gladly,
Ancient Star of holy Vishnu,
Light of Krishna, Buddha, Jesus.

THE TWO MASTERS, SELF AND TRUTH

Upon the battlefield of the human soul two masters are ever contending for the crown of supremacy, for the kingship and dominion of the heart; the master of self, called also the "Prince of this world," and the master of Truth, called also the Father God. The master self is that rebellious one whose weapons are passion, pride, avarice, vanity, self-will, implements of darkness; the master Truth is that meek and lowly one whose weapons are gentleness, patience, purity, sacrifice, humility, love, instruments of Light.

In every soul the battle is waged, and as a soldier cannot engage at once in two opposing armies, so every heart is enlisted either in the ranks of self or of Truth. There is no half-and-half course; "There is self and there is Truth; where self is, Truth is not, where Truth is, self is not." Thus spake Buddha, the teacher of Truth, and Jesus, the manifested Christ, declared that "No man can serve two masters; for either he will hate the one and love the other; or else he will hold to the one, and despise the other. Ye cannot serve God and Mammon."

Truth is so simple, so absolutely undeviating and uncompromising that it admits of no complexity, no turning, no qualification. Self is ingenious, crooked, and, governed by subtle and snaky desire, admits of endless turnings and qualifications, and the deluded worshipers of self vainly imagine that they can gratify every worldly desire, and at the same time possess the Truth. But the lovers of Truth worship Truth with the sacrifice of self, and ceaselessly guard themselves against worldliness and self-seeking.

Do you seek to know and to realize Truth? Then you must be prepared to sacrifice, to renounce to the uttermost, for Truth in all its glory can only be perceived and known when the last vestige of self has disappeared.

The eternal Christ declared that he who would be His disciple must "deny himself daily." Are you willing to deny yourself, to give up your lusts, your prejudices, your opinions? If so, you may enter the narrow way of Truth, and find that peace from which the world is shut out. The absolute denial, the utter extinction, of self is the perfect state of Truth, and all religions and philosophies are but so many aids to this supreme attainment.

Self is the denial of Truth. Truth is the denial of self. As you let self die, you will be reborn in Truth. As you cling to self, Truth will be hidden from you.

Whilst you cling to self, your path will be beset with difficulties, and repeated pains, sorrows, and disappointments will be your lot. There are no difficulties in Truth, and coming to Truth, you will be freed from all sorrow and disappointment.

Truth in itself is not hidden and dark. It is always revealed and is perfectly transparent. But the blind and wayward self cannot perceive it. The light of day is not hidden except to the blind, and the Light of Truth is not hidden except to those who are blinded by self.

Truth is the one Reality in the universe, the inward Harmony, the perfect Justice, the eternal Love. Nothing can be added to it, nor taken from it. It does not depend upon any man, but all men depend upon it. You cannot perceive the beauty of Truth while you are looking out through the eyes of self. If you are vain, you will color everything with your own vanities. If lustful, your heart and mind will be so clouded with the smoke and flames of passion, that everything will appear distorted through them. If proud and opinionative, you will see nothing in the whole universe except the magnitude and importance of your own opinions.

There is one quality which pre-eminently distinguishes the man of Truth from the man of self, and that is humility. To be not only free from vanity, stubbornness and egotism, but to regard one's own opinions as of no value, this indeed is true humility.

He who is immersed in self regards his own opinions as Truth and the opinions of other men as error. But that humble Truth-lover who has learned to distinguish between opinion and Truth, regards all men with the eye of charity, and does not seek to defend his opinions against theirs, but sacrifices those opinions that he may love the more, that he may manifest the spirit of Truth, for Truth in its very nature is ineffable and can only be lived. He who has most of charity has most of Truth.

Men engage in heated controversies, and foolishly imagine they are defending the Truth, when in reality they are merely defending their own petty interests and perishable opinions. The follower of self takes up arms against others. The follower of Truth takes up arms against himself. Truth, being unchangeable and eternal, is independent of your opinion and of mine. We may enter into it, or we may stay outside; but both our defense and our attack are superfluous, and are hurled back upon ourselves.

Men, enslaved by self, passionate, proud, and condemnatory, believe their particular creed or religion to be the Truth, and all other religions to be error; and they proselytize with passionate ardor. There is but one religion, the religion of Truth. There is but one error, the error of self. Truth is not a formal belief; it is an unselfish, holy, and aspiring heart, and he who has Truth is at peace with all, and cherishes all with thoughts of love.

You may easily know whether you are a child of Truth or a worshiper of self, if you will silently examine your mind, heart, and conduct. Do you harbor thoughts of suspicion, enmity, envy, lust, pride, or do you strenuously fight against these? If the former, you are chained to self, no matter what religion you may profess; if the latter, you are a candidate for Truth, even though outwardly you may profess no religion. Are you passionate, self-willed, ever seeking to gain your own ends, self-indulgent, and self-centered; or are you gentle, mild, unselfish, quit of every form of self-indulgence, and are ever ready to give up your own? If the former, self is your master; if the latter, Truth is the object of your affection. Do you strive for riches? Do you fight, with passion, for your party? Do you lust for power and leadership? Are you given to ostentation and self-praise? Or have you given up the love of riches? Have you relinquished all strife? Are you content to take the lowest place, and to be passed by unnoticed? And have you ceased to talk about yourself and to regard yourself with self-complacent pride? If the former, even though you may imagine you worship God, the god of your heart is self. If the latter, even though you may withhold your lips from worship, you are dwelling with the Most High.

The signs by which the Truth-lover is known are unmistakable. Hear the Holy Krishna declare them, in Sir Edwin Arnold's beautiful rendering of the "Bhagavad Gita":--

"Fearlessness, singleness of soul, the will

Always to strive for wisdom; opened hand

And governed appetites; and piety,

And love of lonely study; humbleness,

Uprightness, heed to injure nought which lives

Truthfulness, slowness unto wrath, a mind

That lightly letteth go what others prize;

And equanimity, and charity

Which spieth no man's faults; and tenderness

Towards all that suffer; a contented heart,

Fluttered by no desires; a bearing mild,

Modest and grave, with manhood nobly mixed,

With patience, fortitude and purity;

An unrevengeful spirit, never given

To rate itself too high--such be the signs,

O Indian Prince! Of him whose feet are set

On that fair path which leads to heavenly birth!"

When men, lost in the devious ways of error and self, have forgotten the "heavenly birth," the state of holiness and Truth, they set up artificial standards by which to judge one another, and make acceptance of, and adherence to, their own particular theology, the test of Truth; and so men are divided one against another, and there is ceaseless enmity and strife, and unending sorrow and suffering.

Reader, do you seek to realize the birth into Truth? There is only one way: Let self die. All those lusts, appetites, desires, opinions, limited conceptions and prejudices to which you have hitherto so tenaciously clung, let them fall from you. Let them no longer hold you in bondage, and Truth will be yours. Cease to look upon your own religion as superior to all others, and strive humbly to learn the supreme lesson of charity. No longer cling to the idea, so productive of strife and sorrow, that the Savior whom you worship is the only Savior, and that the Savior whom your brother worships with equal sincerity and ardor, is an impostor; but seek diligently the path of holiness, and then you will realize that every holy man is a savior of mankind.

The giving up of self is not merely the renunciation of outward things. It consists of the renunciation of the inward sin, the inward error. Not by giving up vain clothing; not by relinquishing riches; not by abstaining from certain foods; not by speaking smooth words; not by merely doing these things is the Truth found; but by giving up the spirit of vanity; by relinquishing the desire for riches; by abstaining from the lust of self-indulgence; by giving up all hatred, strife, condemnation, and self-seeking, and becoming gentle and pure at heart; by doing these things is the Truth found. To do the former, and not to do the latter, is pharisaism and hypocrisy, whereas the latter includes the former. You may renounce the outward world, and isolate yourself in a cave or in the depths of a forest, but you will take all your selfishness with you, and unless you renounce that, great indeed will be your wretchedness and deep your delusion. You may remain just where you are, performing all your duties, and yet renounce the world, the inward enemy. To be in the world and yet not of the world is the highest perfection, the most blessed peace, is to achieve the greatest victory. The renunciation of self is the way of Truth, therefore,

"Enter the Path; there is no grief like hate,

No pain like passion, no deceit like sense;

Enter the Path; far hath he gone whose foot

Treads down one fond offense."

As you succeed in overcoming self you will begin to see things in their right relations. He who is swayed by any passion, prejudice, like or dislike, adjusts everything to that particular bias, and sees only his own delusions. He who is absolutely free from all passion, prejudice, preference, and partiality, sees himself as he is; sees others as they are; sees all things in their proper proportions and right relations. Having nothing to attack, nothing to defend, nothing to conceal, and no interests to guard, he is at peace. He has realized the profound simplicity of Truth, for this unbiased, tranquil, blessed state of mind and heart is the state of Truth. He who attains to it dwells with the angels, and sits at the footstool of the Supreme. Knowing the Great Law; knowing the origin of sorrow; knowing the secret of suffering; knowing the way of emancipation in Truth, how can such a one engage in strife or condemnation; for though he knows that the blind, self-seeking world, surrounded with the clouds of its own illusions, and enveloped in the darkness of error and self, cannot perceive the steadfast Light of Truth, and is utterly incapable of comprehending the profound simplicity of the heart that has died, or is dying, to self, yet he also knows that when the suffering ages have piled up mountains of sorrow, the crushed and burdened soul of the world will fly to its final refuge, and that when the ages are completed, every prodigal will come back to the fold of Truth. And so he dwells in goodwill toward all, and regards all with that tender compassion which a father bestows upon his wayward children.

Men cannot understand Truth because they cling to self, because they believe in and love self, because they believe self to be the only reality, whereas it is the one delusion.

When you cease to believe in and love self you will desert it, and will fly to Truth, and will find the eternal Reality.

When men are intoxicated with the wines of luxury, and pleasure, and vanity, the thirst of life grows and deepens within them, and they delude themselves with dreams of fleshly immortality, but when they come to reap the harvest of their own sowing, and pain and sorrow supervene, then, crushed and humiliated, relinquishing self and all the intoxications of self, they come, with aching hearts to the one immortality, the immortality that destroys all delusions, the spiritual immortality in Truth.

Men pass from evil to good, from self to Truth, through the dark gate of sorrow, for sorrow and self are inseparable. Only in the peace and bliss of Truth is all sorrow vanquished. If you suffer disappointment because your cherished plans have been thwarted, or because someone has not come up to your anticipations, it is because you are clinging to self. If you suffer remorse for your conduct, it is because you have given way to self. If you are overwhelmed with chagrin and regret because of the attitude of someone else toward you, it is because you have been cherishing self. If you are wounded on account of what has been done to you or said of you, it is because you are walking in the painful way of self. All suffering is of self. All suffering ends in Truth. When you have entered into and realized Truth, you will no longer suffer disappointment, remorse, and regret, and sorrow will flee from you.

"Self is the only prison that can ever bind the soul;

Truth is the only angel that can bid the gates unroll;

And when he comes to call thee, arise and follow fast;

His way may lie through darkness, but it leads to light at last."

The woe of the world is of its own making. Sorrow purifies and deepens the soul, and the extremity of sorrow is the prelude to Truth.

Have you suffered much? Have you sorrowed deeply? Have you pondered seriously upon the problem of life? If so, you are prepared to wage war against self, and to become a disciple of Truth.

The intellectual who does not see the necessity for giving up self, frame endless theories about the universe, and call them Truth; but do thou pursue that direct line of conduct which is the practice of righteousness, and thou wilt realize the Truth which has no place in theory, and which never changes. Cultivate your heart. Water it continually with unselfish love and deep-felt pity, and strive to shut out from it all thoughts and feelings which are not in accordance with Love. Return good for evil, love for hatred, gentleness for ill-treatment, and remain silent when attacked. So shall you transmute all your selfish desires into the pure gold of Love, and self will disappear in Truth. So will you walk blamelessly among men, yoked with the easy yoke of lowliness and clothed with the divine garment of humility?

O come, weary brother! Thy struggling and striving
End thou in the heart of the Master of ruth;
Across self's drear desert why wilt thou be driving,
A thirst for the quickening waters of Truth
When here, by the path of thy searching and sinning,
Flows Life's gladsome stream, lies Love's oasis green?
Come, turn thou and rest; know the end and beginning,
The sought and the searcher, the seer and seen.
Thy Master sits not in the unapproached mountains,
Nor dwells in the mirage which floats on the air,
Nor shalt thou discover His magical fountains
In pathways of sand that encircle despair.
In selfhood's dark desert cease wearily seeking
The odorous tracks of the feet of thy King;
And if thou wouldst hear the sweet sound of His speaking,
Be deaf to all voices that emptily sing.
Flee the vanishing places; renounce all thou hast;

Leave all that thou lovest, and, naked and bare,
Thyself at the shrine of the Innermost cast;
The Highest, the Holiest, the Changeless is there.
Within, in the heart of the Silence He dwelleth;
Leave sorrow and sin, leave thy wanderings sore;
Come bathe in His Joy, whilst He, whispering, telleth
Thy soul what it seeketh, and wander no more.
Then cease, weary brother, thy struggling and striving;
Find peace in the heart of the Master of ruth.
Across self's dark desert cease wearily driving;
Come; drink at the beautiful waters of Truth.

THE ACQUIREMENT
OF SPIRITUAL POWER

The world is filled with men and women seeking pleasure, excitement, novelty; seeking ever to be moved to laughter or tears; not seeking strength, stability, and power; but courting weakness, and eagerly engaged in dispersing what power they have.

Men and women of real power and influence are few, because few are prepared to make the sacrifice necessary to the acquirement of power, and fewer still are ready to patiently build up character.

To be swayed by your fluctuating thoughts and impulses is to be weak and powerless; to rightly control and direct those forces is to be strong and powerful. Men of strong animal passions have much of the ferocity of the beast, but this is not power. The elements of power are there; but it is only when this ferocity is tamed and subdued by the higher intelligence that real power begins; and men can only grow in power by awakening themselves to higher and ever higher states of intelligence and consciousness.

The difference between a man of weakness and one of power lies not in the strength of the personal will (for the stubborn man is usually weak and foolish), but in that focus of consciousness which represents their states of knowledge.

The pleasure-seekers, the lovers of excitement, the hunters after novelty, and the victims of impulse and hysterical emotion lack that knowledge of principles which gives balance, stability, and influence.

A man commences to develop power when, checking his impulses and selfish inclinations, he falls back upon the higher and calmer consciousness within him, and begins to steady himself upon a principle. The realization of unchanging principles in consciousness is at once the source and secret of the highest power.

When, after much searching, and suffering, and sacrificing, the light of an eternal principle dawns upon the soul, a divine calm ensues and joy unspeakable gladdens the heart.

He who has realized such a principle ceases to wander, and remains poised and self-possessed. He ceases to be "passion's slave," and becomes a master-builder in the Temple of Destiny.

The man that is governed by self, and not by a principle, changes his front when his selfish comforts are threatened. Deeply intent upon defending and guarding his own interests, he regards all means as lawful that will subserve that end. He is continually scheming as to how he may protect himself against his enemies, being too self-centered to perceive that he is his own enemy. Such a man's work crumbles away, for it is divorced from Truth and power. All effort that is grounded upon self, perishes; only that work endures that is built upon an indestructible principle.

The man that stands upon a principle is the same calm, dauntless, self-possessed man under all circumstances. When the hour of trial comes, and he has to decide between his personal comforts and Truth, he gives up his comforts and remains firm. Even the prospect of torture and death cannot alter or deter him. The man of self regards the loss of his wealth, his comforts, or his life as the greatest calamities which can befall him. The man of principle looks upon these incidents as comparatively insignificant, and not to be weighed with loss of character, loss of Truth. To desert Truth is, to him, the only happening which can really be called a calamity.

It is the hour of crisis which decides, who are the minions of darkness and who the children of Light. It is the epoch of threatening disaster, ruin, and persecution which divides the sheep from the goats, and reveals to the reverential gaze of succeeding ages the men and women of power.

It is easy for a man, so long as he is left in the enjoyment of his possessions, to persuade himself that he believes in and adheres to the principles of Peace, Brotherhood, and Universal Love; but if, when his enjoyments are threatened, or he imagines they are threatened, he begins to clamor loudly for war, he shows that he believes in and stands upon, not Peace, Brotherhood, and Love, but strife, selfishness, and hatred.

He who does not desert his principles when threatened with the loss of every earthly thing, even to the loss of reputation and life, is the man of power; is the man whose every word and work endures; is the man whom the afterworld honors, reveres, and worships. Rather than desert that principle of Divine Love on which he

rested, and in which all his trust was placed, Jesus endured the
utmost extremity of agony and deprivation; and today the world
prostrates itself at his pierced feet in rapt adoration.

There is no way to the acquirement of spiritual power except by
that inward illumination and enlightenment which is the realization of spiritual principles; and those principles can only be realized by constant practice and application.

Take the principle of divine Love, and quietly and diligently meditate upon it with the object of arriving at a thorough understanding of it. Bring its searching light to bear upon all your habits,
your actions, your speech and intercourse with others, your every
secret thought and desire. As you persevere in this course, the
divine Love will become more and more perfectly revealed to you,
and your own shortcomings will stand out in more and more vivid
contrast, spurring you on to renewed endeavor; and having once
caught a glimpse of the incomparable majesty of that imperishable
principle, you will never again rest in your weakness, your selfishness, your imperfection, but will pursue that Love until you have
relinquished every discordant element, and have brought yourself
into perfect harmony with it. And that state of inward harmony
is spiritual power. Take also other spiritual principles, such as
Purity and Compassion, and apply them in the same way, and,
so exacting is Truth, you will be able to make no stay, no resting-
place until the inmost garment of your soul is bereft of every stain,
and your heart has become incapable of any hard, condemnatory,
and pitiless impulse.

Only in so far as you understand, realize, and rely upon, these
principles, will you acquire spiritual power, and that power will be
manifested in and through you in the form of increasing dispassion, patience and equanimity.

Dispassion argues superior self-control; sublime patience is the
very hall-mark of divine knowledge, and to retain an unbroken
calm amid all the duties and distractions of life, marks off the man
of power. "It is easy in the world to live after the world's opinion;
it is easy in solitude to live after our own; but the great man is he
who in the midst of the crowd keeps with perfect sweetness the
independence of solitude."

Some mystics hold that perfection in dispassion is the source
of that power by which miracles (so-called) are performed, and
truly he who has gained such perfect control of all his interior

forces that no shock, however great, can for one moment unbalance him, must be capable of guiding and directing those forces with a master-hand.

To grow in self-control, in patience, in equanimity, is to grow in strength and power; and you can only thus grow by focusing your consciousness upon a principle. As a child, after making many and vigorous attempts to walk unaided, at last succeeds, after numerous falls, in accomplishing this, so you must enter the way of power by first attempting to stand alone. Break away from the tyranny of custom, tradition, conventionality, and the opinions of others, until you succeed in walking lonely and erect among men. Rely upon your own judgment; be true to your own conscience; follow the Light that is within you; all outward lights are so many will-o'-the-wisps. There will be those who will tell you that you are foolish; that your judgment is faulty; that your conscience is all awry, and that the Light within you is darkness; but heed them not. If what they say is true the sooner you, as a searcher for wisdom, find it out the better, and you can only make the discovery by bringing your powers to the test. Therefore, pursue your course bravely. Your conscience is at least your own, and to follow it is to be a man; to follow the conscience of another is to be a slave. You will have many falls, will suffer many wounds, will endure many buffetings for a time, but press on in faith, believing that sure and certain victory lies ahead. Search for a rock, a principle, and having found it cling to it; get it under your feet and stand erect upon it, until at last, immovably fixed upon it, you succeed in defying the fury of the waves and storms of selfishness.

For selfishness in any and every form is dissipation, weakness, death; unselfishness in its spiritual aspect is conservation, power, life. As you grow in spiritual life, and become established upon principles, you will become as beautiful and as unchangeable as those principles, will taste of the sweetness of their immortal essence, and will realize the eternal and indestructible nature of the God within.

No harmful shaft can reach the righteous man,

Standing erect amid the storms of hate,

Defying hurt and injury and ban,

Surrounded by the trembling slaves of Fate.

Majestic in the strength of silent power,

Serene he stands, nor changes not nor turns;
Patient and firm in suffering's darkest hour,
Time bends to him, and death and doom he spurns.

Wrath's lurid lightnings round about him play,
And hell's deep thunders roll about his head;
Yet heeds he not, for him they cannot slay
Who stands whence earth and time and space are fled.

Sheltered by deathless love, what fear hath he?
Armored in changeless Truth, what can he know
Of loss and gain? Knowing eternity,
He moves not whilst the shadows come and go.

Call him immortal, call him Truth and Light
And splendor of prophetic majesty
Who bideth thus amid the powers of night,
Clothed with the glory of divinity.

THE REALIZATION
OF SELFLESS LOVE

It is said that Michael Angelo saw in every rough block of stone a thing of beauty awaiting the master-hand to bring it into reality. Even so, within each there reposes the Divine Image awaiting the master-hand of Faith and the chisel of Patience to bring it into manifestation. And that Divine Image is revealed and realized as stainless, selfless Love.

Hidden deep in every human heart, though frequently covered up with a mass of hard and almost impenetrable accretions, is the spirit of Divine Love, whose holy and spotless essence is undying and eternal. It is the Truth in man; it is that which belongs to the Supreme: that which is real and immortal. All else changes and passes away; this alone is permanent and imperishable; and to realize this Love by ceaseless diligence in the practice of the highest righteousness, to live in it and to become fully conscious in it, is to enter into immortality here and now, is to become one with Truth, one with God, one with the central Heart of all things, and to know our own divine and eternal nature.

To reach this Love, to understand and experience it, one must work with great persistency and diligence upon his heart and mind, must ever renew his patience and keep strong his faith, for there will be much to remove, much to accomplish before the Divine Image is revealed in all its glorious beauty.

He who strives to reach and to accomplish the divine will be tried to the very uttermost; and this is absolutely necessary, for how else could one acquire that sublime patience without which there is no real wisdom, no divinity? Ever and anon, as he proceeds, all his work will seem to be futile, and his efforts appear to be thrown away. Now and then a hasty touch will mar his image, and perhaps when he imagines his work is almost completed he will find what he imagined to be the beautiful form of Divine Love utterly destroyed, and he must begin again with his past bitter experience to guide and help him. But he who has resolutely set himself to realize the Highest recognizes no such thing as defeat. All failures are apparent, not real. Every slip, every fall, every return to self-ishness is a lesson learned, an experience gained, from which a golden grain of wisdom is extracted, helping the striver toward the accomplishment of his lofty object. To recognize,

"That of our vices we can frame

A ladder if we will but tread

Beneath our feet each deed of shame,"

is to enter the way that leads unmistakably toward the Divine, and the failings of one who thus recognizes are so many dead selves, upon which he rises, as upon stepping-stones, to higher things.

Once come to regard your failings, your sorrows and sufferings as so many voices telling you plainly where you are weak and faulty, where you fall below the true and the divine, you will then begin to ceaselessly watch yourself, and every slip, every pang of pain will show you where you are to set to work, and what you have to remove out of your heart in order to bring it nearer to the like-ness of the Divine, nearer to the Perfect Love. And as you proceed, day by day detaching yourself more and more from the inward selfishness the Love that is selfless will gradually become revealed to you. And when you are growing patient and calm, when your petulances, tempers, and irritabilities are passing away from you, and the more powerful lusts and prejudices cease to dominate and enslave you, then you will know that the divine is awakening within you, that you are drawing near to the eternal Heart, that you are not far from that selfless Love, the possession of which is peace and immortality.

Divine Love is distinguished from human loves in this supremely important particular, it is free from partiality. Human loves cling to a particular object to the exclusion of all else, and when that object is removed, great and deep is the resultant suffering to the one who loves. Divine Love embraces the whole universe, and, without clinging to any part, yet contains within itself the whole, and he who comes to it by gradually purifying and broadening his human loves until all the selfish and impure elements are burnt out of them, ceases from suffering. It is because human loves are narrow and confined and mingled with selfishness that they cause suffering. No suffering can result from that Love which is so ab-solutely pure that it seeks nothing for itself. Nevertheless, human loves are absolutely necessary as steps toward the Divine, and no soul is prepared to partake of Divine Love until it has become capable of the deepest and most intense human love. It is only by passing through human loves and human sufferings that Divine Love is reached and realized.

All human loves are perishable like the forms to which they cling; but there is a Love that is imperishable, and that does not cling to appearances.

All human loves are counterbalanced by human hates; but there is a Love that admits of no opposite or reaction; divine and free from all taint of self, that sheds its fragrance on all alike.

Human loves are reflections of the Divine Love, and draw the soul nearer to the reality, the Love that knows neither sorrow nor change.

It is well that the mother, clinging with passionate tenderness to the little helpless form of flesh that lies on her bosom, should be overwhelmed with the dark waters of sorrow when she sees it laid in the cold earth. It is well that her tears should flow and her heart ache, for only thus can she be reminded of the evanescent nature of the joys and objects of sense, and be drawn nearer to the eternal and imperishable Reality.

It is well that lover, brother, sister, husband, wife should suffer deep anguish, and be enveloped in gloom when the visible object of their affections is torn from them, so that they may learn to turn their affections toward the invisible Source of all, where alone abiding satisfaction is to be found.

It is well that the proud, the ambitious, the self-seeking, should suffer defeat, humiliation, and misfortune; that they should pass through the scorching fires of affliction; for only thus can the wayward soul be brought to reflect upon the enigma of life; only thus can the heart be softened and purified, and prepared to receive the Truth.

When the sting of anguish penetrates the heart of human love; when gloom and loneliness and desertion cloud the soul of friendship and trust, then it is that the heart turns toward the sheltering love of the Eternal, and finds rest in its silent peace. And whosoever comes to this Love is not turned away comfortless, is not pierced with anguish nor surrounded with gloom; and is never deserted in the dark hour of trial.

The glory of Divine Love can only be revealed in the heart that is chastened by sorrow, and the image of the heavenly state can only be perceived and realized when the lifeless, formless accretions of ignorance and self are hewn away.

Only that Love that seeks no personal gratification or reward, that does not make distinctions, and that leaves behind no heartaches, can be called divine.

Men, clinging to self and to the comfortless shadows of evil, are in the habit of thinking of divine Love as something belonging to a God who is out of reach; as something outside themselves, and that must for ever remain outside. Truly, the Love of God is ever beyond the reach of self, but when the heart and mind are emptied of self then the selfless Love, the supreme Love, the Love that is of God or Good, becomes an inward and abiding reality.

And this inward realization of holy Love is none other than the Love of Christ that is so much talked about and so little comprehended. The Love that not only saves the soul from sin, but lifts it also above the power of temptation.

But how may one attain to this sublime realization? The answer which Truth has always given, and will ever give to this question is,--"Empty thyself, and I will fill thee." Divine Love cannot be known until self is dead, for self is the denial of Love, and how can that which is known be also denied? Not until the stone of self is rolled away from the sepulcher of the soul does the immortal Christ, the pure Spirit of Love, hitherto crucified, dead and buried, cast off the bands of ignorance, and come forth in all the majesty of His resurrection.

You believe that the Christ of Nazareth was put to death and rose again. I do not say you err in that belief; but if you refuse to believe that the gentle spirit of Love is crucified daily upon the dark cross of your selfish desires, then, I say, you err in this unbelief, and have not yet perceived, even afar off, the Love of Christ.

You say that you have tasted of salvation in the Love of Christ. Are you saved from your temper, your irritability, your vanity, your personal dislikes, your judgment and condemnation of others? If not, from what are you saved, and wherein have you realized the transforming Love of Christ?

He who has realized the Love that is divine has become a new man, and has ceased to be swayed and dominated by the old elements of self. He is known for his patience, his purity, his self-control, his deep charity of heart, and his unalterable sweetness.

Divine or selfless Love is not a mere sentiment or emotion; it is a state of knowledge which destroys the dominion of evil and the belief in evil, and lifts the soul into the joyful realization of the supreme Good. To the divinely wise, knowledge and Love are one and inseparable.

It is toward the complete realization of this divine Love that the whole world is moving; it was for this purpose that the universe came into existence, and every grasping at happiness, every reaching out of the soul toward objects, ideas and ideals, is an effort to realize it. But the world does not realize this Love at present because it is grasping at the fleeting shadow and ignoring, in its blindness, the substance. And so suffering and sorrow continue, and must continue until the world, taught by its self-inflicted pains, discovers the Love that is selfless, the wisdom that is calm and full of peace.

And this Love, this Wisdom, this Peace, this tranquil state of mind and heart may be attained to, may be realized by all who are willing and ready to yield up self, and who are prepared to humbly enter into a comprehension of all that the giving up of self involves. There is no arbitrary power in the universe, and the strongest chains of fate by which men are bound are self-forged. Men are chained to that which causes suffering because they desire to be so, because they love their chains, because they think their little dark prison of self is sweet and beautiful, and they are afraid that if they desert that prison they will lose all that is real and worth having.

"Ye suffer from yourselves, none else compels,

None other holds ye that ye live and die."

And the indwelling power, which forged the chains and built around itself the dark and narrow prison, can break away when it desires and wills to do so, and the soul does will to do so when it has discovered the worthlessness of its prison, when long suffering has prepared it for the reception of the boundless Light and Love.

As the shadow follows the form, and as smoke comes after fire, so effect follows cause, and suffering and bliss follow the thoughts and deeds of men. There is no effect in the world around us but has its hidden or revealed cause, and that cause is in accordance with absolute justice. Men reap a harvest of suffering because in the near or distant past they have sown the seeds of evil; they reap a harvest of bliss also as a result of their own sowing of the seeds of good. Let a man meditate upon this, let him strive to understand it and he will then begin to sow only seeds of good, and will burn up the tares and weeds which he has formerly grown in the garden of his heart.

The world does not understand the Love that is selfless because it is engrossed in the pursuit of its own pleasures, and cramped within the narrow limits of perishable interests mistaking, in its ignorance, those pleasures and interests for real and abiding things. Caught in the flames of fleshly lusts, and burning with anguish, it sees not the pure and peaceful beauty of Truth. Feeding upon the swinish husks of error and self-delusion, it is shut out from the mansion of all-seeing Love.

Not having this Love, not understanding it, men institute innumerable reforms which involve no inward sacrifice, and each imagines that his reform is going to right the world for ever, while he himself continues to propagate evil by engaging it in his own heart. That only can be called reform which tends to reform the human heart, for all evil has its rise there, and not until the world, ceasing from selfishness and party strife, has learned the lesson of divine Love, will it realize the Golden Age of universal blessedness.

Let the rich cease to despise the poor, and the poor to condemn the rich; let the greedy learn how to give, and the lustful how to grow pure; let the partisan cease from strife, and the uncharitable begin to forgive; let the envious endeavor to rejoice with others, and the slanderers grow ashamed of their conduct. Let men and women take this course, and, lo! The Golden Age is at hand. He therefore, who purifies his own heart is the world's greatest benefactor.

Yet, though the world is, and will be for many ages to come, shut out from that Age of Gold, which is the realization of selfless Love, you, if you are willing, may enter it now, by rising above your selfish self; if you will pass from prejudice, hatred, and condemnation, to gentle and forgiving love.

Where hatred, dislike, and condemnation are, selfless Love does not abide. It resides only in the heart that has ceased from all condemnation.

You say, "How can I love the drunkard, the hypocrite, the sneak,

the murderer? I am compelled to dislike and condemn such men."
It is true you cannot love such men emotionally, but when you
say that you must perforce dislike and condemn them you show
that you are not acquainted with the Great over-ruling Love; for
it is possible to attain to such a state of interior enlightenment as
will enable you to perceive the train of causes by which these men
have become as they are, to enter into their intense sufferings, and
to know the certainty of their ultimate purification. Possessed of
such knowledge it will be utterly impossible for you any longer to
dislike or condemn them, and you will always think of them with
perfect calmness and deep compassion.

If you love people and speak of them with praise until they in
some way thwart you, or do something of which you disapprove,
and then you dislike them and speak of them with dispraise, you
are not governed by the Love which is of God. If, in your heart, you
are continually arraigning and condemning others, selfless Love is
hidden from you.

He who knows that Love is at the heart of all things and has realized the all-sufficing power of that Love has no room in his heart
for condemnation.

Men, not knowing this Love, constitute themselves judge and executioner of their fellows, forgetting that there is the Eternal Judge
and Executioner, and in so far as men deviate from them in their
own views, their particular reforms and methods, they brand them
as fanatical, unbalanced, lacking judgment, sincerity, and honesty; in so far as others approximate to their own standard do they
look upon them as being everything that is admirable. Such are
the men who are centered in self. But he whose heart is centered
in the supreme Love does not so brand and classify men; does not
seek to convert men to his own views, not to convince them of the
superiority of his methods. Knowing the Law of Love, he lives it,
and maintains the same calm attitude of mind and sweetness of
heart toward all. The debased and the virtuous, the foolish and
the wise, the learned and the unlearned, the selfish and the unselfish receive alike the benediction of his tranquil thought.

You can only attain to this supreme knowledge, this divine Love
by unremitting endeavor in self-discipline, and by gaining victory
after victory over yourself. Only the pure in heart see God, and
when your heart is sufficiently purified you will enter into the New
Birth, and the Love that does not die, nor change, nor end in pain

and sorrow will be awakened within you, and you will be at peace.

He who strives for the attainment of divine Love is ever seeking to overcome the spirit of condemnation, for where there is pure spiritual knowledge, condemnation cannot exist, and only in the heart that has become incapable of condemnation is Love perfected and fully realized.

The Christian condemns the Atheist; the Atheist satirizes the Christian; the Catholic and Protestant are ceaselessly engaged in wordy warfare and the spirit of strife and hatred rules where peace and love should be.

"He that hateth his brother is a murderer," a crucifier of the divine Spirit of Love; and until you can regard men of all religions and of no religion with the same impartial spirit, with all freedom from dislike, and with perfect equanimity, you have yet to strive for that Love which bestows upon its possessor freedom and salvation.

The realization of divine knowledge, selfless Love, utterly destroys the spirit of condemnation, disperses all evil, and lifts the consciousness to that height of pure vision where Love, Goodness, Justice are seen to be universal, supreme, all-conquering, indestructible.

Train your mind in strong, impartial, and gentle thought; train your heart in purity and compassion; train your tongue to silence and to true and stainless speech; so shall you enter the way of holiness and peace, and shall ultimately realize the immortal Love. So living, without seeking to convert, you will convince; without arguing, you will teach; not cherishing ambition, the wise will find you out; and without striving to gain men's opinions, you will subdue their hearts. For Love is all-conquering, all-powerful; and the thoughts, and deeds, and words of Love can never perish.

To know that Love is universal, supreme, all-sufficing; to be freed from the trammels of evil; to be quit of the inward unrest; to know that all men are striving to realize the Truth each in his own way; to be satisfied, sorrowless, serene; this is peace; this is gladness; this is immortality; this is Divinity; this is the realization of selfless Love.

I stood upon the shore, and saw the rocks

Resist the onslaught of the mighty sea,

And when I thought how all the countless shocks

They had withstood through an eternity,
I said, "To wear away this solid main
The ceaseless efforts of the waves are vain."
But when I thought how they the rocks had rent,
And saw the sand and shingles at my feet
(Poor passive remnants of resistance spent)
Tumbled and tossed where they the waters meet,
Then saw I ancient landmarks 'neath the waves,
And knew the waters held the stones their slaves.

I saw the mighty work the waters wrought
By patient softness and unceasing flow;
How they the proudest promontory brought
Unto their feet, and massy hills laid low;
How the soft drops the adamantine wall
Conquered at last, and brought it to its fall.

And then I knew that hard, resisting sin
Should yield at last to Love's soft ceaseless roll
Coming and going, ever flowing in
Upon the proud rocks of the human soul;
That all resistance should be spent and past,
And every heart yield unto it at last.

ENTERING INTO THE INFINITE

From the beginning of time, man, in spite of his bodily appetites and desires, in the midst of all his clinging to earthly and impermanent things, has ever been intuitively conscious of the limited, transient, and illusionary nature of his material existence, and in his sane and silent moments has tried to reach out into a comprehension of the Infinite, and has turned with tearful aspiration toward the restful Reality of the Eternal Heart.

While vainly imagining that the pleasures of earth are real and satisfying, pain and sorrow continually remind him of their unreal and unsatisfying nature. Ever striving to believe that complete satisfaction is to be found in material things, he is conscious of an inward and persistent revolt against this belief, which revolt is at once a refutation of his essential mortality, and an inherent and imperishable proof that only in the immortal, the eternal, the infinite can he find abiding satisfaction and unbroken peace.

And here is the common ground of faith; here the root and spring of all religion; here the soul of Brotherhood and the heart of Love,--that man is essentially and spiritually divine and eternal, and that, immersed in mortality and troubled with unrest, he is ever striving to enter into a consciousness of his real nature.

The spirit of man is inseparable from the Infinite, and can be satisfied with nothing short of the Infinite, and the burden of pain will continue to weigh upon man's heart, and the shadows of sorrow to darken his pathway until, ceasing from his wanderings in the dream-world of matter, he comes back to his home in the reality of the Eternal.

As the smallest drop of water detached from the ocean contains all the qualities of the ocean, so man, detached in consciousness from the Infinite, contains within him its likeness; and as the drop of water must, by the law of its nature, ultimately find its way back to the ocean and lose itself in its silent depths, so must man, by the unfailing law of his nature, at last return to his source, and lose himself in the great ocean of the Infinite.

To re-become one with the Infinite is the goal of man. To enter into perfect harmony with the Eternal Law is Wisdom, Love and Peace. But this divine state is, and must ever be, incomprehensible to the merely personal. Personality, separateness, selfishness are one and the same, and are the antithesis of wisdom and divinity. By the unqualified surrender of the personality, separateness and selfishness cease, and man enters into the possession of his divine heritage of immortality and infinity.

Such surrender of the personality is regarded by the worldly and selfish mind as the most grievous of all calamities, the most irreparable loss, yet it is the one supreme and incomparable blessing, the only real and lasting gain. The mind unenlightened upon the inner laws of being, and upon the nature and destiny of its own life, clings to transient appearances, things which have in them no enduring substantiality, and so clinging, perishes, for the time being, amid the shattered wreckage of its own illusions.

Men cling to and gratify the flesh as though it were going to last forever, and though they try to forget the nearness and inevitability of its dissolution, the dread of death and of the loss of all that they cling to clouds their happiest hours, and the chilling shadow of their own selfishness follows them like a remorseless specter.

And with the accumulation of temporal comforts and luxuries, the divinity within men is drugged, and they sink deeper and deeper into materiality, into the perishable life of the senses, and where there is sufficient intellect, theories concerning the immortality of the flesh come to be regarded as infallible truths. When a man's soul is clouded with selfishness in any or every form, he loses the power of spiritual discrimination, and confuses the temporal with the eternal, the perishable with the permanent, mortality with immortality, and error with Truth. It is thus that the world has come to be filled with theories and speculations having no foundation in human experience. Every body of flesh contains within itself, from the hour of birth, the elements of its own destruction, and by the unalterable law of its own nature must it pass away.

The perishable in the universe can never become permanent; the permanent can never pass away; the mortal can never become immortal; the immortal can never die; the temporal cannot become eternal nor the eternal become temporal; appearance can never become reality, nor reality fade into appearance; error can never become Truth, nor can Truth become error. Man cannot immortalize the flesh, but, by overcoming the flesh, by relinquishing all its inclinations, he can enter the region of immortality. "God alone hath immortality," and only by realizing the God state of consciousness does man enter into immortality.

All nature in its myriad forms of life is changeable, impermanent, un-enduring. Only the informing Principle of nature endures. Nature is many, and is marked by separation. The informing Principle is One and is marked by unity. By overcoming the senses and the selfishness within, which is the overcoming of nature, man emerges from the chrysalis of the personal and illusory, and wings himself into the glorious light of the impersonal, the region of universal Truth, out of which all perishable forms come.

Let men, therefore, practice self-denial; let them conquer their animal inclinations; let them refuse to be enslaved by luxury and pleasure; let them practice virtue, and grow daily into high and ever higher virtue, until at last they grow into the Divine, and enter into both the practice and the comprehension of humility, meekness, forgiveness, compassion, and love, which practice and comprehension constitute Divinity.

"Good-will gives insight," and only he who has so conquered his personality that he has but one attitude of mind, that of good-will, toward all creatures, is possessed of divine insight, and is capable of distinguishing the true from the false. The supremely good man is, therefore, the wise man, the divine man, the enlightened seer, the knower of the Eternal. Where you find unbroken gentleness, enduring patience, sublime lowliness, graciousness of speech, self-control, self-forgetfulness, and deep and abounding sympathy, look there for the highest wisdom, seek the company of such a one, for he has realized the Divine, he lives with the Eternal, he has become one with the Infinite. Believe not him that is impatient, given to anger, boastful, who clings to pleasure and refuses to renounce his selfish gratifications, and who practices not good-will and far-reaching compassion, for such a one hath not wisdom, vain is all his knowledge, and his works and words will perish, for they are grounded on that which passes away.

Let a man abandon self, let him overcome the world, let him deny the personal; by this pathway only can he enter into the heart of the Infinite.

The world, the body, the personality are mirages upon the desert of time; transitory dreams in the dark night of spiritual slumber, and those who have crossed the desert, those who are spiritually awakened, have alone comprehended the Universal Reality where all appearances are dispersed and dreaming and delusion are destroyed.

There is one Great Law which exacts unconditional obedience, one unifying principle which is the basis of all diversity, one eternal Truth wherein all the problems of earth pass away like shadows. To realize this Law, this Unity, this Truth, is to enter into the Infinite, is to become one with the Eternal.

To center one's life in the Great Law of Love is to enter into rest, harmony, peace. To refrain from all participation in evil and discord; to cease from all resistance to evil, and from the omission of that which is good, and to fall back upon unswerving obedience to the holy calm within, is to enter into the inmost heart of things, is to attain to a living, conscious experience of that eternal and infinite principle which must ever remain a hidden mystery to the merely perceptive intellect. Until this principle is realized, the soul is not established in peace, and he who so realizes is truly wise; not wise with the wisdom of the learned, but with the simplicity of a blameless heart and of a divine manhood.

To enter into a realization of the Infinite and Eternal is to rise superior to time, and the world, and the body, which comprise the kingdom of darkness; and is to become established in immortality, Heaven, and the Spirit, which make up the Empire of Light.

Entering into the Infinite is not a mere theory or sentiment. It is a vital experience which is the result of assiduous practice in inward purification. When the body is no longer believed to be, even remotely, the real man; when all appetites and desires are thoroughly subdued and purified; when the emotions are rested and calm, and when the oscillation of the intellect ceases and perfect poise is secured, then, and not till then, does consciousness become one with the Infinite; not until then is childlike wisdom and profound peace secured.

Men grow weary and gray over the dark problems of life, and finally pass away and leave them unsolved because they cannot see their way out of the darkness of the personality, being too much engrossed in its limitations. Seeking to save his personal life, man forfeits the greater impersonal Life in Truth; clinging to the perishable, he is shut out from a knowledge of the Eternal.

By the surrender of self all difficulties are overcome, and there is no error in the universe but the fire of inward sacrifice will burn it up like chaff; no problem, however great, but will disappear like a shadow under the searching light of self-abnegation. Problems exist only in our own self-created illusions, and they vanish away when self is yielded up. Self and error are synonymous. Error is involved in the darkness of unfathomable complexity, but eternal simplicity is the glory of Truth.

Love of self shuts men out from Truth, and seeking their own personal happiness they lose the deeper, purer, and more abiding bliss. Says Carlyle--"There is in man a higher than love of happiness. He can do without happiness, and instead thereof find blessedness.

... Love not pleasure, love God. This is the Everlasting Yea, wherein all contradiction is solved; wherein whoso walks and works, it is well with him."

He who has yielded up that self, that personality that men most love, and to which they cling with such fierce tenacity, has left behind him all perplexity, and has entered into a simplicity so profoundly simple as to be looked upon by the world, involved as it is in a network of error, as foolishness. Yet such a one has realized the highest wisdom, and is at rest in the Infinite. He "accomplishes without striving," and all problems melt before him, for he has entered the region of reality, and deals, not with changing effects, but with the unchanging principles of things. He is enlightened with a wisdom which is as superior to ratiocination, as reason is to animality. Having yielded up his lusts, his errors, his opinions and prejudices, he has entered into possession of the knowledge of God, having slain the selfish desire for heaven, and along with it the ignorant fear of hell; having relinquished even the love of life itself, he has gained supreme bliss and Life Eternal, the Life which bridges life and death, and knows its own immortality. Having yielded up all without reservation, he has gained all, and rests in peace on the bosom of the Infinite.

Only he who has become so free from self as to be equally content to be annihilated as to live, or to live as to be annihilated, is fit to enter into the Infinite. Only he who, ceasing to trust his perishable self has learned to trust in boundless measure the Great Law, the Supreme Good, is prepared to partake of undying bliss.

For such a one there is no more regret, nor disappointment, nor remorse, for where all selfishness has ceased these sufferings cannot be; and whatever happens to him he knows that it is for his own good, and he is content, being no longer the servant of self, but the servant of the Supreme. He is no longer affected by the changes of earth, and when he hears of wars and rumors of wars his peace is not disturbed, and where men grow angry and cynical and quarrelsome, he bestows compassion and love. Though appearances may contradict it, he knows that the world is progressing, and that

"Through its laughing and its weeping,

Through its living and its keeping,

Through its follies and its labors, weaving in and out of sight,

   To the end from the beginning,

Through all virtue and all sinning,

Reeled from God's great spool of Progress, runs the golden

   thread of light."

When a fierce storm is raging none are angered about it, because they know it will quickly pass away, and when the storms of contention are devastating the world, the wise man, looking with the eye of Truth and pity, knows that it will pass away, and that out of the wreckage of broken hearts which it leaves behind the immortal Temple of Wisdom will be built.

Sublimely patient; infinitely compassionate; deep, silent, and pure, his very presence is a benediction; and when he speaks men ponder his words in their hearts, and by them rise to higher levels of attainment. Such is he who has entered into the Infinite, who by the power of utmost sacrifice has solved the sacred mystery of life.

Questioning Life and Destiny and Truth,

I sought the dark and labyrinthine Sphinx,

Who spake to me this strange and wondrous thing:--

"Concealment only lies in blinded eyes,

And God alone can see the Form of God."

I sought to solve this hidden mystery

Vainly by paths of blindness and of pain,

But when I found the Way of Love and Peace,

Concealment ceased, and I was blind no more:

Then saw I God e'en with the eyes of God.

SAINTS, SAGES, AND SAVIORS: THE LAW OF SERVICE

The spirit of Love which is manifested as a perfect and rounded life is the crown of being and the supreme end of knowledge upon this earth.

The measure of a man's truth is the measure of his love, and Truth is far removed from him whose life is not governed by Love. The intolerant and condemnatory, even though they profess the highest religion, have the smallest measure of Truth; while those who exercise patience, and who listen calmly and dispassionately to all sides, and both arrive themselves at, and incline others to, thoughtful and unbiased conclusions upon all problems and issues, have Truth in fullest measure. The final test of wisdom is this,--how does a man live? What spirit does he manifest? How does he act under trial and temptation? Many men boast of being in possession of Truth who are continually swayed by grief, disappointment, and passion, and who sink under the first little trial that comes along. Truth is nothing if not unchangeable, and in so far as a man takes his stand upon Truth does he become steadfast in virtue, does he rise superior to his passions and emotions and changeable personality.

Men formulate perishable dogmas, and call them Truth. Truth cannot be formulated; it is ineffable, and ever beyond the reach of intellect. It can only be experienced by practice; it can only be manifested as a stainless heart and a perfect life.

Who, then, in the midst of the ceaseless pandemonium of schools and creeds and parties, has the Truth? He who lives it. He who practices it. He who, having risen above that pandemonium by overcoming himself, no longer engages in it, but sits apart, quiet, subdued, calm, and self-possessed, freed from all strife, all bias, all condemnation, and bestows upon all the glad and unselfish love of the divinity within him.

He, who is patient, calm, gentle, and forgiving under all circumstances, manifests the Truth. Truth will never be proved by wordy arguments and learned treatises, for if men do not perceive the Truth in infinite patience, undying forgiveness, and all-embracing compassion, no words can ever prove it to them.

It is an easy matter for the passionate to be calm and patient when they are alone, or are in the midst of calmness. It is equally easy for the uncharitable to be gentle and kind when they are dealt kindly with, but he who retains his patience and calmness under all trial, who remains sublimely meek and gentle under the most trying circumstances, he, and he alone, is possessed of the spotless Truth. And this is so because such lofty virtues belong to the Divine, and can only be manifested by one who has attained to the highest wisdom, who has relinquished his passionate and self-seeking nature, who has realized the supreme and unchangeable Law, and has brought himself into harmony with it.

Let men, therefore, cease from vain and passionate arguments about Truth, and let them think and say and do those things which make for harmony, peace, love, and good-will. Let them practice heart-virtue, and search humbly and diligently for the Truth which frees the soul from all error and sin, from all that blights the human heart, and that darkens, as with unending night, the pathway of the wandering souls of earth.

There is one great all-embracing Law which is the foundation and cause of the universe, the Law of Love. It has been called by many names in various countries and at various times, but behind all its names the same unalterable Law may be discovered by the eye of Truth. Names, religions, personalities pass away, but the Law of Love remains. To become possessed of a knowledge of this Law, to enter into conscious harmony with it, is to become immortal, invincible, indestructible.

It is because of the effort of the soul to realize this Law that men come again and again to live, to suffer, and to die; and when realized, suffering ceases, personality is dispersed, and the fleshly life and death are destroyed, for consciousness becomes one with the Eternal.

The Law is absolutely impersonal, and its highest manifested expression is that of Service. When the purified heart has realized Truth it is then called upon to make the last, the greatest and holiest sacrifice, the sacrifice of the well-earned enjoyment of Truth. It is by virtue of this sacrifice that the divinely-emancipated soul comes to dwell among men, clothed with a body of flesh, content to dwell among the lowliest and least, and to be esteemed the servant of all mankind. That sublime humility which is manifested by the world's saviors is the seal of Godhead, and he who has annihilated the personality, and has become a living, visible manifestation of the impersonal, eternal, boundless Spirit of Love, is alone singled out as worthy to receive the unstinted worship of posterity. He only who succeeds in humbling himself with that divine humility which is not only the extinction of self, but is also the pouring out upon all the spirit of unselfish love, is exalted above measure, and given spiritual dominion in the hearts of mankind.

All the great spiritual teachers have denied themselves personal luxuries, comforts, and rewards, have abjured temporal power, and have lived and taught the limitless and impersonal Truth. Compare their lives and teachings, and you will find the same simplicity, the same self-sacrifice, the same humility, love, and peace both lived and preached by them. They taught the same eternal Principles, the realization of which destroys all evil. Those who have been hailed and worshiped as the saviors of mankind are manifestations of the Great impersonal Law, and being such, were free from passion and prejudice, and having no opinions, and no special letter of doctrine to preach and defend, they never sought to convert and to proselytize. Living in the highest Goodness, the supreme Perfection, their sole object was to uplift mankind by manifesting that Goodness in thought, word, and deed. They stand between man the personal and God the impersonal, and serve as exemplary types for the salvation of self-enslaved mankind.

Men who are immersed in self, and who cannot comprehend the Goodness that is absolutely impersonal, deny divinity to all saviors except their own, and thus introduce personal hatred and doctrinal controversy, and, while defending their own particular views with passion, look upon each other as being heathens or infidels, and so render null and void, as far as their lives are concerned, the unselfish beauty and holy grandeur of the lives and teachings of their own Masters. Truth cannot be limited; it can never be the special prerogative of any man, school, or nation, and when personality steps in, Truth is lost.

The glory alike of the saint, the sage, and the savior is this,--that he has realized the most profound lowliness, the most sublime unselfishness; having given up all, even his own personality, all his works are holy and enduring, for they are freed from every taint of self. He gives, yet never thinks of receiving; he works without regretting the past or anticipating the future, and never looks for reward.

When the farmer has tilled and dressed his land and put in the seed, he knows that he has done all that he can possibly do, and that now he must trust to the elements, and wait patiently for the course of time to bring about the harvest, and that no amount of expectancy on his part will affect the result. Even so, he who has realized Truth goes forth as a sower of the seeds of goodness, purity, love and peace, without expectancy, and never looking for results, knowing that there is the Great Over-ruling Law which brings about its own harvest in due time, and which is alike the source of preservation and destruction.

Men, not understanding the divine simplicity of a profoundly unselfish heart, look upon their particular savior as the manifestation of a special miracle, as being something entirely apart and distinct from the nature of things, and as being, in his ethical excellence, eternally unapproachable by the whole of mankind. This attitude of unbelief (for such it is) in the divine perfectibility of man, paralyzes effort, and binds the souls of men as with strong ropes to sin and suffering. Jesus "grew in wisdom" and was "perfected by suffering." What Jesus was, he became such; what Buddha was, he became such; and every holy man became such by unremitting perseverance in self-sacrifice. Once recognize this, once realize that by watchful effort and hopeful perseverance you can rise above your lower nature, and great and glorious will be the vistas of attainment that will open out before you. Buddha vowed that he would not relax his efforts until he arrived at the state of perfection, and he accomplished his purpose.

What the saints, sages, and saviors have accomplished, you likewise may accomplish if you will only tread the way which they trod and pointed out, the way of self-sacrifice, of self-denying service.

Truth is very simple. It says, "Give up self," "Come unto Me" (away from all that defiles) "and I will give you rest." All the mountains of commentary that have been piled upon it cannot hide it from the heart that is earnestly seeking for Righteousness. It does not require learning; it can be known in spite of learning. Disguised under many forms by erring self-seeking man, the beautiful simplicity and clear transparency of Truth remains unaltered and undimmed, and the unselfish heart enters into and partakes of its

shining radiance. Not by weaving complex theories, not by building up speculative philosophies is Truth realized; but by weaving
the web of inward purity, by building up the Temple of a stainless
life is Truth realized.

He who enters upon this holy way begins by restraining his passions. This is virtue, and is the beginning of saintship, and saintship is the beginning of holiness. The entirely worldly mangratifies
all his desires, and practices no more restraint than the law of
the land in which he lives demands; the virtuous man restrains
his passions; the saint attacks the enemy of Truth in its stronghold within his own heart, and restrains all selfish and impure
thoughts; while the holy man is he who is free from passion and all
impure thought, and to whom goodness and purity have become
as natural as scent and color are to the flower. The holy man is
divinely wise; he alone knows Truth in its fullness, and has entered into abiding rest and peace. For him evil has ceased; it has
disappeared in the universal light of the All-Good. Holiness is the
badge of wisdom. Said Krishna to the Prince Arjuna--

"Humbleness, truthfulness, and harmlessness,

Patience and honor, reverence for the wise,

Purity, constancy, control of self,

Contempt of sense-delights, self-sacrifice,

Perception of the certitude of ill

In birth, death, age, disease, suffering and sin;

An ever tranquil heart in fortunes good

And fortunes evil, ...

... Endeavors resolute

To reach perception of the utmost soul,

And grace to understand what gain it were

So to attain--this is true wisdom, Prince!

And what is otherwise is ignorance!"

Whoever fights ceaselessly against his own selfishness, and
strives to supplant it with all-embracing love, is a saint, whether
he live in a cottage or in the midst of riches and influence; or
whether he preaches or remains obscure.

To the worldling, who is beginning to aspire towards higher things, the saint, such as a sweet St. Francis of Assisi, or a conquering St. Anthony, is a glorious and inspiring spectacle; to the saint, an equally enrapturing sight is that of the sage, sitting serene and holy, the conqueror of sin and sorrow, no more tormented by regret and remorse, and whom even temptation can never reach; and yet even the sage is drawn on by a still more glorious vision, that of the savior actively manifesting his knowledge in selfless works, and rendering his divinity more potent for good by sinking himself in the throbbing, sorrowing, aspiring heart of mankind.

And this only is true service--to forget oneself in love towards all, to lose oneself in working for the whole. O thou vain and foolish man, who thinkest that thy many works can save thee; who, chained to all error, talkest loudly of thyself, thy work, and thy many sacrifices, and magnifiest thine own importance; know this, that though thy fame fill the whole earth, all thy work shall come to dust, and thou thyself be reckoned lower than the least in the Kingdom of Truth!

Only the work that is impersonal can live; the works of self are both powerless and perishable. Where duties, howsoever humble, are done without self-interest, and with joyful sacrifice, there is true service and enduring work. Where deeds, however brilliant and apparently successful, are done from love of self, there is ignorance of the Law of Service, and the work perishes.

It is given to the world to learn one great and divine lesson, the lesson of absolute unselfishness. The saints, sages, and saviors of all time are they who have submitted themselves to this task, and have learned and lived it. All the Scriptures of the world are framed to teach this one lesson; all the great teachers reiterate it. It is too simple for the world which, scorning it, stumbles along in the complex ways of selfishness.

A pure heart is the end of all religion and the beginning of divinity. To search for this Righteousness is to walk the Way of Truth and Peace, and he who enters this Way will soon perceive that Immortality which is independent of birth and death, and will realize that in the Divine economy of the universe the humblest effort is not lost.

The divinity of a Krishna, a Gautama, or a Jesus is the crowning glory of self-abnegation, the end of the soul's pilgrimage in matter

and mortality, and the world will not have finished its long journey
until every soul has become as these, and has entered into the
blissful realization of its own divinity.

Great glory crowns the heights of hope by arduous struggle won;
Bright honor rounds the hoary head that mighty works hath done;
Fair riches come to him who strives in ways of golden gain. And
fame enshrines his name who works with genius-glowing brain;
but greater glory waits for him who, in the bloodless strife against
self and wrong, adopts, in love, the sacrificial life. And brighter
honor rounds the brow of him who, 'mid the scorns of blind idola-
ters of self, accepts the crown of thorns. And fairer purer riches
come to him who greatly strives to walk in ways of love and truth
to sweeten human lives. And he who serveth well mankind exchanges fleeting fame for Light eternal, Joy and Peace, and robes
of heavenly flame.

THE REALIZATION OF PERFECT PEACE

In the external universe there is ceaseless turmoil, change, and unrest; at the heart of all things there is undisturbed repose; in this deep silence dwelleth the Eternal.

Man partakes of this duality, and both the surface change and disquietude, and the deep-seated eternal abode of Peace, are contained within him.

As there are silent depths in the ocean which the fiercest storm cannot reach, so there are silent, holy depths in the heart of man which the storms of sin and sorrow can never disturb. To reach this silence and to live consciously in it is peace.

Discord is rife in the outward world, but unbroken harmony holds sway at the heart of the universe. The human soul, torn by discordant passion and grief, reaches blindly toward the harmony of the sinless state, and to reach this state and to live consciously in it is peace.

Hatred severs human lives, fosters persecution, and hurls nations into ruthless war, yet men, though they do not understand why, retain some measure of faith in the overshadowing of a Perfect Love; and to reach this Love and to live consciously in it is peace.

And this inward peace, this silence, this harmony, this Love, is the Kingdom of Heaven, which is so difficult to reach because few are willing to give up themselves and to become as little children.

"Heaven's gate is very narrow and minute,

It cannot be perceived by foolish men

Blinded by vain illusions of the world;

E'en the clear-sighted who discern the way,

And seek to enter, find the portal barred,

And hard to be unlocked. Its massive bolts

Are pride and passion, avarice and lust."

Men cry peace! Peace! Where there is no peace, but on the contrary, discord, disquietude and strife. Apart from that Wisdom which is inseparable from self-renunciation, there can be no real and abiding peace.

The peace which results from social comfort, passing gratification, or worldly victory is transitory in its nature, and is burnt up in the heat of fiery trial. Only the Peace of Heaven endures through all trial, and only the selfless heart can know the Peace of Heaven.

Holiness alone is undying peace. Self-control leads to it, and the ever-increasing Light of Wisdom guides the pilgrim on his way. It is partaken of in a measure as soon as the path of virtue is entered upon, but it is only realized in its fullness when self disappears in the consummation of a stainless life.

"This is peace,

To conquer love of self and lust of life,

To tear deep-rooted passion from the heart

To still the inward strife."

If, O reader! You would realize the Light that never fades, the Joy that never ends, and the tranquility that cannot be disturbed; if you would leave behind for ever your sins, your sorrows, your anxieties and perplexities; if, I say, you would partake of this salvation, this supremely glorious Life, then conquer yourself. Bring every thought, every impulse, every desire, into perfect obedience to the divine power resident within you. There is no other way to peace but this, and if you refuse to walk it, your much praying and your strict adherence to ritual will be fruitless and unavailing, and neither gods nor angels can help you. Only to him that overcometh is given the white stone of the regenerate life, on which is written the New and Ineffable Name.

Come away, for awhile, from external things, from the pleasures of the senses, from the arguments of the intellect, from the noise and the excitements of the world, and withdraw yourself into the inmost chamber of your heart, and there, free from the sacrilegious intrusion of all selfish desires, you will find a deep silence, a holy calm, a blissful repose, and if you will rest awhile in that holy place, and will meditate there, the faultless eye of Truth will open within you, and you will see things as they really are. This holy place within you is your real and eternal self; it is the divine within you; and only when you identify yourself with it can you be said to be "clothed and in your right mind." It is the abode of peace, the temple of wisdom, the dwelling-place of immortality. Apart from this inward resting-place, this Mount of Vision, there can be no true peace, no knowledge of the Divine, and if you can remain there for one minute, one hour, or one day, it is possible for you to remain there always. All your sins and sorrows, your fears and anxieties are your own, and you can cling to them or you can give them up. Of your own accord you cling to your unrest; of your own accord you can come to abiding peace. No one else can give up sin for you; you must give it up yourself. The greatest teacher can do no more than walk the way of Truth for himself, and point it out to you; you yourself must walk it for yourself. You can obtain freedom and peace alone by your own efforts, by yielding up that which binds the soul, and which is destructive of peace.

The angels of divine peace and joy are always at hand, and if you do not see them, and hear them, and dwell with them, it is because you shut yourself out from them, and prefer the company of the spirits of evil within you. You are what you will to be, what you wish to be, what you prefer to be. You can commence to purify yourself, and by so doing can arrive at peace, or you can refuse to purify yourself, and so remain with suffering.

Step aside, then; come out of the fret and the fever of life; away from the scorching heat of self, and enter the inward resting-place where the cooling airs of peace will calm, renew, and restore you.

Come out of the storms of sin and anguish. Why be troubled and tempest-tossed when the haven of Peace of God is yours!

Give up all self-seeking; give up self, and lo! The Peace of God is yours!

Subdue the animal within you; conquer every selfish uprising, every discordant voice; transmute the base metals of your selfish nature into the unalloyed gold of Love, and you shall realize the Life of Perfect Peace. Thus subduing, thus conquering, thus transmuting, you will, O reader! While living in the flesh, cross the dark waters of mortality, and will reach that Shore upon which the storms of sorrow never beat, and where sin and suffering and dark uncertainty cannot come. Standing upon that Shore, holy, compassionate, awakened, and self-possessed and glad with unending gladness, you will realize that

"Never the Spirit was born, the Spirit will cease to be never; Never was time it was not, end and beginning are dreams; Birthless and deathless and changeless remaineth the Spirit for ever; Death hath not touched it at all, dead though the house of it seems."

You will then know the meaning of Sin, of Sorrow, of Suffering, and that the end thereof is Wisdom; will know the cause and the issue of existence.

And with this realization you will enter into rest, for this is the bliss of immortality, this, the unchangeable gladness, this the untrammeled knowledge, undefiled Wisdom, and undying Love; this, and this only, is the realization of Perfect Peace.

O thou who wouldst teach men of Truth!

Hast thou passed through the desert of doubt?

Art thou purged by the fires of sorrow? Hath Truth

The fiends of opinion cast out

Of thy human heart? Is thy soul so fair

That no false thought can ever harbor there?

O thou who wouldst teach men of Love!

Hast thou passed through the place of despair?

Hast thou wept through the dark night of grief?

Does it move

(Now freed from its sorrow and care)

Thy human heart to pitying gentleness,

Looking on wrong, and hate, and ceaseless stress?

O thou who wouldst teach men of Peace!

Hast thou crossed the wide ocean of strife?

Hast thou found on the Shores of the Silence,

Release from all the wild unrest of life?

From thy human heart hath all striving gone,

Leaving but Truth, and Love, and Peace alone?

Above Life's Turmoil

Foreword

We cannot alter external things, nor shape other people to our liking, nor mould the world to our wishes but we can alter internal things, our desires, passions, thoughts, we can shape our liking to other people, and we can mould the inner world of our own mind in accordance with wisdom, and so reconcile it to the outer world of men and things. The turmoil of the world we cannot avoid, but the disturbances of mind we can overcome. The duties and difficulties of life claim our attention, but we can rise above all anxiety concerning them. Surrounded by noise, we can yet have a quiet mind; involved in responsibilities, the heart can be at rest; in the midst of strife, we can know the abiding peace. The twenty pieces which comprise this book, unrelated as some of them are in the letter, will be found to be harmonious in the spirit, in that they point the reader towards those heights of self-knowledge and self-conquest which, rising above the turbulence of the world, lift their peaks where the Heavenly Silence reigns.

James Allen

True Happiness

To maintain an unchangeable sweetness of disposition, to think only thoughts that are pure and gentle, and to be happy under all circumstances,- such blessed conditions and such beauty of character and life should be the aim of all, and particularly so of those who wish to lessen the misery of the world. If anyone has failed to lift himself above ungentleness, impurity, and unhappiness, he is greatly deluded if he imagines he can make the world happier by the propagation of any theory or theology. He who is daily living in harshness, impurity, or unhappiness is day by day adding to the sum of the world's misery; whereas he who continually lives in goodwill, and does not depart from happiness, is day by day increasing the sum of the world's happiness, and this independently of any religious beliefs which these may or may not hold.

He who has not learned how to be gentle, or giving, loving and happy, has learned very little, great though his book-learning and profound his acquaintance which the letter of Scripture may be, for it is in the process of becoming gentle, pure, and happy that the deep, real and enduring lessons of life are learned. Unbroken sweetness of conduct in the face of all outward antagonism is the infallible indication of a self-conquered soul, the witness of wisdom, and the proof of the possession of Truth.

A sweet and happy soul is the ripened fruit of experience and wisdom, and it sheds abroad the invisible yet powerful aroma of its influence, gladdening the hearts of others, and purifying the world. And all who will, and who have not yet commenced, may begin this day, if they will so resolve, to live sweetly and happily, as becomes the dignity of a true manhood or womanhood. Do not say that your surroundings are against you. A man's surroundings are never against him; they are there to aid him, and all those outward occurrences over which you lose sweetness and peace of mind are the very conditions necessary to your development, and it is only by meeting and overcoming them that you can learn, and grow, and ripen. The fault is in yourself.

Pure happiness is the rightful and healthy condition of the soul, and all may possess it if they will live purely and unselfish.

"Have goodwill

To all that lives, letting unkindness die,

And greed and wrath, so that your lives be made

Like soft airs passing by."

Is this too difficult for you? Then unrest and unhappiness will continue to dwell with you. Your belief and aspiration and resolve are all that are necessary to make it easy, to render it in the near future a thing accomplished, a blessed state realised.

Despondency, irritability, anxiety and complaining, condemning and grumbling- all these are thought-cankers, mind-diseases; they are the indications of a wrong mental condition, and those who suffer therefrom would do well to remedy their thinking and conduct. It is true there is much sin and misery in the world, so that all our love and compassion are needed, but our misery is not needed- there is already too much of that. No, it is our cheerfulness and happiness that are needed for there is too little of that. We can give nothing better to the world than beauty of life and character; without this, all other things are vain; this is pre-eminently excellent; it is enduring, real, and not to be overthrown, and it includes all joy and blessedness.

Cease to dwell pessimistically upon the wrongs around you; dwell no more in complaints about, and revolt against, the evil in others, and commence to live free from all wrong and evil yourself. Peace of mind, pure religion, and true reform lie this way. If you would have others true, be true; if you would have the world emancipated from misery and sin, emancipate yourself; if you would have your home and your surroundings happy, be happy. You can transform everything around you if you will transform yourself.

"Don't bewail and bemoan.....

Don't waste yourself in rejection, nor bark against the bad,

  but chant the beauties of the good."

And this you will naturally and spontaneously do as you realise the good in yourself.

The Immortal Man

Immortality is here and now, and is not a speculative something beyond the grave. It is a lucid state of consciousness in which the sensations of the body, the varying and unrestful states of mind, and the circumstances and events of life are seen to be of a fleeting and therefore of an illusory character.

Immortality does not belong to time, and will never be found in time; it belongs to Eternity; and just as time is here and now, so is Eternity here and now, and a man may find that Eternity and establish in it, if he will overcome the self that derives its life from the unsatisfying and perishable things of time.

Whilst a man remains immersed in sensation, desire, and the passing events of his day-by-day existence, and regards those sensations, desires, and passing events as of the essence of himself, he can have no knowledge of immortality. The thing which such a man desires, and which he mistakes for immortality, is persistence; that is, a continous succession of sensations and events in time. Living in, loving and clinging to, the things which stimulate and minister to his immediate gratification, and realising no state of consciousness above and independent of this, he thirsts for its continuance, and strives to banish the thought that he will at last have to part from those earthly luxuries and delights to which he has become enslaved, and which he regards as being inseparable from himself.

Persistence is the antithesis of immortality; and to be absorbed in it is spiritual death. Its very nature is change, impermanence. It is a continual living and dying.

The death of the body can never bestow upon a man immortality. Spirits are not different from men, and live their little feverish life of broken consciousness, and are still immersed in change and mortality. The mortal man, he who thirsts for the persistence of his pleasure-loving personality is still mortal after death, and only lives another life with a beginning and an end without memory of the past, or knowledge of the future.

The immortal man is he who has detached himself from the

things of time by having ascended into that state of consciousness which is fixed and unvariable, and is not affected by passing events and sensations. Human life consists of an evermoving procession of events, and in this procession the mortal man is immersed, and he is carried along with it; and being so carried along, he has no knowledge of what is behind and before him. The immortal man is he who has stepped out of this procession, and he stands by unmoved and watches it; and from his fixed place he sees both the before, the behind and the middle of the moving thing called life. No longer identifying himself with the sensations and fluctuations of the personality, or with the outward changes which make up the life in time, he has become the passionless spectator of his own destiny and of the destinies of the men and nations.

The mortal man, also, is one who is caught in a dream, and he neither knows that he was formerly awake, nor that he will wake again; he is a dreamer without knowledge, nothing more. The immortal man is as one who has awakened out of his dream, and he knows that his dream was not an enduring reality, but a passing illusion. He is a man with knowledge, the knowledge of both states- that of persistence, and that of immortality,- and is in full possession of himself.

The mortal man lives in the time or world state of consciousness which begins and ends; the immortal man lives in the cosmic or heaven state of consciousness, in which there is neither beginning nor end, but an eternal now. Such a man remains poised and steadfast under all changes, and the death of his body will not in any way interrupt the eternal consciousness in which he abides. Of such a one it is said, "He shall not taste of death", because he has stepped out of the stream of mortality, and established himself in the abode of Truth. Bodies, personalities, nations, and worlds pass away, but Truth remains, and its glory is undimmed by time. The immortal man, then, is he who has conquered himself; who no longer identifies himself with the self-seeking forces of the personality, but who has trained himself to direct those forces with the hand of a master, and so has brought them into harmony with the causal energy and source of all things.

The fret and fever of life has ceased, doubt and fear are cast out, and death is not for him who has realised the fadeless splendour of that life of Truth by adjusting heart and mind to the eternal and unchangeable verities.

The Overcoming of Self

Many people have very confused and erroneous ideas concerning the terms "the overcoming of self", "the eradication of desire", and "the annihilation of the personality." Some (particularly the intellectual who are prone to theories) regard it as a metaphysical theory altogether apart from life and conduct; while others conclude that it is the crushing out of all life, energy and action, and the attempt to idealise stagnation and death. These errors and confusions, arising as they do in the minds of individuals, can only be removed by the individuals themselves; but perhaps it may make their removal a little less difficult (for those who are seeking Truth) by presenting the matter in another way.

The doctrine of the overcoming or annihilation of self is simplicity itself; indeed, so simple, practical, and close at hand is it that a child of five, whose mind has not yet become clouded with theories, theological schemes and speculative philosophies, would be far more likely to comprehend it than many older people who have lost their hold upon simple and beautiful truths by the adoption of complicated theories.

The annihilation of self consists in weeding out and destroying all those elements in the soul which lead to division, strife, suffering, disease and sorrow. It does not mean the destruction of any good and beautiful and peace-producing quality. For instance, when a man is tempted to irritability or anger, and by a great effort overcomes the selfish tendency, casts it from him, and acts from the spirit of patience and love, in that moment of self-conquest he practises the annihilation of self. Every noble man practises it in part, though he may deny it in his words, and he who carries out this practice to its completion, eradicating every selfish tendency until only the divinely beautiful qualities remain, he is said to have annihilated the personality (all the personal elements) and to have arrived at Truth.

The self which is to be annihilated is composed of the following ten worthless and sorrow-producing elements:

Lust

Hatred

Avarice

Self-indulgence

Self-seeking

Vanity

Pride

Doubt

Dark belief

Delusion

It is the total abandonment, the complete annihilation of these ten elements, for they comprise the body of desire. On the other hand it teaches the cultivation, practice, and preservation of the following ten divine qualities:

Purity

Patience

Humility

Self-sacrifice

Self-reliance

Fearlessness

Knowledge

Wisdom

Compassion

Love

These comprise the Body of Truth, and to live entirely in them is to be a doer and knower of the Truth, is to be an embodiment of Truth. The combination of the ten elements is called Self or the Personality; the combination of the ten qualities produces what is called Truth; the Impersonal; the abiding, real and immortal Man.

It will thus be seen that it is not the destruction of any noble, true, and enduring quality that is taught, but only the destruction of those things that are ignoble, false and evanescent. Neither is this overcoming of self the deprivation of gladness, happiness and joy, but rather is it the constant possession of these things by living in the joy-begetting qualities. It is the abandonment of the lust for enjoyment, but not of enjoyment itself; the destruction of the thirst for pleasure, but not of pleasure itself; the annihilation of the selfish longing for love, and power, and possessions themselves. It is the preservation of all those things which draw and bind men together in unity and concord, and, far from idealising stagnation and death, urges men to the practice of those qualities which lead to the highest, noblest, most effective, and enduring action. He whose actions proceed from some or all of the ten elements wastes his energies upon negations, and does not preserve his soul; but he whose actions proceed from some or all of the ten qualities, he truly and wisely acts and so preserves his soul.

He who lives largely in the ten earthly elements, and who is blind and deaf to the spiritual verities, will find no attraction in the doctrine of self-surrender, for it will appear to him as the complete extinction of his being; but he who is endeavouring to live in the ten heavenly qualities will see the glory and beauty of the doctrine, and will know it as the foundation of Life Eternal. He will also see that when men apprehend and practise it, industry, commerce, government, and every worldly activity will be purified; and action, purpose and intelligence, instead of being destroyed, will be intensified and enlarged, but freed from strife and pain.

The Uses of Temptation

The soul, in its journey towards perfection, passes through three distinct stages. The first is the animal stage, in which the man is content to live, in the gratification of his senses, unawakened to the knowledge of sin, or of his divine inheritance, and altogether unconscious of the spiritual possibilities within himself.

The second is the dual stage, in which the mind is continually oscillating between its animal and divine tendencies having become awakened to the consciousness of both. It is during this stage that temptation plays its part in the progress of the soul. It is a stage of continual fighting, of falling and rising, of sinning and repenting, for the man, still loving, and reluctant to leave, the gratifications in which he has so long lived, yet also aspires to the purity and excellence of the spiritual state, and he is continually mortified by an undecided choice.

Urged on by the divine life within him, this stage becomes at last one of deep anguish and suffering, and then the soul is ushered into the third stage, that of knowledge , in which the man rises above both sin and temptation, and enters into peace.

Temptation, like contentment in sin, is not a lasting condition,as the majority of people suppose; it is a passing phase, an experience through which the soul must pass; but as to whether a man will pass through that condition in this present life, and realise holiness and heavenly rest here and now, will depend entirely upon the strength of his intellectual and spiritual exertions, and upon the intensity and ardour with which he searches for Truth.

Temptation, with all its attendant torments can be overcome here and now, but it can only be overcome by knowledge. It is a condition of darkness or of semi-darkness. The fully enlightened soul is proof against all temptation. When a man fully understands the source, nature, and meaning of temptation, in that hour he will conquer it, and will rest from his long travail; but whilst he remains in ignorance, attention to religious observances, and much praying and reading of Scripture will fail to bring him peace.

If a man goes out to conquer an enemy, knowing nothing of his

enemy's strength, tactics, or place of ambush, he will not only ig-
nominiously fail, but will speedily fall into the hands of the enemy.
He who would overcome his enemy the tempter, must discover his
stronghold and place of concealment, and must also find out the
unguarded gates in his own fortress where his enemy effects so
easy an entrance. This necessitates continual meditation, ceaseless watchfulness, and constant and rigid introspection which lays
bare, before the spiritual eyes of the tempted one, the vain and
selfish motives of his soul. This is the holy warfare of the saints; it
is the fight upon which every soul enters when it awakens out of
its long sleep of animal indulgence.

Men fail to conquer, and the fight is indefinitely prolonged, because they labour, almost universally, under two delusions: first,
that all temptations come from without; and second, that they are
tempted because of their goodness. Whilst a man is held in bondage by these two delusions, he will make no progress; when he has
shaken them off, he will pass on rapidly from victory to victory,
and will taste of spiritual joy and rest.

Two searching truths must take the place of these two delusions, and those truths are: first, that all temptation comes from
within; and second, that a man is tempted because of the evil that
is within him. The idea that God, a devil, evil spirits, or outward
objects are the source of temptation must be dispelled.

The source and cause of all temptation is in the inward desire;
that being purified or eliminated, outward objects and extraneous
powers are utterly powerless to move the soul to sin or to temptation. The outward object is merely the occasion of the temptation, never the cause; this is in the desire of the one tempted. If
the cause existed in the object, all men would be tempted alike,
temptation could never be overcome, and men would be hopelessly doomed to endless torment; but seated, as it is, in his own
desires, he has the remedy in his own hands, and can become
victorious over all temptation by purifying those desires. A man is
tempted because there are within him certain desires or states of
mind which he has come to regard as unholy. Thes desires may lie
asleep for a long time, and the man may think that he has got rid
of them, when suddenly, on the presentation of an outward object,
the sleeping desire wakes up and thirsts of immediate gratification; and this is the state of temptation.

The good in a man is never tempted. Goodness destroys temptation. It is the evil in a man that is aroused and tempted. The measure of a man's temptations is the exact register of his own unholiness. As a man purifies his heart, temptation ceases, for when a certain unlawful desire has been taken out of the heart, the object which formerly appealed to it can no longer do so, but becomes dead and powerless, for there is nothing left in the heart that can respond to it.The honest man cannot be tempted to steal, let the occasion be ever so opportune; the man of purified appeties cannot be tempted to gluttony and drunkenness, though the viands and wines be the most luscious; he of an enlightened understanding, whose mind is calm in the strength of inward virtue, can never be tempted to anger, irritability or revenge, and the wiles and charms of the wanton fall upon the purified heart as empty meaningless shadows.

Temptation shows a man just where he is sinful and ignorant, and is a means of urging him on to higher altitudes of knowledge and purity. Without temptation the soul cannot grow and become strong, there could be no wisdom, no real virtue; and though there would be lethargy and death, there could be no peace and no fulness of life. When temptation is understood and conquered, perfection is assured, and such perfection may bcome any man's who is willing to cast every selfish and impure desire by which he is possessed, into the sacrificial fire of knowledge. Let men, therefore, search diligently for Truth, realising that whilst they are subject to temptation, they have not comprehended Truth, and have much to learn.

Ye who are tempted know, then, that ye are tempted of yourselves. "For every man is tempted when he is drawn away of his own lusts," says the Apostle James. You are tempted because you are clinging to the animal within you and are unwilling to let go; because you are living in the false mortal self which is ever devoid of all true knowledge, knowing nothing, seeking nothing, but its own immediate gratification, ignorant of every Truth, and of every divine Principle. Clinging to that self, you continually suffer the pains of three separate torments; the torment of desire, the torment of repletion, and the torment of remorse.

"So flameth Trishna, lust and thirst of things.

Eager, ye cleave to shadows, dote on dreams;

A false self in the midst ye plant, and make

A World around which seems;

Blind to the height beyond; deaf to the sound

Of sweet airs breathed from far past Indra's sky;

Dumb to the summons of the true life kept

For him who false puts by,

So grow the strifes and lusts which make earth's war,

So grieve poor cheated hearts and flow salt tears;

So wax the passions, envies, angers, hates;

So years chase blood-stained years

With wild red feet."

In that false self lies the germ of every suffering, the blight of every hope, the substance of every grief. When you are ready to give it up; when you are willing to have laid bare before you all its selfishness, impurity, and ignorance, and to confess its darkness to the uttermost, then will you enter upon the life of self-knowledge and self-mastery; you will become conscious of the god within you, of that divine nature which, seeking no gratification, abides in a region of perpetual joy and peace where suffering cannot come and where temptation can find no foothold. Establishing yourself, day by day, more and more firmly in that inward Divinity, the time will at last come when you will be able to say with Him whom millions worship, few understand and fewer still follow, - "The Prince of this world cometh and hath nothing in me."

The Man of Integrity

There are times in the life of every man who takes his stand on high moral principles when his faith in, and knowledge of, those principles is tested to the uttermost, and the way in which he comes out of the fiery trial decides as to whether he has sufficient strength to live as a man of Truth, and join the company of the free, or shall still remain a slave and a hireling to the cruel task-master, Self.

Such times of trial generally assume the form of a temptation to do a wrong thing and continue in comfort and prosperity, or to stand by what is right and accept poverty and failure; and so powerful is the trial that, to the tempted one, it plainly appears on the face of things as though, if he chooses the wrong, his material success will be assured for the remainder of his life, but if he does what is right, he will be ruined for ever.

Frequently the man at once quails and gives way before this appalling prospect which the Path of Righteousness seems to hold out for him, but should he prove sufficiently strong to withstand this onslaught of temptation, then the inward seducer the spirit of self, assumes the garb of an Angel of Light, and whispers, "Think of your wife and children; think of those who are dependent upon you; will you bring them down to disgrace and starvation?"

Strong indeed and pure must be the man who can come triumphant out of such a trial, but he who does so, enters at once a higher realm of life, where his spiritual eyes are opened to see beautiful things; and then poverty and ruin which seemed inevitable do not come, but a more abiding success comes, and a peaceful heart and a quiet conscience. But he who fails does not obtain the promised prosperity, and his heart is restless and his conscience troubled.

The right-doer cannot ultimately fail, the wrong-doer cannot ultimately succeed, for...

"Such is the Law which moves to Righteousness

Which none at last can turn aside or stay,"

and it is because justice is at the heart of things- because the

Great Law is good- that the man of integrity is superior to fear, and failure, and poverty, and shame, and disgrace.As the poet further says of this Law:

"The heart of its Love, the end of it

Is peace and cosummation sweet-obey."

The man who fearing the loss of present pleasures or material comforts, denies the Truth within him, can be injured, and robbed, and degraded, and trampled upon, because he has first injured, robbed and degraded, and trampled upon his own nobler self; but the man of steadfast virtue, of unblemished integrity, cannot be subject to such conditions, because he has denied the craven self within him and has taken refuge in Truth. It is not the scourge and the chains which make a man a slave, but the fact that he is a slave.

Slander, Accusation, and malice cannot affect the righteous man, nor call from him any bitter response, nor does he need to go about to defend himself and prove his innocence. His innocence and integrity alone are a sufficient answer to all that hatred may attempt against him. Nor can he ever be subdued by the forces of darkness, having subdued all those forces within himself; but he turns all evil things to good account - out of darkness he brings light, out of hatred love, out of dishonour honour; and slanders, envies, and misrepresentations only serve to make more bright the jewel of Truth within him, and to glorify his high and holy destiny.

Let the man of integrity rejoice and be glad when he is severely tried; let him be thankful that he has been given an opportunity of proving his loyalty to the noble principles which he has espoused; and let him think: "Now is the hour of holy opportunity! Now is the day of triumph for Truth! Though I lose the whole world I will not desert the right!" So thinking, he will return good for evil, and will think compassionately of the wrong-doer.

The slanderer, the backbiter, and the wrong-doer may seem to succeed for a time, but the Law of Justice prevails; the man of integrity may seem to fail for a time, but he is invincible, and in none of the worlds, visible or invisible, can there be forged a weapon that shall prevail against him.

Discrimination

There is one quality which is pre-eminently necessary to spiritual development, the quality of discrimination.

A man's spiritual progress will be painfully slow and uncertain until there opens with him the eye of discrimination, for without this testing, proving, searching quality, he will but grope in the dark, will be unable to distinguish the real from the unreal, the shadow from the substance, and will so confuse the false with the true as to mistake the inward promptings of his animal nature for those of the spirit of Truth.

A blind man left in a strange place may go grope his way in darkness, but not without much confusion and many painful falls and bruisings. Without discrimination a man is mentally blind, and his life is a painful groping in darkness, a confusion in which vice and virtue are indistinguishable one from the other, where facts are confounded with truths; opinions with principles, and where ideas, events, men, and things appear to be out of all relation to each other.

A man's mind and life should be free from confusion. He should be prepared to meet every mental, material and spritual difficulty, and should not be inextricably caught (as many are) in the meshes of doubt, indecision and uncertainity when troubles and so-called misfortunes come along. He should be fortified against every emergency that can come against him; but such mental preparedness and strength cannot be attained in any degree without discrimination, and discrimination can only be developed by bringing into play and constantly exercising the analytical faculty.

Mind, like muscle, is developed by use, and the assiduous exercise of the mind in any given direction will develop, in that direction, mental capacity and power. The merely critical faculty is developed and strengthened by continuously comparing and analysing the ideas and opinions of others. But discrimination is something more and greater than criticism; it is a spiritual quality from which the cruelty and egotism which so frequently accompany criticism are eliminated, and by virtue of which a man sees things as they are, and not as he would like them to be.

Discrimination, being a spiritual quality, can only be developed by spiritual methods, namely, by questioning, examining, and analysing one's own ideas, opinions, and conduct. The critical, fault finding faculty must be withdrawn from its merciless application to the opinions and conduct of others, and must be applied, with undiminished severity, to oneself. A man must be prepared to question his every opinion, his every thought, and his every line of conduct, and rigorously and logically test them; only in this way can the discrimination which destroys confusion will be developed.

Before a man can enter upon such mental exercise, he must make himself of a teachable spirit. This does not mean that he must allow himself to be led by others; it means that he must be prepared to yield up any cherished thoughts to which he clings, if it will not bear the penetrating light of reason, if it shrivels up before the pure flames of searching aspirations. The man who says, "I am right!" and who refuses to question his position in order to discover whether he is right, will continue to follow the line of his passions and prejudices, and will not acquire discrimination. The man who humbly asks, "Am I right?" and then proceeds to test and prove his position by earnest thought and the love of Truth, will always be able to discover the true and to distinguish it from the false, and he will acquire the priceless possession of discrimination.

The man who is afraid to think searchingly upon his opinions, and to reason critically upon his position, will have to develop moral courage before he can acquire discrimination.

A man must be true to himself, fearless with himself, before he can perceive the Pure Principles of Truth, before he can receive the all-revealing Light of Truth.

The more Truth is inquired of, the brighter it shines; it cannot suffer under examination and analysis.

The more error is questioned, the darker it grows; it cannot survive the entrance of pure and searching thought.

To "prove all things" is to find the good and throw the evil.

He who reasons and meditates learns to discriminate; he who discriminates discovers the eternally True.

Confusion, suffering and spiritual darkness follow the thoughtless.

Harmony, blessedness and the Light of Truth attend upon the thoughtful.

Passion and prejudice are blind, and cannot discriminate: they are still crucifying the Christ and releasing Barabbas.

Belief, The Basis of Action

Belief is an important word in the teachings of the wise, and it figures prominently in all religions. According to Jesus, a certain kind of belief is necessary to salvation or regeneration, and Buddha definitely taught that right belief is the first and most essential step in the Way of Truth, as without right belief there cannot be right conduct, and he who has not learned how to rightly govern and conduct himself, has not yet comprehended the simplest rudiments of Truth.

Belief as laid down by the Great Teachers, is not belief in any particualr school, philosophy, or religion, but consists of an altitude of mind determining the whole course of one's life. Belief and conduct are, therefore inseparable, for the one determines the other.

Belief is the basis of all action, and, this being so, the belief which dominates the hearts or mind is shown in the life. Every man acts, thinks, lives in exact accordance with the belief which is rooted in his innermost being, and such is the mathematical nature of the laws which govern mind that it is absolutely impossible for anyone to believe in two opposing conditions at the same time. For instance, it is impossible to believe in justice and injustice, hatred and love, peace and strife, self and truth. Every man believes in one or the other of these opposites, never in both, and the daily conduct of every man indicates the nature of his belief. The man who believes in justice, who regards it as an eternal and indestructible Principle, never boils over with righteous indignation, does not grow cynical and pessimistic over the inequalities of life, and remains calm and untroubled through all trials and difficulties. It is impossible for him to act otherwise, for he believes that justice reigns, and that, therefore, all that is called injustice is fleeting and illusory.

The man who is continually getting enraged over the injustice of his fellow men, who talks about himself being badly treated, or who mourns over the lack of justice in the world around him, shows by his conduct, his attitude of mind, that he believes in injustice. However he may protest to the contrary, in his inmost heart he believes that confusion and chaos are dominant in the universe, the result being that he dwells in misery and unrest, and his conduct is faulty.

Again, he who believes in love, in its stability and power, practises it under all circumstances, never deviates from it, and bestows it alike upon enemies as upon friends. He who slanders and condemns, who speaks disparagingly of others, or regards them with contempt, believes not in love, but hatred; all his actions prove it, even though with tongue or pen he may eulogise love.

The believer in peace is known by his peaceful conduct. It is impossible for him to engage in strife. If attacked he does not retaliate, for he has seen the majesty of the angel of peace, and he can no longer pay homage to the demon of strife. The stirrer-up of strife, the lover of argument, he who rushes into self-defence upon any or every provocation, believes in strife, and will have naught to do with peace.

Further, he who believes in Truth renounces himself- that is, he refuses to centre his life in those passions, desires, and characteristics which crave only their own gratification, and by thus renouncing he becomes steadfastly fixed in Truth, and lives a wise, beautiful, and blameless life. The believer in self is known by his daily indulgences, gratifications, and vanities, and by the disappointments, sorrows, and mortifications which he continually suffers.

The believer in Truth does not suffer, for he has given up that self which is the cause of such suffering.

It will be seen by the foregoing that every man believes either in permanent and eternal Principles directing human life towards law and harmony, or in the negation of those Principles, with the resultant chaos in human affairs and in his own life.

Belief in the divine Principles of Justice, Compassion, Love, constitutes the right belief laid down by Buddha as being the basis of right conduct, and also the belief unto salvation as emphasised in the Christian Scriptures, for he who so believes cannot do otherwise than build his whole life upon these Principles, and so purifies his heart, and perfects his life.

Belief in the negation of this divine principle constitutes what is called in all religious unbelief and this unbelief is manifested as a sinful, troubled, and imperfect life.

Where there is Right Belief there is a blameless and perfect life; where there is false belief there is sin, there is sorrow, the mind and life are improperly governed, and there is affliction and unrest. "By their fruits ye shall know them."

There is much talk about, "belief in Jesus," but what does belief in Jesus mean? It means belief in his words, in the Principles he enunciated and lived, in his commandments and in his exemplary life of perfection. He who declares belief in Jesus, and yet is all the time living in his lusts and indulgences, or in the spirit of hatred and condemnation, is self deceived. He believes not in Jesus. He believes in his own animal self. As a faithful servant delights in carrying out the commands of his master, so he who believes in Jesus carries out his commandments, and so is saved from sin. The supreme test of belief in Jesus is this: Do I keep his commandments? And this test is applied by St.John himself in the following words: "He that saith. I know him (Jesus), and keepeth not His Commandments, is a liar, and the truth is not in him. But whoso keepeth his word, in him verily is the word of God perfected."

It will be found after a rigid and impartial analysis, that belief lies at the root of all human conduct. Every thought, every act, every habit, is the direct outcome of a certain fixed belief, and one's conduct alters only as one's beliefs are modified. What we cling to, in that we believe; what we practise, in that we believe. When our belief in a thing ceases, we can no longer cling to or practise it; it falls away from us as a garment out-worn. Men cling to their lusts, and lies, and vanities, because they believe in them, believe there is gain and happiness in them. When they transfer their belief to the divine qualities of purity and humility, those sins trouble them no more.

Men are saved from error by belief in the supremacy of Truth. They are saved from sin by belief in Holiness or Perfection. They are saved from evil by belief in Good, for every belief is manifested in the life. It is not necessary to inquire as to a man's theological belief, for that is of little or no account, for what can it avail a man to believe that Jesus died for him, or that Jesus is God, or that he is "justified by faith," if he continues to live in his lower, sinful nature? All that is necessary to ask is this: "How does a man live?" "How does he conduct himself under trying circumstances?" The answer to these questions will show whether a man believes in the power of evil or in the power of Good.

He who believes in the power of Good, lives a good, spiritual, or godly life, for Goodness is God, yea, verily is God Himself, and he will soon leave behind him all sins and sorrows who believes, with steadfast and unwavering faith, in the Supreme Good.

The Belief That Saves

It has been said that a man's whole life and character is the out-come of his belief, and also that his belief has nothing whatever to do with his life. Both statements are true. The confusion and contradiction of these two statements are only apparent, and are quickly dispelled when it is remembered that there are two entirely distinct kinds of beliefs, namely, Head-belief and Heart-belief .

Head, or intellectual belief, is not fundamental and causative, but it is superficial and consequent, and that it has no power in the moulding of a man's character, the most superficial observer may easily see. Take, for instance, half a dozen men from any creed. They not only hold the same theological belief, but confess the same articles of faith in every particular, and yet their char-acters are vastly different. One will be just as noble as another is ignoble; one will be mild and gentle, another coarse and irascible; one will be honest, another dishonest; one will indulge certain habits which another will rigidly abjure, and so on, plainly indicat-ing that theological belief is not an influential factor in a man's life.

A man's theological belief is merely his intellectual opinion or view of the universe. God, The Bible, etc., and behind and under-neath this head-belief there lies, deeply rooted in his innermost being, the hidden, silent, secret belief of his heart, and it is this belief which moulds and makes his whole life. It is this which makes those six men who, whilst holding the same theology, are yet so vastly at variance in their deeds- they differ in the vital belief of the heart.

What, then, is this heart-belief?

It is that which a man loves and clings to and fosters in his soul; for he thus loves and clings to and fosters in his heart, because he believes in them, and believing in them and loving them, he practises them; thus is his life the effect of his belief , but it has no relation to the particular creed which comprises his intellectual belief. One man clings to impure and immoral things because he believes in them; another does not cling to them because he has ceased to believe in them. A man cannot cling to anything unless he believes in it; belief always precedes action, therefore a man's deeds and life are the fruits of his belief.

The Priest and the Levite who passed by the injured and helpless man, held, no doubt, very strongly to the theological doctrines of their fathers- that was their intellectual belief,- but in their hearts they did not believe in mercy, and so lived and acted accordingly. The good Samaritan may or may not have had any theological beliefs nor was it necessary that he should have; but in his heart he believed in mercy, and acted accordingly.

Strictly speaking, there are only two beliefs which vitally affect the life, and they are, belief in good and belief in evil.

He who believes in all those things that are good, will love them, and live in them; he who believes in those things that are impure and selfish, will love them, and cling to them. The tree is known by its fruits.

A man's beliefs about God, Jesus, and the Bible are one thing; his life, as bound up in his actions, is another; therefore a man's theological belief is of no consequence; but the thoughts which he harbours, his attitude of mind towards others, and his actions, these, and these only, determine and demonstrate whether the belief of a man's heart is fixed in the false or true.

Thought And Action

As the fruit to the tree and the water to the spring, so is action to thought. It does not come into manifestation suddenly and without a cause. It is the result of a long and silent growth; the end of a hidden process which has long been gathering force. The fruit of the tree and the water gushing from the rock are both the effect of a combination of natural processes in air and earth which have long worked together in secret to produce the phenomenon; and the beautiful acts of enlightenment and the dark deeds of sin are both the ripened effects of trains of thought which have long been harboured in the mind.

The sudden falling, when greatly tempted, into some grievous sin by one who was believed, and who probably believed himself, to stand firm, is seen neither to be a sudden nor a causeless thing when the hidden process of thought which led up to it are revealed. The falling was merely the end, the outworking, the finished result of what commenced in the mind probably years before. The man had allowed a wrong thought to enter his mind; and a second and a third time he had welcomed it, and allowed it to nestle in his heart. Gradually he became accustomed to it, and cherished, and fondled, and tended it; and so it grew, until at last it attained such strength and force that it attracted to itself the opportunity which enabled it to burst forth and ripen into act. As falls the stately building whose foundations have been gradually undermined by the action of water, so at last falls the strong man who allows corrupt thoughts to creep into his mind and secretly undermine his character.

When it is seen that all sin and temptation are the natural outcome of the thoughts of the individual, the way to overcome sin and temptation becomes plain, and its achievement a near possibility, and, sooner or later, a certain reality; for if a man will admit, cherish, and brood upon thoughts that are pure and good, those thoughts, just as surely as the impure, will grow and gather force, and will at last attract to themselves the opportunities which will enable them to ripen into act.

"There is nothing hidden that shall not be revealed," and every thought that is harboured in the mind must, by virtue of the impelling force which is inherent in the universe, at last blossom into act good or bad according to its nature. The divine Teacher and the sensualist are both the product of their own thoughts, and have become what they are as the result of the seeds of thought which they have implanted, are allowed to fall, into the garden of the heart, and have afterwards watered, tended, and cultivated.

Let no man think he can overcome sin and temptation by wrestling with opportunity; he can only overcome them by purifying his thoughts; and if he will, day by day, in the silence of his soul, and in the performance of his duties, strenuously overcome all erroneous inclination, and put in its place thoughts that are true and that will endure the light, opportunity to do evil will give place to opportunity for accomplishing good, for a man can only attarct that to him which is in harmony with his nature, and no temptation can gravitate to a man unless there is that in his heart which is capable of responding to it.

Guard well your thoughts, reader, for what you really are in your secret thoughts today, be it good or evil, you will, sooner or later, become in actual deed. He who unwearingly guards the portals of his mind against the intrusion of sinful thoughts, and occupies himself with loving thoughts, with pure, strong, and beautiful thoughts, will, when the season of their ripening comes, bringforth the fruits of gentle and holy deeds, and no temptation that can come against him shall find him unarmed or unprepared.

Your Mental Attitude

As a being of thought, your dominant mental attitude will determine your condition in life. It will also be the gauge of your knowledge and the measures of your attainment. The so-called limitations of your nature are the boundary lines of your thoughts; they are self-erected fences, and can be drawn to a narrower circle, extended to a wider, or be allowed to remain.

You are the thinker of your thoughts and as such you are the maker of yourself and condition. Thought is causal and creative, and appears in your character and life in the form of results. There are no accidents in your life. Both its harmonies and antagonisms are the responsive echoes of your thoughts. A man thinks, and his life appears.

If your dominant mental attitude is peaceable and lovable, bliss and blessedness will follow you; if it be resistant and hateful, trouble and distress will cloud your pathway. Out of ill-will will come grief and disaster; out of good-will, healing and reparation.

You imagine your circumstances as being separate from yourself, but they are intimately related to your thought world. Nothing appears without an adequate cause. Everything that happens is just. Nothing is fated, everything is formed.

As you think, you travel; as you love, you attract. You are today where your thoughts have brought you; you will be tomorrow where your thoughts take you. You cannot escape the result of your thoughts, but you can endure and learn, can accept and be glad.

You will always come to the place where your love (your most abiding and intense thought) can receive its measure of gratification. If your love be base, you will come to a base place; if it be beautiful, you will come to a beautiful place.

You can alter your thoughts, and so alter your condition. Strive to perceive the vastness and grandeur of your responsibility. You are powerful, not powerless. You are as powerful to obey as you are to disobey; as strong to be pure as to be impure; as ready for wisdom as for ignorance. You can learn what you will, can remain as ignorant as you choose. If you love knowledge you will obtain it; if you love wisdom you will secure it; if you love purity you will realise it. All things await your acceptance, and you choose by the thoughts which you entertain.

A man remains ignorant because he loves ignorance, and chooses ignorant thoughts; a man becomes wise because he loves wisdom and chooses wise thoughts. No man is hindered by another; he is only hindered by himself. No man suffers because of another; he suffers only because of himself. By the noble Gateway of Pure Thought you can enter the highest Heaven; by the ignoble doorway of impure thought you can descend into the lowest hell.

Your mental attitude towards others will faithfully react upon yourself, and will manifest itself in every relation of your life. Every impure and selfish thought that you send out comes back to you in your circumstances in some form of suffering; every pure and unselfish thought returns to you in some form of blessedness. Your circumstances are effects of which the cause is inward and invisible. As the father-mother of your thoughts you are the maker of your state and condition. When you know yourself, you will perceive, that every event in your life is weighed in the faultless balance of equity. When you understand the law within your mind you will cease to regard yourself as the impotent and blind tool of circumstances, and will become the strong and seeing master.

Sowing And Reaping

Go into the fields and country lanes in the spring-time, and you will see farmers and gardeners busy sowing seeds in the newly prepared soil. If you were to ask any one of those gardeners or farmers what kind of produce he expected from the seed he was sowing, he would doubtless regard you as foolish, and would tell you that he does not "expect" at all, that it is a matter of common knowledge that his produce will be of the kind which he is sowing, and that he is sowing wheat, or barley, or turnips, as the case may be, in order to reproduce that particular kind.

Every fact and process in Nature contains a moral lesson for the wise man. There is no law in the world of Nature around us which is not to be found operating with the same mathematical certainty in the mind of man and in human life. All the parables of Jesus are illustrative of this truth, and are drawn from the simple facts of Nature. There is a process of seed-sowing in the mind and life a spiritual sowing which leads to a harvest according to the kind of seed sown. Thoughts, words, and acts are seeds sown, and, by the inviolable law of things, they produce after their kind.

The man who thinks hateful thoughts brings hatred upon himself. The man who thinks loving thoughts is loved. The man whose thoughts, words and acts are sincere, is surrounded by sincere friends; the insincere man is surrounded by insincere friends. The man who sows wrong thoughts and deeds, and prays that God will bless him, is in the position of a farmer who, having sown tares, asks God to bring forth for him a harvest of wheat.

"That which ye sow, ye reap; see yonder fields

The sesamum was sesamum, the corn

Was corn; the silence and the darkness knew;

So is a man's fate born."

"He cometh reaper of the things he sowed."

He who would be blest, let him scatter blessings. He who would be happy, let him consider the happiness of others.

Then there is another side to this seed sowing. The farmer must scatter all his seed upon the land, and then leave it to the elements. Were he to covetously hoard his seed, he would lose both it and his produce, for his seed would perish. It perishes when he sows it, but in perishing it brings forth a great abundance. So in life, we get by giving; we grow rich by scattering. The man who says he is in possession of knowledge which he cannot give out because the world is incapable of receiving it, either does not possess such knowledge, or, if he does, will soon be deprived of it - if he is not already so deprived. To hoard is to lose; to exclusively retain is to be dispossessed.

Even the man who would increase his material wealth must be willing to part with (invest) what little capital he has, and then wait for the increase. So long as he retains his hold on his precious money, he will not only remain poor, but will be growing poorer everyday. He will, after all, lose the thing he loves, and will lose it without increase. But if he wisely lets it go; if, like the farmer, he scatters his seeds of gold, then he can faithfully wait for, and reasonably expect, the increase.

Men are asking God to give them peace and purity, and righteousness and blessedness, but are not obtaining these things; and why not? Because they are not practising them, not sowing them. I once heard a preacher pray very earnestly for forgiveness, and shortly afterwards, in the course of his sermon, he called upon his congregation to "show no mercy to the enemies of the church." Such self-delusion is pitiful, and men have yet to learn that the way to obtain peace and blessedness is to scatter peaceful and blessed thoughts, words, and deeds.

Men believe that they can sow the seeds of strife, impurity, and unbrotherliness, and then gather in a rich harvest of peace, purity and concord by merely asking for it. What more pathetic sight than to see an irritable and quarrelsome man praying for peace. Men reap that which they sow, and any man can reap all blessedness now and at once, if he will put aside selfishness, and sow broadcast the seeds of kindness, gentleness, and love.

If a man is troubled, perplexed, sorrowful, or unhappy, let him ask:

"What mental seeds have I been sowing?"

"What seeds am I sowing?"

"What have I done for others?"

"What is my attitude towards others?"

"What seeds of trouble and sorrow and unhappiness have I sown that I should thus reap these bitter weeds?"

Let him seek within and find, and having found, let him abandon all the seeds of self, and sow, henceforth, only the seeds of Truth.

Let him learn of the farmer the simple truths of wisdom.

The Reign Of Law

The little party gods have had their day. The arbitrary gods, creatures of human caprice and ignorance, are falling into disrepute. Men have quarrelled over and defended them until they have grown weary of the strife, and now, everywhere, they are relinquishing and breaking up these helpless idols of their long worship.

The god of revenge, hatred and jealousy, who gloats over the downfall of his enemies; the partial god who gratifies all our narrow and selfish desires; the god who saves only the creatures of his particular special creed; the god of exclusiveness and favouritism; such were the gods (miscalled by us God) of our soul's infancy, gods base and foolish as ourselves, the fabrications of our selfish self. And we relinquished our petty gods with bitter tears and misgivings, and broke our idols with bleeding hands. But in so doing we did not lose sight of God; nay we drew nearer to the great, silent Heart of Love. Destroying the idols of self, we began to comprehend somewhat of the Power which cannot be destroyed, and entered into a wider knowledge of the God of Love, of Peace, of Joy; the God in whom revenge and partiality cannot exist; the God of Light, from whose presence the darkness of fear and doubt and selfishness cannot choose but flee.

We have reached one of those epochs in the world's progress which witnesses the passing of the false gods; the gods of human selfishness and human illusion. The new-old revelation of one universal impersonal Truth has again dawned upon the world, and its searching light has carried consternation to the perishable gods who take shelter under the shadow of self.

Men have lost faith in a god who can be cajoled, who rules arbitrarily and capriciously, subverting the whole order of things to gratify the wishes of his worshippers, and are turning, with a new light in their eyes and a new joy in their hearts, to the God of Law.

And to Him they turn, not for personal happiness and gratification, but for knowledge, for understanding, for wisdom, for liberation from the bondage of self. And thus turning, they do not seek in vain, nor are they sent away empty and discomfited. They find within themselves the reign of Law, that every thought, every impulse, every act and word brings about a result in exact accordance with its own nature; that thoughts of love bring about beautiful and blissful conditions, that hateful thoughts bring about distorted and painful conditions, that thoughts and acts good and evil are weighed in the faultless balance of the Supreme Law, and receive their equal measure of blessedness on the one hand, and misery on the other. And thus finding they enter a new Path, the Path of Obedience to the Law. Entering that Path they no longer accuse, no longer doubt, no longer fret and despond, for they know that God is right, the universal laws are right, the cosmos is right, and that they themselves are wrong, if wrong there is, and that their salvation depends upon themselves, upon their own efforts, upon their personal acceptance of that which is good and deliberate rejection of that which is evil. No longer merely hearers, they become doers of the Word, and they acquire knowledge, they receive understanding, they grow in wisdom, and they enter into the glorious life of liberation from the bondage of self.

"The Law of the Lord is perfect, enlightening the eyes." Imperfection lies in man's ignorance, in man's blind folly. Perfection, which is knowledge of the Perfect Law, is ready for all who earnestly seek it; it belongs to the order of things; it is yours and mine now if we will only put self-seeking on one side, and adopt the life of self-obliteration.

The knowledge of Truth, with its unspeakable joy, its calmness and quiet strength, is not for those who persist in clinging to their "rights," defending their "interests," and fighting for their "opinions"; whose works are imbued with the personal "I," and who build upon the shifting sands of selfishness and egotism. It is for those who renounce these causes of strife, these sources of pain and sorrow; and they are, indeed, Children of Truth, disciples of the Master, worshippers of the most High.

The Children of Truth are in the world today; they are thinking, acting, writing, speaking; yea, even prophets are amongst us, and their influence is pervading the whole earth. An undercurrent of holy joy is gathering force in the world, so that men and women are moved with new aspirations and hopes, and even those who neither see nor hear, feel within themselves strange yearnings after a better and fuller life.

The Law reigns, and it reigns in men's hearts and lives; and they have come to understand the reign of Law who have sought out the Tabernacle of the true God by the fair pathway of unselfishness.

God does not alter for man, for this would mean that the perfect must become imperfect; man must alter for God, and this implies that the imperfect must become perfect. The Law cannot be broken for man, otherwise confusion would ensue; man must obey the Law; this is in accordance with harmony, order, justice.

There is no more painful bondage than to be at the mercy of one's inclinations; no greater liberty than utmost obedience to the Law of Being. And the Law is that the heart shall be purified, the mind regenerated, and the whole being brought in subjection to Love till self is dead and Love is all in all, for the reign of Law is the reign of Love. And Love waits for all , rejecting none. Love may be claimed and entered into now, for it is the heritage of all.

Ah, beautiful Truth! To know that now man may accept his divine heritage, and enter the Kingdom of Heaven!

Oh, pitiful error! To know that man rejects it because of love of self!

Obedience to the Law means the destruction of sin and self, and the realisation of unclouded joy and undying peace.

Clinging to one's selfish inclinations means the drawing about one's soul clouds of pain and sorrow which darken the light of Truth; the shutting out of oneself from all real blessedness; for "whatsoever a man sows that shall he also reap."

Verily the Law reigneth, and reigneth for ever, and Justice and Love are its eternal ministers.

The Supreme Justice

The material universe is maintained and preserved by the equilibrium of its forces.

The moral universe is sustained and protected by the perfect balance of its equivalents.

As in the physical world Nature abhors a vaccum, so in the spiritual world disharmony is annulled.

Underlying the disturbances and destructions of Nature, and behind the mutability of its forms, there abides the eternal and perfect mathematical symmetry; and at the heart of life, behind all its pain, uncertainty, and unrest, there abide the eternal harmony, the unbroken peace, and inviolable Justice.

Is there, then, no injustice in the universe? There is injustice, and there is not. It depends upon the kind of life and the state of consciousness from which a man looks out upon the world and judges. The man who lives in his passions sees injustice everywhere; the man who has overcome his passions, sees the operations of Justice in every department of human life. Injustice is the confused, feverish dream of passion, real enough to those who are dreaming it; Justice is the permanent reality in life, gloriously visible to those who have wakened out of the painful nightmare of self.

The Divine Order cannot be perceived until passion and self are transcended; the Faultless Justice cannot be apprehended until all sense of injury and wrong is consumed in the pure flames of all-embracing Love.

The man who thinks, "I have been slighted, I have been injured, I have been insulted, I have been treated unjustly," cannot know what Justice is; blinded by self, he cannot perceive the pure Principles of Truth, and brooding upon his wrongs, he lives in continual misery.

In the region of passion there is a ceaseless conflict of forces causing suffering to all who are involved in them. There is action and reaction, deed and consequence, cause and effect; and within and above all is the Divine Justice regulating the play of forces with the utmost mathematical accuracy, balancing cause and effect with the finest precision. But this Justice is not perceived - cannot be perceived - by those who are engaged in the conflict; before this can be done, the fierce warfare of passion must be left behind.

The world of passion is the abode of schisms, quarrellings, wars, law-suits, accusations, condemnations, impurities, weaknesses, follies, hatreds, revenges, and resentments. How can a man perceive Justice or understand Truth who is even partly involved in the fierce play of its blinding elements? As well expect a man caught in the flames of a burning building to sit down and reason out the cause of the fire.

In this realm of passion, men see injustice in the actions of others because, seeing only immediate appearances, they regard every act as standing by itself, undetached from cause and consequence. Having no knowledge of cause and effect in the moral sphere, men do not see the exacting and balancing process which is momentarily proceeding, nor do they ever regard their own actions as unjust, but only the actions of others. A boy beats a defenceless animal, then a man beats the defenceless boy for his cruelty, then a stronger man attacks the man for his cruelty to the boy. Each believes the other to be unjust and cruel, and himself to be just and humane; and doubtless most of all would the boy justify his conduct toward the animal as altogether necessary. Thus does ignorance keep alive hatred and strife; thus do men blindly inflict suffering upon themselves, living in passion and resentment, and not finding the true way in life. Hatred is met with hatred, passion with passion, strife with strife. The man who kills is himself killed; the thief who lives by depriving others is himself deprived; the beast that preys on others is hunted and killed; the accuser is accused, the condemner is condemned, the denouncer is persecuted.

"By this the slayer's knife doth stab himself,

The unjust judge has lost his own defender,

The false tongue dooms its lie, the creeping thief

And spoiler rob to render.

Such is the Law."

Passion, also has its active and passive sides. Fool and fraud, oppressor and slave, aggressor and retaliator, the charlatan and the superstitious, complement each other, and come together by the operation of the Law of Justice. Men unconsciously cooperate in the mutual production of affliction; "the blind lead the blind, and both fall together into the ditch." Pain, grief, sorrow, and misery are the fruits of which passion is the flower.

Where the passion-bound soul sees only injustice, the good man, he who has conquered passion, sees cause and effect, sees the Supreme Justice. It is impossible for such a man to regard himself as treated unjustly, because he has ceased to see injustice. He knows that no one can injure or cheat him, having ceased to injure or cheat himself. However passionately or ignorantly men may act towards him, it cannot possibly cause him any pain, for he knows that whatever comes to him (it may be abuse and persecution) can only come as the effect of what he himself has formerly sent out. He therefore regards all things as good, rejoices in all things, loves his enemies and blesses them that curse him, regarding them as the blind but beneficent instruments by which he is enabled to pay his moral debts to the Great Law.

The good man, having put away all resentment, retaliation, self-seeking, and egotism, has arrived at a state of equilibrium,and has thereby become identified with the Eternal and Universal Equilibrium. Having lifted himself above the blind forces of passion, he understands those forces, contemplates them with a calm penetrating insight, like the solitary dweller upon a mountain who looks down upon the conflict of the storms beneath his feet. For him, injustice has ceased, and he sees ignorance and suffering on the one hand and enlightenment and bliss on the other. He sees that not only do the fool and the slave need his sympathy, but that the fraud and the oppressor are equally in need of it, and so his compassion is extended towards all.

The Supreme Justice and the Supreme Love are one. Cause and effect cannot be avoided; consequences cannot be escaped.

While a man is given to hatred, resentment, anger and condemnation, he is subject to injustice as the dreamer to his dream, and cannot do otherwise than see injustice; but he who has overcome those fiery and binding elements, knows that unerring Justice presides over all, that in reality there is no such thing as injustice in the whole of the universe.

The Use Of Reason

We have heard it said that reason is a blind guide, and that it draws men away from Truth rather than leads them to it. If this were true, it were better to remain, or to become, unreasonable, and to persuade others so to do. We have found, however, that the diligent cultivation of the divine faculty of reason brings about calmness and mental poise, and enables one to meet cheerfully the problems and difficulties of life.

It is true there is a higher light than reason; even that of the Spirit of Truth itself, but without the aid of reason, Truth cannot be apprehended. They who refuse to trim the lamp of reason will never, whilst they so refuse, perceive the light of Truth, for the light of reason is a reflection of that Light.

Reason is a purely abstract quality, and comes midway between the animal and divine consciousness in man, and leads, if rightly employed, from the darkness of one to the Light of the other. It is true that reason may be enlisted in the service of the lower, self-seeking nature, but this is only a result of its partial and imperfect exercise. A fuller development of reason leads away from the selfish nature, and ultimately allies the soul with the highest, the divine.

That spiritual perceival who, searching for the Holy Grail of the Perfect Life, is again and again...

"left alone,

And wearying in a land of sand and thorns,"

is not so stranded because he has followed reason, but because he is still clinging to, and is reluctant to leave, some remnants of his lower nature. He who will use the light of reason as a torch to search for Truth will not be left at last in comfortless darkness.

"Come, now, and let us reason together, saith the Lord; though your sins be as scarlet, they shall be as white as snow."

Many men and women pass through untold sufferings, and at last die in their sins, because they refuse to reason; because they cling to those dark delusions which even a faint glimmer of the light of reason would dispel; and all must use their reason freely, fully, and faithfully, who would exchange the scarlet robe of sin and suffering for the white garment of blamelessness and peace.

It is because we have proved and know these truths that we exhort men to...

"tread the middle road, whose course

Bright reason traces, and soft quiet

smooths,"

for reason leads away from passion and selfishness into the quiet ways of sweet persuasion and gentle forgiveness, and he will never be led astray, nor will he follow blind guides, who faithfully adheres to the Apostolic injunction, "Prove all things, and hold fast that which is good." They, therefore, who despise the light of reason, despise the Light of Truth.

Large numbers of people are possessed of the strange delusion that reason is somehow intimately connected with the denial of the existence of God. This is probably due to the fact that those who try to prove that there is no God usually profess to take their stand upon reason, while those who try to prove the reverse generally profess to take their stand on faith. Such argumentative combatants, however, are frequently governed more by prejudice than either reason or faith, their object being not to find Truth, but to defend and confirm a preconceived opinion.

Reason is concerned, not with ephemeral opinions, but with the established truth of things, and he who is possessed of the faculty of reason in its purity and excellence can never be enslaved by prejudice, and will put from him all preconceived opinions as worthless. He will neither attempt to prove nor disprove, but after balancing extremes and bringing together all apparent contradictions, he will carefully and dispassionately weigh and consider them, and so arrive at Truth.

Reason is, in reality, associated with all that is pure and gentle, moderate and just. It is said of a violent man that he is "unreasonable," of a kind and considerate man that he is "reasonable," and of an insane man that he has "lost his reason." Thus it is seen that the word is used, even to a great extent unconsciously, though none the less truly, in a very comprehensive sense, and though reason is not actually love and thoughtfulness and gentleness and sanity, it leads to and is intimately connected with these divine qualities, and cannot, except for purposes of analysis, be dissociated from them.

Reason represents all that is high and noble in man. It distinguishes him from the brute which blindly follows its animal inclinations, and just in the degree that man disobeys the voice of reason and follows his inclinations does he become brutish. As Milton says:

"Reason in man obscured, or not obeyed,

Immediately inordinate desires

And upstart passions catch the government

From reason, and to servitude reduce

Man till then free."

The following definition of "reason" from Nuttall's Dictionary will give some idea of the comprehensiveness of the word:

The cause, ground, principle, or motive of anything said or done; efficient cause; final cause; the faculty of intelligence in man; especially the faculty by which we arrive at necessary truth. It will thus be seen that "reason" is a term, the breadth of which is almost sufficient to embrace even Truth itself, and Archbishop Trench tells us in his celebrated work On the Study of Words that the terms Reason and Word "are indeed so essentially one and the same that the Greek language has one word for them both," so that the Word of God is the Reason of God; and one of the renderings of Lao-tze's "Tao" is Reason, so that in the chinese translation of our New Testament, St.John's Gospel runs; "In the beginning was the Tao."

To the undeveloped and uncharitable mind all words have narrow applications, but as a man enlarges his sympathies and broadens his intelligence, words become filled with rich meanings and assume comprehensive proportions. Let us therefore cease from foolish quarrelings about words, and, like reasonable beings, search for principles and practise those things which make for...

Self-Discipline

A man does not live until he begins to discipline himself; he merely exists. Like an animal he gratifies his desires and pursues his inclinations just where they may lead him. He is happy as a beast is happy, because he is not conscious of what he is depriving himself; he suffers as the beast suffers, because he does not know the way out of suffering. He does not intelligently reflect upon life, and lives in a series of sensations, longings, and confused memories which are unrelated to any central idea or principle. A man whose inner life is so ungoverned and chaotic must necessarily manifest this confusion in the visible conditions of his outer life in the world; and though for a time, running with the stream of his desires, he may draw to himself a more or less large share of the outer necessities and comforts of life, he never achieves any real success nor accomplishes any real good, and sooner or later wordly failure and disaster are inevitable, as the direct result of the inward failure to properly adjust and regulate those mental forces which make the outer life.

Before a man accomplish anything of an enduring nature in the world he must first of all acquire some measure of success in the management of his own mind. This is as mathematical a truism as that two and two are four, for, "out of the heart are the issues of life." If a man cannot govern the forces within himself, he cannot hold a firm hand upon the outer activities which form his visible life. On the other hand, as a man succeeds, in governing himself he rises to higher and higher levels of power and usefulness and success in the world.

The only difference between the life of the beast and that of the undisciplined man is that the man has a wider variety of desires, and experiences a greater intensity of suffering. It may be said of such a man that he is dead, being truly dead to self-control, chastity, fortitude, and all the nobler qualities which constitute life. In the consciousness of such a man the crucified Christ lies entombed, awaiting that resurrection which shall revivify the mortal sufferer, and wake him up to a knowledge of tha realities of his existence.

With the practice of self-discipline a man begins to live, for he then commences to rise above the inward confusion and to adjust his conduct to a steadfast centre within himself. He ceases to follow where inclination leads him, reins in the steed of his desires, and lives in accordance with the dictates of reason and wisdom. Hitherto his life has been without purpose or meaning, but now he begins to consciously mould his own destiny; he is "clothed and in his right mind."

In the process of self-discipline there are three stages namely;

Control

Purification

Relinquishment

A man begins to discipline himself by controlling those passions which have hitherto controlled him; he resists temptation and guards himself against all those tendencies to selfish gratifications which are so easy and natural, and which have formerly dominated him. He brings his appetite into subjection, and begins to eat as a reasonable and responsible being, practising moderation and thoughtfulness in the selection of his food, with the object of making his body a pure instrument through which he may live and act as becomes a man, and no longer degarding that body by pandering to gustatory pleasure. He puts a check upon his tongue, his temper, and, in fact, his every animal desire and tendency, and this he does by referring all his acts to a fixed centre within himself. It is a process of living from within outward, instead of, as formerly, from without inward. He conceives of an ideal, and, enshrining that ideal in the sacred recesses of his heart, he regulates his conduct in accordance with its exaction and demands.

There is a philosophical hypothesis that at the heart of every atom and every aggregation of atoms in the universe there is a motionless center which is the sustaining source of all the universal activities. Be this as it may, there is certainly in the heart of every man and woman a selfless centre without which the outer man could not be, and the ignoring of which leads to suffering and confusion. This selfless center which takes the form, in the mind, of an ideal of unselfishness and spotless purity, the attainment of which is desirable, is man's eternal refuge from the storms of passion and all the conflicting elements of his lower nature. It is the Rock of Ages, the Christ within, the divine and immortal in all men.

As a man practises self-control he approximates more and more to this inward reality, and is less and less swayed by passion and grief, pleasure and pain, and lives a steadfast and virtuous life, manifesting manly strength and fortitude. The restraining of the passions, however, is merely the initial stage in self-discipline, and is immediately followed by the process of Purification. By this a man so purifies himself as to take passion out of the heart and mind altogether; not merely restraining it when it rises within him, but preventing it from rising altogether. By merely restraining his passions a man can never arrive at peace, can never actualise his ideal; he must purify those passions.

It is in the purification of his lower nature that a man becomes strong and god-like, standing firmly upon the ideal centre within, and rendering all temptations powerless and ineffectual. This purification is effected by thoughtful care, earnest meditation, and holy aspiration; and as success is achieved confusion of mind and life pass away, and calmness of mind and spiritualized conduct ensure.

True strength and power and usefulness are born of self-purification, for the lower animal forces are not lost, but are transmuted into intellectual and spiritual energy. The pure life (Pure in thought and deed) is a life of conservation of energy; the impure life (even should the impurity not extent beyond thought) is a life of dissipation of energy. The pure man is more capable, and therefore more fit to succeed in his plans and to accomplish his purposes than the impure. Where the impure man fails, the pure man will step in and be victorious, because he directs his energies with a calmer mind and a greater definiteness and strength of purpose.

With the growth in purity; all the elements which constitute a strong and virtuous manhood are developed in an increasing degree of power, and as a man brings his lower nature into subjection, and makes his passions do his bidding, just so much will he mould the outer circumstances of his life, and influence others for good.

The third stage of self-discipline, that of Relinquishment, is a process of letting the lower desires and all impure and unworthy thoughts drop out of the mind, and also refusing to give them any admittance, leaving them to perish. As a man grows purer, he perceives that all evil is powerless, unless it receives his encouragement, and so he ignores it, and lets it pass out of his life. It is by pursuing this aspect of self-discipline that a man enters into and realises the divine life, and manifests those qualities which are distinctly divine, such as wisdom, patience, non-resistance, compassion, and love. It is here, also, where a man becomes consciously immortal, rising above all the fluctuations and uncertainties of life, and living in and intelligent and unchangeable peace.

By self-discipline a man attains to every degree of virtue and holiness, and finally becomes a purified son of God, realising his oneness with the central heart of all things.

Without self-discipline a man drifts lower and lower, approximating more and more nearly to the beast, until at last he grovels, a lost creature, in the mire of his own befoulment. By self-discipline a man rises higher and higher, approximating more and more nearly to the divine, until at last he stands erect in his divine dignity, a saved soul, glorified by the radiance of his purity. Let a man discipline himself, and he will live; let a man cease to discipline himself, and he will perish. As a tree grows in beauty, health, and fruitfulness by being carefully pruned and tended, so a man grows in grace and beauty of life by cutting away all the branches of evil from his mind, and as he tends and develops the good by constant and unfailing effort.

As a man by practice acquires proficiency in his craft, so the earnest man acquires proficiency in goodness and wisdom. Men shrink from self-discipline because in its early stages it is painful and repellent, and the yielding to desire is, at first, sweet and inviting; but the end of desire is darkness and unrest, whereas the fruits of discipline are immortality and peace.

Resolution

Resolution is the directing and impelling force in individual progress. Without it no substantial work can be accomplished. Not until a man brings resolution to bear upon his life does he consciously and rapidly develop, for a life without resolution is a life without aims, and a life without aims is a drifting and unstable thing.

Resolution may of course be linked to downward tendencies, but it is usually the companion of noble aims and lofty ideals, and I am dealing with it in this, its highest use and application.

When a man makes a resolution, it means that he is dissatisfied with his condition, and is commencing to take himself in hand with a view to producing a better piece of workmanship out of the mental materials of which his character and life are composed, and in so far as he is true to his resolution he will succeed in accomplishing his purpose.

The vows of the saintly ones are holy resolutions directed toward some victory over self, and the beautiful achievements of holy men and the glorious conquests of the Divine Teachers were rendered possible and actual by the pursuit of unswerving resolution.

To arrive at the fixed determination to walk a higher path than heretofore, although it reveals the great difficulties which have to be surmounted, it yet makes possible the treading of that path, and illuminates its dark places with the golden halo of success.

The true resolution is the crisis of long thought, protracted struggle, or fervent but unsatisfied aspiration. It is no light thing, no whimsical impulse or vague desire, but a solemn and irrevocable determination not to rest nor cease from effort until the high purpose which is held in view is fully accomplished.

Half-hearted and premature resolution is no resolution at all, and is shattered at the first difficulty.

A man should be slow to form a resolution. He should searchingly examine his position and take into consideration every circumstance and difficulty connected with his decision, and should be fully prepared to meet them. He should be sure that he completely understands the nature of his resolution, that his mind is finally made up, and that he is without fear and doubt in the matter. With the mind thus prepared, the resolution that is formed will not be departed from, and by the aid of it a man will, in due time, accomplish his strong purpose.

Hasty resolutions are futile.

The mind must be fortified to endure.

Immediately the resolution to walk a higher path is made, temptation and trial begin. Men have found that no sooner have they decided to lead a truer and nobler life than they have been overwhelmed with such a torrent of new temptations and difficulties as make their position almost unendurable, and many men, because of this, relinquish their resolution.

But these temptations and trials are a necessary part of the work of regeneration upon which the man has decided and must be hailed as friends and met with courage if the resolution is to do its work. For what is the real nature of a resolution? Is it not the sudden checking of a particular stream of conduct, and the endeavour to open up an entirely new channel? Think of an engineer who decides to turn the course of a powerfully running stream or river in another direction. He must first cut his new channel, and must take every precaution to avoid failure in the carrying out of his undertaking. But when he comes to the all-important task of directing the stream into its new channel, then the flowing force, which for ages has steadily pursued its accustomed course, becomes refractory, and all the patience and care and skill of the engineer will be required for the successful completion of the work. It is even so with the man who determines to turn his course of conduct in another and higher direction. Having prepared his mind, which is the cutting of a new channel, he then proceeds to the work of redirecting his mental forces - which have hitherto flowed on uninterruptedly - into the new course. Immediately this is attempted, the arrested energy begins to assert itself in the form of powerful temptations and trials hitherto unknown and unencountered. And this is exactly as it should be; it is the law; and the same law that is in the water is in the mind. No man can improve upon the established law of things, but he can learn to understand the law instead of complaining, and wishing things were different. The man who understands all that is involved in the regeneration of his mind will "glory in tribulations," knowing that only by passing through them can he gain strength, obtain purity of heart, and arrive at peace. And as the engineer at last (perhaps after many mistakes and failures) succeeds in getting the stream to flow on peacefully in the broader and better channel, and the turbulence of the water is spent, and all dams can be removed, so the man of resolution at last succeeds in directing his thoughts and acts into the better and nobler way to which he aspires, and temptations and trials give place to steadfast strength and settled peace.

He whose life is not in harmony with his conscience and who is anxious to remedy his mind and conduct in a particular direction, let him first mature his purpose by earnest thought and self-examination, and having arrived at a final conclusion, let him frame his resolution, and having done so let him not swerve from it, let him remain true to his decision under all circumstances, and he cannot fail to achieve his good purpose; for the Great Law ever shields and protects him who, no matter how deep his sins, or how great and many his failures and mistakes, has, deep in his heart, resolved upon the finding of a better way, and every obstacle must at last give way before a matured and unshaken resolution.

The Glorious Conquest

Truth can only be apprehended by the conquest of self.

Blessedness can only be arrived at by overcoming the lower nature.

The way of Truth is barred by a man's self.

The only enemies that can actually hinder him are his own passions and delusions.

Until a man realises this, and commences to cleanse his heart, he has not found the Path which leads to knowledge and peace.

Until passion is transcended, Truth remains unknown. This is the Divine Law.

A man cannot keep his passions and have Truth as well.

Error is not slain until selfishness is dead.

The overcoming of self is no mystical theory, but a very real and practical thing.

It is a process which must be pursued daily and hourly, with unswerving faith and undaunted resolution if any measure of success is to be achieved.

The process is one of orderly growth, having its sequential stages, like the growth of a tree; and as fruit can only be produced by carefully and patiently training the tree even so the pure and satisfying fruits of holiness can only be obtained by faithfully and patiently training the mind in the growth of right thought and conduct.

There are five steps in the overcoming of passion (which includes all bad habits and particular forms of wrong-doing) which I will call:

Repression

Endurance

Elimination

Understanding

Victory

When men fail to overcome their sins, it is because they try to begin at the wrong end. They want to have the stage of Victory without passing through the previous four stages. They are in the position of a gardener who wants to produce good fruit without training and attending to his trees.

Repression consists in checking and controlling the wrong act (such as an outburst of temper, a hasty or unkind word, a selfish indulgence etc.), and not allowing it to take actual form. This is equivalent to the gardener nipping off the useless buds and branches from his tree. It is a necessary process, but a painful one. The tree bleeds while undergoing the process, and the gardener knows that it must not be taxed too severely. The heart also bleeds when it refuses to return passion for passion, whan it ceases to defend and justify itself. It is the process of "mortifying the members" of which St. Paul speaks.

But this repression is only the beginning of self-conquest. When it is made an end in itself, and there is no object of finally purifying the heart, that is a stage of hypocrisy; a hiding of one's true nature, and striving to appear better in the eyes of others than one really is. In that case it is an evil, but when adopted as the first stage toward complete purification, it is good. Its practice leads to the second stage of Endurance, or forbearance, in which one silently endures the pain which arises in the mind when it is brought in contact with certain actions and attitudes of other minds toward one. As success is attained in this stage, the striver comes to see that all his pain actually arises in his own weaknesses, and not in the wrong attitudes of others toward him, these latter being merely the means by which his sins are brought to the surface and revealed to him. He thus gradually exonerates all others from blame in his falls and lapses of conduct, and accuses only himself, and so learns to love those who thus unconsciously reveal to him his sins and shortcomings.

Having passed through these two stages of self-crucifixion, the disciple enters the third, that of Elimination, in which the wrong thought which lay behind the wrong act is cast from the mind immediately it appears. At this stage, conscious strength and holy joy begin to take the place of pain, and the mind having become comparatively calm, the striver is enabled to gain a deeper insight into the complexities of his mind, and thus to understand the inception, growth, and outworking of sin. This is the stage of Understanding.

Perfection in understanding leads to the final conquest of self, a conquest so complete that the sin can no more rise in the mind even as a thought or impression; for when the knowledge of sin is complete; when it is known in its totality, from its inception as a seed in the mind to its ripened outgrowth as act and consequence, then it can no more be allowed a place in life, but it is abandoned for ever. Then the mind is at peace. The wrong acts of others no longer arouse wrong and pain in the mind of the disciple. He is glad and calm and wise. He is filled with Love, and blessedness abides with him. And this is Victory!

Contentment In Activity

The confounding of a positive spiritual virtue or principle with a negative animal vice is common amongst writers even of what is called the "Advance Thought School," and much valuable energy is frequently expended in criticising and condemning, where a little calm reasoning would have revealed a greater light, and led to the exercise of a broader charity.

The other day I came across a vigorous attack upon the teaching of "Love," wherein the writer condemned such teaching as weakly, foolish, and hypocritical. Needless to say, that which he was condemning as "Love," was merely weak sentimentality and hypocrisy.

Another writer in condemning "meekness" does not know that what he calls meekness is only cowardice, while another who attacks "chastity" as "a snare," is really confusing painful and hypocritical restraint with the virtue of chastity. And just lately I received a long letter from a correspondent who took great pains to show me that "contentment" is a vice, and is the source of innumerable evils.

That which my correspondent called "contentment" is, of course animal indifference. The spirit of indifference is incompatible with progress, whereas the spirit of contentment may, and does, attend the highest form of activity, the truest advancement and development. Indolence is the twin sister of indifference, but cheerful and ready action is the friend of contentment.

Contentment is a virtue which becomes lofty and spiritual in its later developments, as the mind is trained to perceive and the heart to receive the guidance, in all things, of a merciful law.

To be contented does not mean to forego effort; it means to free effort from anxiety; it does not mean to be satisfied with sin and ignorance and folly, but to rest happily in duty done, work acomplished.

A man may be said to be content to lead a grovelling life, to remain in sin and in debt, but such a man's true state is one of indifference to his duty, his obligations, and the just claims of his fellow-men. He cannot truly be said to possess the virtue of contentment; he does not experience the pure and abiding joy which is the accompaniment of active contentment; so far as his true nature is concerned he is a sleeping soul, and sooner or later will be awakened by intense suffering, having passed through which he will find that true contentment which is the outcome of honest effort and true living.

There are three things with which a man should be content:

With whatever happens.

With his friendships and possessions.

With his pure thoughts.

Contented with whatever happens, he will escape grief; with his friends and possessions, he will avoid anxiety and wretchedness; and with his pure thoughts, he will never go back to suffer and grovel in impurities.

There are three things with which a man should not be content:

With his opinions.

With his character.

With his spiritual condition.

Not content with his opinions, he will continually increase in intelligence; not content with his character, he will ceaselessly grow in strength and virtue; and not content with his spiritual condition, he will, everyday, enter into a larger wisdom and fuller blessedness. In a word, a man should be contented, but not indifferent to his development as a responsible and spiritual being.

The truly contented man works energetically and faithfully, and accepts all results with an untroubled spirit, trusting, at first, that all is well, but afterwards, with the growth of enlightenment, knowing that results exactly correspond with efforts. Whatsoever material possessions come to him, come not by greed and anxiety and strife, but by right thought, wise action, and pure exertion.

The Temple of Brotherhood

Universal Brotherhood is the supreme Ideal of Humanity, and towards that Ideal the world is slowly but surely moving.

Today, as never before, numbers of earnest men and women are striving to make this Ideal tangible and real; Fraternities are springing up on every hand, and Press and Pulpit, the world over, are preaching the Brotherhood of Man.

The unselfish elements in all such efforts cannot fail to have their effect upon the race, and are with certainty urging it towards the goal of its noblest aspirations; but the ideal state has not yet manifested through any outward organisation, and societies formed for the purpose of propagating Brotherhood are continually being shattered to pieces by internal dissension.

The Brotherhood for which Humanity sighs is withheld from actuality by Humanity itself; nay, more, it is frustrated even by men who work zealously for it is a desirable possibility; and this because the purely spiritual nature of Brotherhood is not perceived, and the principles involved, as well as the individual course of conduct necessary to perfect unity, are not comprehended.

Brotherhood as a human organisation cannot exist so long as any degree of self-seeking reigns in the hearts of men and women who band themselves together for any purpose, as such self-seeking must eventually rend the Seamless Coat of loving unity. But although organised Brotherhood has so far largely failed, any man may realise Brotherhood in its perfection, and know it in all its beauty and completion, if he will make himself of a wise, pure, and loving spirit, removing from his mind every element of strife, and learning to practise those divine qualities without which Brotherhood is but a mere theory, opinion, or illusive dream.

For Brotherhood is at first spiritual, and its outer manifestation in the world must follow as a natural sequence.

As a spiritual reality it must be discovered by each man for himself, and in the only place where spiritual realities can be found - within himself, and it rests with each whether he shall choose or refuse it.

There are four chief tendencies in the human mind which are destructive of Brotherhood, and which bar the way to its comprehension, namely:

Pride

Self-love

Hatred

Condemnation

Where these are there can be no Brotherhood; in whatsoever heart these hold sway, discord rules, and Brotherhood is not realised, for these tendencies are, in their very nature, dark and selfish amd always make for disruption and destruction. From these four things proceeds that serpent brood of false actions and conditions which poison the heart of man, and fill the world with suffering and sorrow.

Out of the spirit of pride proceed envy, resentment, and opinionativeness. Pride envies the position, influence, or goodness of others; it thinks, "I am more deserving than this man or this woman"; it also continually finds occasion for resenting the actions of others, and says, "I have been snubbed," "I have been insulted," and thinking altogether of his own excellence, it sees no excellence in others.

From the spirit of self-love proceed egotism, lust for power, and disparagement and contempt. Self-love worships the personality in which it moves; it is lost in the adoration and glorification of that "I", that "self" which has no real existence, but is a dark dream and a delusion. It desires pre-eminence over others, and thinks, "Iam great," "I am more important than others"; it also disparages others, and bestows upon them contempt, seeing no beauty in them, being lost in the contemplation of its own beauty.

From the spirit of hatred proceed slander, cruelty, reviling, and anger. It strives to overcome evil by adding evil to it. It says, "This man has spoken of me ill, I will speak still more ill of him and thus teach him a lesson." It mistakes cruelty for kindness, and causes its possessor to revile a reproving friend. It feeds the flames of anger with bitter and rebellious thoughts.

From the spirit of condemnation proceed accusation, false pity, and false judgement. It feeds itself on the contemplation of evil, and cannot see the good. It has eyes for evil only, and finds it in almost every thing and every person. It sets up an arbitrary standard of right and wrong by which to judge others, and it thinks, "This man does not do as I would have him do, he is therefore evil, and I will denounce him." So blind is the spirit of condemnation that whilst rendering its possessor incapable of judging himself, it causes him to set himself up as the judge of all the earth.

From the four tendencies enumerated, no element of brotherliness can proceed. They are deadly mental poisons, and he who allows them to rankle in his mind, cannot apprehend the peaceful principles on which Brotherhood rests.

Then there are chiefly four divine qualities which are productive of Brotherhood; which are, as it were, the foundation stones on which it rests, namely:

Humility

Self-surrender

Love

Compassion

Wheresoever these are, there Brotherhood is active. In whatsoever heart these qualities are dominant, there Brotherhood is an established reality, for they are, in their very nature, unselfish and are filled with the revealing Light of Truth. There is no darkness in them, and where they are, so powerful is their light, that the dark tendencies cannot remain, but are dissolved and dissipated.

Out of these four qualities proceed all those angelic actions and conditions which make for unity and bring gladness to the heart of man and to the world.

From the spirit of Humility proceed meekness and peacefulness; from self-surrender come patience, wisdom, and true judgment; from Love spring kindness, joy, and harmony; and from Compassion proceed gentleness and forgiveness.

He who has brought himself into harmony with these four qualities is divinely enlightened; he sees whence the actions of men proceed and whither they tend, and therefore can no longer live in the exercise of the dark tendencies. He has realised Brotherhood in its completion as freedom from malice; from envy, from bitterness, from contention, from condemnation. All men are his brothers, those who live in the dark tendencies, as well as those who live in the enlightened qualities, for he knows that when they have perceived the glory and beauty of the Light of Truth, the dark tendencies will be dispelled from their minds. He has but one attitude of mind towards all, that of good-will.

Of the four dark tendencies are born ill-will and strife; of the four divine qualities are born good-will and peace.

Living in the four tendencies a man is a strife-producer. Living in the four qualities a man is a peace-maker.

Involved in the darkness of the selfish tendencies, men believe that they can fight for peace, kill to make alive, slay injury by injuring, restore love by hatred, unity by contention, kindness by cruelty, and establish brotherhood by erecting their own opinions (which they themselves will, in the course of time, abandon as worthless) as objects of universal adoration.

The wished-for Temple of Brotherhood will be erected in the world when its four foundation stones of Humility, Self-surrender, Love, and Compassion are firmly laid in the hearts of men, for Brotherhood consists, first of all, in the abandonment of self by the individual, and its after-effects is unity between man and man.

Theories and schemes for propagating Brotherhood are many, but Brotherhood itself is one and unchangeable and consists in the complete cessation from egotism and strife, and in practising good-will and peace; for Brotherhood is a practice and not a theory. Self-surrender and Good-will are its guardian angels, and peace is its habitation.

Where two are determined to maintain an opposing opinion, the clinging to self and ill-will are there, and Brotherhood is absent.

Where two are prepared to sympathise with each other, to see no evil in each other, to serve and not to attack each other; the Love of Truth and Good-will are there, and Brotherhood is present.

All strifes, divisions, and wars inhere in the proud, unyielding self; all peace, unity, and concord inhere in the Principles which the yielding up of self reveals.

Brotherhood is only practised and known by him whose heart is at peace with all the world.

Pleasant Pastures Of Peace

He who aspires to the bettering of himself and humanity should ceaselessly strive to arrive at the exercise of that blessed attitude of mind by which he is enabled to put himself, mentally and sympathetically in the place of others, and so, instead of harshly and falsely judging them, and thereby making himself unhappy without adding to the happiness of those others, he will enter into their experience, will understand their particular frame of mind, and will feel for them and sympathise with them.

One of the great obstacles to the attainment of such an attitude of mind is, prejudice, and until this is removed it is impossible to act toward others as we would wish others to act toward us.

Prejudice is destructive of kindness, sympathy, love and true judgment, and the strength of a man's prejudice will be the measure of his harshness and unkindness toward others, for prejudice and cruelty are inseparable.

There is no rationality in prejudice, and, immediately it is aroused in a man he ceases to act as a reasonable being, and gives way to rashness, anger, and injurious excitement. He does not consider his words nor regard the feelings and liberties of those against whom his prejudices are directed. He has, for the time being, forfeited his manhood, and has descended to the level of an irrational creature.

While a man is determined to cling to his preconceived opinions, mistaking them for Truth, and refuses to consider dispassionately the position of others, he cannot escape hatred nor arrive at blessedness.

The man who strives after gentleness, who aspires to act unselfishly toward others, will put away all his passionate prejudice and petty opinions, and will gradually acquire the power of thinking and feeling for others, of understanding their particular state of ignorance or knowledge, and thereby entering fully into their hearts and lives, sympathizing with them and seeing them as they are.

Such a man will not oppose himself to the prejudices of others by introducing his own, but will seek to allay prejudice by introducing sympathy and love, striving to bring out all that is good in men, encouraging the good by appealing to it, and discouraging the evil by ignoring it. He will realise the good in the unselfish efforts of others, though their outward methods may be very different from his own, and will so rid his heart of hatred, and will fit it with love and blessedness.

When a man is prone to harshly judge and condemn others, he should inquire how far he falls short himself; he should also reconsider those periods of suffering when he himself was misjudged and misunderstood, and, gathering wisdom and love from his own bitter experience, should studiously and self-sacrificingly refrain from piercing with anguish hearts that are as yet too weak to ignore, too immature and uninstructed to understand.

Sympathy is not required towards those who are purer and more enlightened than one's self, as the purer one lives above the necessity for it. In such a case reverence should be exercised, with a striving to lift one's self up to the purer level, and so enter into possession of the larger life. Nor can a man fully understand one who is wiser than himself, and before condemning, he should earnestly ask himself whether he is, after all, better than the man whom he has singled out as the object of his bitterness. If he is, let him bestow sympathy. If he is not, let him exercise reverence.

For thousands of years the sages have taught, both by precept and example, that evil is only overcome by good, yet still that lesson for the majority, remains unlearned. It is a lesson profound in its simplicity, and difficult to learn because men are blinded by the illusions of self. Men are still engaged in resenting, condemning, and fighting the evil in their own fellow-men, thereby increasing the delusion in their own hearts, and adding to the world's sum of misery and suffering. When they find out that their own resentment must be eradicated, and love put in its place, evil will perish for lack of sustenance.

"With burning brain and heart of hate,

I sought my wronger, early, late,

And all the wretched night and day

My dream and thought was slay, and slay.

My better self rose uppermost,

The beast within my bosom lost

Itself in love; peace from afar

Shone o'er me radiant like a star.

I Slew my wronger with a deed,

A deed of love; I made him bleed

With kindness, and I filled for years

His soul with tenderness and tears."

Dislike, resentment, and condemnation are all forms of hatred, and evil cannot cease until these are taken out of the heart.

But the obliterating of injuries from the mind is merely one of the beginnings in wisdom. There is a still higher and better way. And that way is so to purify the heart and enlighten the mind that, far from having to forget injuries, there will be none to remember. For it is only pride and self that can be injured and wounded by the actions and attitudes of others; and he who takes pride and self out of his heart can never think the thought, "I have been injured by another" or "I have been wronged by another."

From a purified heart proceeds the right comprehension of things; and from the right comprehension of things proceeds the life that is peaceful, freed from bitterness and suffering, calm and wise. He who thinks, "This man has injured me," has not perceived the Truth in life; falls short of that enlightenment which disperses the erroneous idea of evil as a thing to be hatefully resented. He who is troubled and disturbed about the sins of others is far from Truth; he who is troubled and disturbed about his own sins is very near to the Gate of Wisdom. He in whose heart the flames of resentment burn, cannot know Peace nor understand Truth; he who will banish resentment from his heart, will know and understand.

He who has taken evil out of his own heart cannot resent or resist it in others, for he is enlightened as to its origin and nature, and knows it as a manifestation of the mistakes of ignorance. With the increase of enlightenment, sin becomes impossible. He who sins, does not understand; he who understands does not sin.

The pure man maintains his tenderness of his heart toward those who ignorantly imagine they can do him harm. The wrong attitude of others toward him does not trouble him; his heart is at rest in Compassion and Love.

Blessed is he who has no wrongs to remember, no injuries to forget; in whose pure heart no hateful thought about another can take root and flourish.

Let those who aim at the right life, who believe that they love Truth, cease to passionately oppose themselves to others, and let them strive to calmly and wisely understand them, and in thus acting toward others they will be conquering themselves; and while sympathizing with others, their own souls will be fed with the heavenly dews of kindness, and their hearts be strengthened and refreshed in the Pleasant Pastures of Peace.

The Eight Pillars
of Prosperity

Preface

It is popularly supposed that a greater prosperity for individuals or nations can only come through a political and social reconstruction. This cannot be true apart from the practice of the moral virtues in the individuals that comprise a nation. Better laws and social conditions will always follow a higher realisation of morality among the individuals of a community, but no legal enactment can give prosperity to, nay it cannot prevent the ruin of, a man or a nation that has become lax and decadent in the pursuit and practice of virtue.

The moral virtues are the foundation and support of prosperity as they are the soul of greatness. They endure forever, and all the works of man which endure are built upon them. Without them there is neither strength, stability nor substantial reality, but only ephemeral dreams. To find moral principles is to have found prosperity, greatness, truth, and is therefore to be strong, valiant, joyful and free.

JAMES ALLEN

"Bryngoleu,"

Ilfracombe,

England.

Chapter 1

Eight pillars

Prosperity rests upon a moral foundation. It is popularly supposed to rest upon an immoral foundation - that is, upon trickery, sharp practice, deception and greed. One commonly hears even an otherwise intelligent man declare that "No man can be successful in business unless he is dishonest," thus regarding business prosperity - a good thing - as the effect of dishonesty - a bad thing. Such a statement is superficial and thoughtless, and reveals a total lack of knowledge of moral causation, as well as a very limited grasp of the facts of life. It is as though one should sow henbane and reap spinach, or erect a brick house on a quagmire - things impossible in the natural order of causation, and therefore not to be attempted. The spiritual or moral order of causation is not different in principle, but only in nature. The same law obtains in things unseen - in thoughts and deeds - as in things seen - in natural phenomena. Man sees the processes in natural objects, and acts in accordance with them, but not seeing the spiritual processes, he imagines that they do not obtain, and so he does not act in harmony with them.

Yet these spiritual processes are just as simple and just as sure as the natural processes. They are indeed the same natural modes manifesting in the world of mind. All the parables and a large number of the sayings of the Great Teachers are designed to illustrate this fact. The natural world is the mental world made visible. The 'seen' is the mirror of the unseen. The upper half of a circle is in no way different from the lower half, but its sphericity is reversed. The material and the mental are not two detached arcs in the universe they are the two halves of a complete circle. The natural and the spiritual are not at eternal enmity, but in the true order of the universe are eternally at one. It is in the unnatural - in the abuse of function and faculty - where division arises, and where main is wrested back, with repeated sufferings, from the perfect circle from which he has tried to depart. Every process in matter is also a process in mind. Every natural law has its spiritual counterpart.

Take any natural object, and you will find its fundamental processes in the mental sphere if you rightly search. Consider, for
instance, the germination of a seed and its growth into a plant
with the final development of a flower, and back to seed again.
This also is a mental process. Thoughts are seeds which, falling
in the soil of the mind, germinate and develop until they reach the
completed stage, blossoming into deeds good or bad, brilliant or
stupid, according to their nature, and ending as seeds of thought
to be again sown in other minds. A teacher is a sower of seed, a
spiritual agriculturist, while he who teaches himself is the wise
farmer of his own mental plot. The growth of a thought is as the
growth of a plant. The seed must be sown seasonably, and time is
required for its full development into the plant of knowledge and
the flower of wisdom.

While writing this, I pause, and turn to look through my study
window, and there, a hundred yards away, is a tall tree in the top
of which some enterprising rook from a rookery hard by, has, for
the first time, built its nest. A strong, north-east wind is blowing,
so that the top of the tree is swayed violently to and fro by the on-
set of the blast; yet there is no danger to that frail thing of sticks
and hair, and the mother bird, sitting upon her eggs, has no fear
of the storm. Why is this? It is because the bird has instinctively
built her nest in harmony with principles which ensure the maximum strength and security. First, a fork is chosen as the foundation for the nest, and not a space between two separate branches,
so that, however great may be the swaying of the tree top, the position of the nest is not altered, nor its structure disturbed; then the
nest is built on a circular plan so as to offer the greatest resistance
to any external pressure, as well as to obtain more perfect com-
pactness within, in accordance with its purpose; and so, however
the tempest may rage, the birds rest in comfort and security. This
is a very simple and familiar object, and yet, in the strict obedience of its structure to mathematical law, it becomes, to the wise,
a parable of enlightenment, teaching them that only by ordering
one's deeds in accordance with fixed principles is perfect surety,
perfect security, and perfect peace obtained amid the uncertainty
of events and the turbulent tempests of life.

A house or a temple built by man is a much more complicated
structure than a bird's nest, yet it is erected in accordance with
those mathematical principles which are everywhere evidenced in
nature. And here is seen how man, in material things, obeys uni-

versal principles. He never attempts to put up a building in defiance of geometrical proportions, for he knows that such a building would be unsafe, and that the first storm would, in all probability, level it to the ground, if, indeed, it did not fall about his ears during the process of erection. Man in his material building scrupulously obeys the fixed principles of circle, square and angle, and, aided by rule, plumb line and compasses, he raises a structure which will resist the fiercest storms, and afford him a secure shelter and safe protection.

All this is very simple, the reader may say. Yes, it is simple because it is true and perfect; so true that it cannot admit the smallest compromise, and so perfect that no man can improve upon it. Man, through long experience, has learned these principles of the material world, and sees the wisdom of obeying them, and I have thus referred to them in order to lead up to a consideration of those fixed principles in the mental or spiritual world which are just as simple, and just as eternally true and perfect, yet are at present so little understood by man that he daily violates them, because ignorant of their nature, and unconscious of the harm he is all the time inflicting upon himself.

In mind as in matter, in thoughts as in things, in deeds as in natural processes, there is a fixed foundation of law which, if consciously or ignorantly ignored leads to disaster, and defeat. It is, indeed, the ignorant violation of this law which is the cause of the world's pain and sorrow. In matter, this law is presented as mathematical; in mind, it is perceived as moral. But the mathematical and the moral are not separate and opposed; they are but two aspects of a united whole. The fixed principles of mathematics, to which all matter is subject, are the body of which the spirit is ethical; while the eternal principles of morality are mathematical truisms operating in the universe of mind. It is as impossible to live successfully apart from moral principles, as to build successfully while ignoring mathematical principles. Characters, like houses, only stand firmly when built on a foundation of moral law - and they are built up slowly and laboriously, deed by deed, for in the building of character, the bricks are deeds. Business and all human enterprises are not exempt from the eternal order, but can only stand securely by the observance of fixed laws. Prosperity, to be stable and enduring, must rest on a solid foundation of moral principle, and be supported by the adamantine pillars of sterling character and moral worth. In the attempt to run a business in defiance of moral principles, disaster, of one kind or another, is inevitable. The permanently prosperous men in any community are not its tricksters and deceivers, but its reliable and upright men. The Quakers are acknowledged to be the most upright men in the British community, and, although their numbers are small, they are the most prosperous. The Jains in India are similar both in numbers and sterling worth, and they are the most prosperous people in India.

Men speak of "building up a business," and, indeed, a business is as much a building as is a brick house or a stone church, albeit the process of building is a mental one. Prosperity, like a house, is a roof over a man's head, affording him protection and comfort. A roof presupposes a support, and a support necessitates a foundation. The roof of prosperity, then, is supported by the following eight pillars which are cemented in a foundation of moral consistency:-

1. Energy
2. Economy
3. Integrity
4. System
5. Sympathy
6. Sincerity
7. Impartiality
8. Self-reliance

A business built up on the faultless practice of all these principles would be so firm and enduring as to be invincible. Nothing could injure it; nothing could undermine its prosperity, nothing could interrupt its success, or bring it to the ground; but that success would be assured with incessant increase so long as the principles were adhered to. On the other hand, where these principles were all absent, there could be no success of any kind; there could not even be a business at all, for there would be nothing to produce the adherence of one part with another; but there would be that lack of life, that absence of fiber and consistency which animates and gives body and form to anything whatsoever. Picture a man with all these principles absent from his mind, his daily life, and even if your knowledge of these principles is but slight and imperfect, yet you could not think of such a man as doing any successful work. You could picture him as leading the confused life of a shiftless tramp but to imagine him at the head of a business, as the centre of an organisation, or as a responsible and controlling agent in any department of life - this you could not do, because you realise its impossibility. The fact that no one of moderate morality and intelligence can think of such a man as commanding any success, should, to all those who have not yet grasped the import of these principles, and therefore declare that morality is not a factor, but rather a hindrance, in prosperity, be a sound proof to them that their conclusion is totally wrong, for if it was right, then the greater the lack of these moral principles, the greater would be the success.

These eight principles, then, in greater or lesser degree, are the causative factors in all success of whatsoever kind. Underneath all prosperity they are the strong supports, and, howsoever appearances may be against such a conclusion, a measure of them informs and sustains every effort which is crowned with that excellence which men name success.

It is true that comparatively few successful men practice, in their entirety and perfection, all these eight principles, but there are those who do, and they are the leaders, teachers, and guides of men, the supports of human society, and the strong pioneers in the van of human evolution.

But while few achieve that moral perfection which ensures the acme of success, all lesser successes come from the partial observance of these principles which are so powerful in the production of good results that even perfection in any two or three of them alone is sufficient to ensure an ordinary degree of prosperity, and maintain a measure of local influence at least for a time, while the same perfection in two or three with partial excellence in all, or nearly all, the others, will render permanent that limited success and influence which will, necessarily, grow and extend in exact ratio with a more intimate knowledge and practice of those principles which, at present, are only partially incorporated in the character.

The boundary lines of a man's morality mark the limits of his success. So true is this that to know a man's moral status would be to know - to mathematically gauge - his ultimate success or failure. The temple of prosperity only stands in so far as it is supported by its moral pillars; as they are weakened, it becomes insecure; in so far as they are withdrawn, it crumbles away and totters to ruin.

Ultimate failure and defeat are inevitable where moral principles are ignored or defied - inevitable in the nature of things as cause and effect. As a stone thrown upward returns to the earth, so every deed, good or bad, returns upon him that sent it forth. Every unmoral or immoral act frustrates the end at which it aims, and every such succeeding act puts it further and further away as an achieved realisation. On the other hand, every moral act is another solid brick in the temple of prosperity, another round of strength and sculptured beauty in the pillars which support it.

Individuals, families, nations grow and prosper in harmony with their growth in moral strength and knowledge; they fall and fail in accordance with their moral decadence.

Mentally, as physically, only that which has form and solidity can stand and endure. The unmoral is nothingness, and from it nothing can be formed. It is the negation of substance. The immoral is destruction. It is the negation of form. It is a process of spiritual denudation. While it undermines and disintegrates, it leaves the scattered material ready for the wise builder to put it into form again; and the wise builder is Morality. The moral is substance, form, and building power in one. Morality always builds up and preserves, for that is its nature, being the opposite of immorality, which always breaks down and destroys. Morality is the master-builder everywhere, whether in individuals or nations.

Morality is invincible, and he who stands upon it to the end, stands upon an impregnable rock, so that his defeat is impossible, his triumph certain. He will be tried, and that to the uttermost, for without fighting there can be no victory, and so only can his moral powers be perfected, and it is in the nature of fixed principles, as of everything finely and perfectly wrought, to have their strength tested and proved. The steel bars which are to perform the strongest and best uses in the world must be subjected to a severe strain by the ironmaster, as a test of their texture and efficiency, before they are sent from his foundry. The brick maker throws aside the bricks which have given way under the severe heat. So he who is to be greatly and permanently successful will pass through the strain of adverse circumstances and the fire of temptation with his moral nature, not merely, not undermined, but strengthened and beautified. He will be like a bar of well-wrought steel, fit for the highest use, and the universe will see, as the ironmaster his finely-wrought steel, that the use does not escape him.

Immorality is assailable at every point, and he who tries to stand upon it, sinks into the morass of desolation. Even while his efforts seem to stand, they are crumbling away. The climax of failure is inevitable. While the immoral man is chuckling over his ill-gotten gains, there is already a hole in his pocket through which his gold is falling. While he who begins with morality, yet deserts it for gain in the hour of trial, is like the brick which breaks on the first application of heat; he is not fit for use, and the universe casts him aside, yet not finally, for he is a being, and not a brick; and he can live and learn, can repent and be restored.

Moral force is the life of all success, and the sustaining element in all prosperity; but there are various kinds of success, and it is frequently necessary that a man should fail in one direction that he may reach up to a greater and more far-reaching success. If, for instance, a literary, artistic, or spiritual genius should begin by trying to make money, it may be, and often is, to his advantage and the betterment of his genius that he should fail therein, so that he may achieve that more sublime success wherein, lies his real power. Many a millionaire would doubtless be willing to barter his millions for the literary success of a Shakespeare or the spiritual success of a Buddha, and would thereby consider that he had made a good bargain. Exceptional spiritual success is rarely accompanied with riches, yet financial success cannot in any way compare with it in greatness and grandeur. But I am not, in this book, dealing with the success of the saint or spiritual genius but with that success which concerns the welfare, well-being, and happiness of the broadly average man and woman, in a word, with the prosperity which, while being more or less connected with money - being present and temporal - yet is not confined thereto, but extends to and embraces all human activities, and which particularly relates to that harmony of the individual with his circumstances which produces that satisfaction called happiness and that comfort known as prosperity. To the achievement of this end, so desirable to the mass of mankind, let us now see how the eight principles operate, how the roof of prosperity is raised and made secure upon the pillars by which it is supported.

Chapter 2

First pillar - Energy

Energy is the working power in all achievement. Inert coal it converts into fire, and water it transmutes into steam; it vivifies and intensifies the commonest talent until it approaches to genius, and when it touches the mind of the dullard, it turns into a living fire that which before was sleeping in inertia.

Energy is a moral virtue, its opposing vice being laziness. As a virtue, it can be cultivated, and the lazy man can become energetic by forcibly arousing himself to exertion. Compared with the energetic man, the lazy man is not half alive. Even while the latter is talking about the difficulty of doing a thing, the former is doing it. The active man has done a considerable amount of work before the lazy man has roused himself from sleep. While the lazy man is waiting for an opportunity, the active man has gone out, and met and utilized half a dozen opportunities. He does things while the other is rubbing his eyes.

Energy is one of the primary forces: without it nothing can be accomplished. It is the basic element in all forms of action. The entire universe is a manifestation of tireless, though inscrutable energy. Energy is, indeed, life, and without it there would be no universe, no life. When a man has ceased to act, when the body lies inert, and all the functions have ceased to act, then we say he is dead; and in so far as a man fails to act, he is so far dead. Man, mentally and physically, is framed for action, and not for swinish ease. Every muscle of the body (being a lever for exertion) is a rebuke to the lazy man. Every bone and nerve is fashioned for resistance; every function and faculty is there for a legitimate use. All things have their end in action; all things are perfected in use.

This being so, there is no prosperity for the lazy man, no happiness, no refuge and no rest; for him, there is not even the ease which he covets, for he at last becomes a homeless outcast, a troubled, harried, despised man, so that the proverb wisely puts it that "The lazy man does the hardest work", in that, avoiding the systematic labour of skill, he brings upon himself the hardest lot.

Yet energy misapplied is better than no energy at all. This is powerfully put by St. John in the words: "I would have you either hot or cold; if you are lukewarm I will spew you out of my mouth". The extremes of heat and cold here symbolize the transforming agency of energy, in its good and bad aspects.

The lukewarm stage is colourless, lifeless, useless; it can scarcely be said to have either virtue or vice, and is merely barren empty, fruitless. The man who applies his abounding energy to bad ends has at the very power with which he strives to acquire his selfish ends, will bring upon him such difficulties, pains, and sorrows, that will compel him to learn by experience, and so at last to re-fashion his base of action. At the right moment, when his mental eyes open to better purposes, he will turn round and cut new and proper channels for the outflow of his power, and will then be just as strong in good as he formerly was in evil. This truth is beautifully crystallized in the old proverb, "The greater the sinner, the greater the saint".

Energy is power, and without it there will be no accomplishment; there will not even be virtue, for virtue does not only consist of not doing evil, but also, primarily, of doing good. There are those who try, yet fail through insufficient energy. Their efforts are too feeble to produce positive results. Such are not vicious, and because they never do any deliberate harm, are usually spoken of as good men that fail. But to lack the initiative to do harm is not to be good; it is only to be weak and powerless. He is the truly good man who, having the power to do evil yet chooses to direct his energies in ways that are good. Without a considerable degree of energy, therefore, there will be no moral power. What good there is will be latent and sleeping; there will be no going forth of good, just as there can be no mechanical motion without the motive power.

Energy is the informing power in all doing in every department of life, and whether it be along material or spiritual lines. The call to action, which comes not only from the soldier but from the lips or pen of every teacher in every grade of thought, is a call to men to rouse their sleeping energy, and to do vigorously the task in hand. Even the men of contemplation and mediation never cease to rouse their disciples to exertion in meditative thought, is a call to men to rouse their sleeping energy, and to do vigorously the task in hand. Even the men of contemplation and meditation never cease to rouse their disciples to exertion in meditative thought. Energy is alike needed in all spheres of life, and not only are the rules of the soldier, the engineer and the merchant rules of action, but nearly all the percepts of the saviors, sages, and saints are precepts of doing.

The advice of one of the Great Teachers to his disciples - "Keep wide awake", tersely expresses the necessity for tireless energy if one's purpose is to be accomplished, and is equally good advice to the salesman as to the saint. "Eternal vigilance is the price of liberty", and liberty is the reaching of one's fixed end. It was the same Teacher that said: "If anything is to be done, let a man do it at once; let him attack it vigorously!" The wisdom of this advice is seen when it is remembered that action is creative, that increase and development follow upon legitimate use. To get more energy we must use to the full that which we already possess. Only to him that that is given. Only to him that puts his hand vigorously to some task, does power and freedom come.

But energy, to be productive, must not only be directed towards good ends, it must be carefully controlled and conserved. "The conservation of energy" is a modern term expressive of that principle in nature by which no energy is wasted or lost, and the man whose energies are to be fruitful in results must work intelligently upon this principle. Noise and hurry are so much energy running to waste. "More haste, less speed". The maximum of noise usually accompanies the minimum of accomplishment. With much talk, there is little doing. Working steam is not heard. It is the escaping steam which makes a great noise. It is the concentrated powder which drives the bullet to its mark.

In so far as a man intensifies his energies by conserving them and concentrating them upon the accomplishment of his purpose just so far does he gain quietness and silence in response and calmness. It is great delusion that noise means power. There is no greater baby than the blustering boaster. Physically a man, he is but an infant mentally, and having no strength to anything, and no work to show, he tries to make up for it by loudly proclaiming what he has done, or could do.

"Still waters run deep," and the great universal forces are inaudible. Where calmness is, there is the greatest power. Calmness is the sure indication of a strong, well trained, patiently disciplined mind. The calm man knows his business, be sure of it. His words are few, but they tell. His schemes are well planned, and they work true, like a well balanced machine. He sees a long way ahead, and makes straight for his object. The enemy, Difficulty, he converts into a friend, and makes profitable use of him, for he has studied well how to "agree with his adversary while he is in the way with him". Like a wise general, he has anticipated all emergencies. Indeed, he is the man who is prepared beforehand. In his meditations, in the counsels of his judgment, he has conferred with causes, and has caught the bent of all contingencies. He is never taken by surprise; is never in a hurry, is safe in the keeping of his own steadfastness, and is sure of his ground. You may think you have got him, only to find, the next moment, that you have tripped in your haste, and that he has got you, or rather that you, wanting calmness, have hurried yourself into the dilemma which you had prepared for him. Your impulse cannot do battle with his deliberation, but is foiled at the first attack; your uncurbed energy cannot turn aside the wisely directed steam of his concentrated power. He is "armed at all points". By a mental Ju-Jitsu acquired through self discipline, he meets opposition in such a way that it destroys itself. Upbraid him with angry words, and the reproof hidden in his gentle reply searches to the very heart of your folly, and the fire of your anger sinks into the ashes of remorse. Approach him with a vulgar familiarity and his look at once, fill you with shame and bring you back to your senses. As he is prepared for all events, so he is ready for all men; though no men are ready for him. All weaknesses are betrayed in his presence, and he commands by an inherent force which calmness has rendered habitual and unconscious.

Calmness, as distinguished from the dead placidity of languor, is the acme of concentrated energy. There is a focused mentality behind it. In agitation and excitement the mentality is dispersed. It is irresponsible, and is without force or weight. The fussy, peevish, irritable man has no influence. He repels, and not attracts. He wonders why his "easy going" neighbour succeeds, and is sought after, while he who is always hurrying, worrying and troubling the miscalls is striving, falls and is avoided. His neighbour being a calmer man, not more easy going but more deliberate, gets through more work, does it more skillfully, and is more self possessed and manly. This is the reason of his success and influence. His energy is controlled and used, while the other man's energy is dispersed and abused.

Energy, then, is the first pillar in the temple of prosperity, and without it, as the first and most essential equipment, there can be no prosperity. No energy means, no capacity; there is no manly self respect and independence. Amongst the unemployed will be found many who are unemployable through sheer lack of this first essential of work energy. The man that stands many hours a day at a street corner with his hands in his pockets and a pipe in his mouth, waiting for someone to treat him to a glass of beer, is little likely to find employment, or to accept it should it come to him. Physically flabby and mentally inert, he is every day becoming more some, is making himself more unfit to work, and therefore unfit to live. The energetic man may pass through temporary periods of unemployment and suffering, but it is impossible for him to become one of the permanently unemployed. He will either find work or make it, for inertia is painful to him, and work is a delight; and he who delights in work will not long remain unemployed.

The lazy man does not wish to be employed. He is in his element when doing nothing. His chief study is how to avoid exertion. To vegetate in semi torpor is his idea of happiness. He is unfit and unemployable. Even the extreme Socialist, who places all unemployment, at the door of the rich, would discharge a lazy, neglectful and unprofitable servant, and so add one more to the arm of the unemployed; for laziness is one of the lowest vices repulsive to all active, right minded men.

But energy is a composite power. It does not stand alone. Involved in it are qualities which go to the making of vigorous character and the production of prosperity. Mainly, these qualities are contained in the four following characteristics:

1. Promptitude
2. Vigilance
3. Industry
4. Earnestness

The pillar of energy is therefore a concrete mass composed of these four tenacious elements. They are through, enduring, and are calculated to withstanding the wildest weather of adversity. They all make for life, power, capacity, and progress.

Promptitude is valuable possession. It begets reliability. People who are alert, prompt, and punctual are relied upon. They can be trusted to do their duty, and to do it vigorously and well. Masters who are prompt are a tonic to their employees, and a whip to those who are inclined to shirk. They are a means of wholesome discipline to those who would not otherwise discipline themselves. Thus while aiding their own usefulness and success, they contribute to the usefulness and success of others. The perfunctory worker, who is ever procrastinating, and is always behind time, becomes a nuisance, if not to himself, to others, and his services come to be regarded as of little economic value. Deliberation and dispatch, handmaids of promptitude, are valuable aids in the achievement of prosperity. In ordinary business channels, alacrity is a saving power, and promptness spells profit. It is doubtful whether a confirmed procrastinator ever succeeded in business. I have not yet met one such, though I have known many who have failed.

Vigilance is the guard of all the faculties and powers of the mind. It is the detective that prevents the entrance of any violent and destructive element. It is the close companion and protector of all success, liberty, and wisdom. Without this watchful attitude of mind, a man is a fool, and there is no prosperity for a fool. The fool allows his mind to be ransacked and robbed of its gravity, serenity, and judgment by mean thoughts and violent passions as they come along to molest him. He is never on his guard, but leaves open the doors of his mind to every nefarious intruder. He is so weak and unsteady as to be swept off his balance by every gust of impulse that overtakes him. He is an example to others of what they should not be. He is always a failure, for the fool is an offence to all men, and there is no society that can receive him with respect. As wisdom is the acme of strength, so folly is the other extreme of weakness.

The lack of vigilance is shown in thoughtlessness and in a general looseness in the common details of life. Thoughtlessness is built another name for folly. It lies at the root of a great deal of failure and misery. No one who aims at any kind of usefulness and prosperity (for usefulness in the body politic and prosperity to one's self cannot be served) can afford to be asleep with regard to his actions and the effect of those actions on other and reactively on himself. He must, at the outset of his career, wake up to a sense of his personnel responsibility. He must know that wherever he is - in the home, the counting-house, the pulpit, the store, in the schoolroom or behind the counter, in company or alone, at work or at play--his conduct will materially affect his career for good or bad; for there is a subtle influence in behavior which leaves its impression every man, woman, and child that it touches, and that impress is the determining factor in the attitude of persons towards one another. It is for the reason that the cultivation of good manners plays such an important part in all coherent society. If you carry about with you a disturbing or disagreeable mental defect, it needs not to be named and known to work its poison upon your affairs. Its corrosive influence will eat into all your efforts, and disfigure your happiness and prosperity, as powerful acid eats into and disfigures the finest steel. On the other hand, if you carry about an assuring and harmonious mental excellence, it needs no assurance that those about you understand it to be influenced by it. They will be drawn towards you in good will, often without knowing why, and that good quality will be the most powerful sport in all your affairs, bringing you friends and opportunities, and greatly aiding in the success of all your enterprises. It will even right your minor incapacities, covering a multitude of faults.

Thus we receive at the hands of the world according to the measure of our giving. For bad, bad; for good, good. For defective conduct, indifferent influence and imperfect success; for superior conduct lasting power and consummate achievement. We act, and the world responds. When the foolish man fails, he blames other, and sees no error in himself; but the wise man watches and corrects himself, and so is assured of success.

The man whose mind is vigilant and alert, has thereby a valuable equipment in the achievement of his aims; and if he be fully alive and wide-awake on all occasions, to all opportunities, and against all marring defects of character, what event, what circumstance, what enemy shall overtake him and find him unprepared? What shall prevent him from achieving the legitimate and at which he aims?

Industry brings cheerfulness and plenty. Vigorously industrious people are the happiest members of the community. They are not always the richest, if by riches is meant a superfluity of money; but they are always the most lighthearted and joyful, and the most satisfied with what they do and have, and are therefore the richer, if by richer we mean more abundantly blessed. Active people have no time for moping and brooding, or for dwelling selfishly upon their ailments and troubles. Things most used are kept the brightest, and people most employed best retain their brightness and buoyancy of spirit. Things unused tarnish quickest; and the time

killer is attacked with ennui and morbid fancies. To talk of having to "kill time" is almost like a confession of imbecility; for who,
in the short life at his disposal, and in a world so flooded with
resources of knowledge with sound heads and good hearts can fill
up every moment of every day usefully and happily, and if they
refer to time at all, it is to the effect that it is all too short to enable
them to do all that they would like to do.

Industry too, promoted health and well being. The active man
goes to bed tired every night; his rest is sound and sweet, and he
wakes up early in the morning, fresh and strong for another day's
delightful toil. His appetite and digestion are good. He has an excellent sauce in recreation, and a good tonic in toil. What compan-
ionship can such a man have with moping and melancholy? Such
morbid spirits hang around those who do little and dine excessively. People, who make themselves useful to the community, receive
back from the community their full share of health, happiness,
and prosperity. They brighten the daily task, and keep the world
moving. They are the gold of the nation and the salt of the earth.

"Earnestness", said a Great Teacher "is the path of immortality.
They who are in earnest do not die; they who are not in earnest are
as if dead already". Earnestness is the dedication of the entire mind
to its task. We live only in what we do. Earnest people are dissatisfied with anything short of the highest excellence in whatever they
do, and they always reach that excellence. There are so many that
are careless and half hearted; so satisfied with a poor performance
that the earnest ones shine apart as it were, in their excellence.
They are always plenty of "vacancies" in the ranks of usefulness
and service for earnest people. There never was, and never will be,
a deeply earnest man or woman who did not fill successfully some
suitable sphere. Such people are scrupulous, conscientious, and
painstaking, and cannot rest in ease until the very best is done,
and the whole world is always on the lookout to reward the best. It
always stands ready to pay the full price, whether in money, fame,
friends, influence, happiness, scope or life, for that which is of
surpassing excellence, whether it be in things material, intellectual, or spiritual. Whatever you are - whether shopkeeper or saintly
teacher you can safely give the very best to the world without any
doubt or misgiving. If the indelible impress of your earnestness be
on your goods in the one case, or on your words in the other, your
business will flourish, or your precepts will live.

Earnest people make rapid progress both in their work and their character. It is thus that they live, and "do not die", for stagnation only is death, and where there is incessant progress and ever ascending excellence, stagnation and health are swallowed up in activity and life.

Thus is the making and masonry of the First pillar explained. He who builds it well, and sets it firm and straight, will have a powerful and enduring support in the business of his life.

Chapter 3

Second pillar - Economy

It is said of Nature that she knows no vacuum. She also knows no waste. In the divine economy Nature is conserved and turned to good account. Even excreta are chemically transmitted, and utilized in the building up of new forms. Nature destroys every foulness not by annihilation but by transmutation, by sweetening and purifying it, and making it serve the ends of things beautiful, useful and good.

That economy, which in nature is a universal principle, is in man a moral quality and it is that quality by which he preserves his energies, and sustains his place as a working unit in the scheme of things.

Financial economy is merely a fragment of this principle or rather it is a material symbol of that economy which is purely mental, and its transmutations spiritual. The financial economist exchanges coppers for silver, silver for gold, gold for notes, and the notes he converts into the figures of a bank account. By these conversions of money into more readily transmissible forms he is the gainer in the financial management of his affairs. The spiritual economist transmutes passions into intelligence, intelligence into principles, principles into wisdom, and wisdom is manifested in actions which are few but of powerful effect. By all these transmutations he is the gainer in character and in the management of his life.

True economy is the middle way in all things, whether material or mental, between waste and undue retention. That which is wasted, whether money or mental energy, is rendered powerless; that which is selfishly retained and hoarded up, is equally powerless. To secure power, whether of capital or mentality, there must be concentration, but concentration must be followed by legitimate use. The gathering up of money or energy is only a means; the end is use; and it is use only that produces power.

An all round economy consists in finding the middle way in the following seven things: Money, Food, Clothing, Recreation, Rest, Time and Energy.

Money is the symbol of exchange, and represents purchasing power. He who is anxious to acquire financial wealth as well as he who wishes to avoid debt - must study how to apportion his expenditure in accordance with his income, so as to leave a margin of ever increasing working capital, or to have a little store ready in hand for any emergency. Money spent in thoughtless expenditure - in worthless pleasures or harmful luxuries - is money wasted and power destroyed; for, although a limited and subordinate power, the means and capacity for legitimate and virtuous purchase is, nevertheless, a power, and one that enters largely into the details of our everyday life. The spendthrift can never become rich, but if he begins with riches, must soon become poor. The miser, with all his stored-away gold, cannot be said to be rich, for he is in want, and his gold, lying idle, is deprived of its power of purchase. The thrifty and prudent are on the way to riches, for while they spend wisely they save carefully, and gradually enlarge their spheres as their growing means allow.

The poor man who is to become rich must begin at the bottom, and must not wish, nor try to appear affluent by attempting something far beyond his means. There is always plenty of room and scope at the bottom, and it is a safe place from which to begin, as there is nothing below, and everything above. Many a young business man comes at once to grief by swagger and display which he foolishly imagines are necessary to success, but which, deceiving no one but himself, lead quickly to ruin. A modest and true beginning, in any sphere, will better ensure success than an exaggerated advertisement of one's standing and importance. The smaller the capital, the smaller should be the sphere of operations. Capital and scope are hand and glove, and they should fit. Concentrate your capital within the circle of its working power, and however circumscribed that circle may be it will continue to widen and extend as the gathering momentum of power presses for expression.

Above all take care always to avoid the two extremes of parsimony and prodigality.

Food represents life, vitality, and both physical and mental strength. There is a middle way in eating and drinking, as in all else. The man who is to achieve prosperity must be well nourished, but not overfed. The man that starves his body, whether through miserliness or asceticism (both forms of false economy), diminishes his mental energy, and renders his body too enfeebled to be the instrument for any strong achievement. Such a man courts sickly mindedness, a condition conducive only to failure.

The glutton, however, destroys himself by excess. His bestialized body becomes a stored up reservoir of poisons, which attract disease and corruption, while his mind becomes more and more brutalized and confused, and therefore more incapable. Gluttony is one of the lowest and most animal vices, and is obnoxious to all who pursue a moderate course.

The best workers and most successful men are they who are most moderate in eating and drinking. By taking enough nourishment, but not too much, they attain the maximum physical and mental fitness. Beings thus well equipped by moderation, they are enabled to vigorously and joyfully fight the battle of life.

Clothing is covering and protection for the body, though it is frequently wrested from this economic purpose, and made a means of vain display. The two extremes to be avoided here are negligence and vanity. Custom cannot, and need not, be ignored; and cleanliness is all important. The ill-dressed, unkempt man or woman invites failure and loneliness. A man's dress should harmonize with his station in life, and it should be of good quality, and be well made and appropriate. Clothing should not be cast aside while comparatively new, but should be well worn. If a man be poor, he will not lose in either self respect or the respect of others by wearing threadbare clothing if it be clean and his whole body be clean and neat. But vanity, leading to excessive luxury in clothing, is a vice which should be studiously avoided by virtuous people. I know a lady who had forty dresses in her wardrobe; also a man who had twenty walking-sticks, about the same number of hats, and some dozen mackintoshes; while another had some twenty or thirty pairs of boots. Rich people, who thus squander money on piles of superfluous clothing, are courting poverty, for it is waste, and waste leads to want. The money so heedlessly spent could be better used, for suffering abounds and charity is noble.

An obtrusive display in clothing and jewelry bespeaks a vulgar and empty mind. Modest and cultured people are modest and becoming in their dress and their spare money is wisely used in further enhancing their culture and virtue. Education and progress are of more importance to them than vain and needless apparel;

and literature, art, and science are encouraged thereby. A true refinement is in the mind and behaviour, and a mind adorned with virtue and intelligence cannot add to its attractiveness though it may detract from it) by an ostentatious display of the body. Time spent in uselessly adorning the body could be more fruitfully employed. Simplicity in dress, as in other things, is the best. It touches the point of excellence in usefulness, comfort, and bodily grace, and bespeaks true taste and cultivated refinement.

Recreation is one of the necessities of life. Every man and women should have some definitive work as the main object of life, and to which a considerable amount of time should be devoted, and he should only turn from it at given and limited periods for recreation and rest. The object of recreation is greater buoyancy of both body and mind, with an increase of power in one's serious work. It is, therefore, a means, not an end; and this should ever be born in mind, for, to many, some forms of recreation innocent and good in themselves - become so fascinating that they are in danger of making them the end of life, and of thus abandoning duty for pleasure. To make of life a ceaseless round of games and pleasures, with no other object in life, is to turn living upside down, as it were, and it produces monotony and enervation. People who do it are the most unhappy of mortals and suffer from languor, ennui, and peevishness. As sauce is an aid to digestion, and can only lead to misery when made the work of life. When a man has done his day's duty he can turn to his recreation with a free mind and a light heart, and both his work and his pleasure will be to him a source of happiness.

It is a true economy in this particular neither to devote the whole of one's time to work nor to recreation, but to apportion to each its time and place; and so fill out life with those changes which are necessary to a long life and a fruitful existence.

All agreeable changes is recreation and the mental worker will gain both in the quality and, quantity of his work by laying it down at the time appointed for restful and refreshing recreation; while the physical worker will improve in every way by turning to some form of study as a hobby or means of education.

As we do not spend all our time in eating or sleeping or resting, neither should we spend it in exercise or pleasure, but should give recreation its proper place as a natural tonic in the economic scheme of our life.

Rest is for recuperation after toil. Every self respecting human being should do sufficient work every day to make his sleep restful and sweet, and his rising up fresh and bright.

Enough sleep should be taken, but not too much, over indulgence on the one hand, or deprivation on the other, are both harmful. It is an easy matter to find out how much sleep one requires. By going to bed early, and getting up early (rising a little earlier every morning if one has been in the habit of spending long hours in bed), one can very soon accurately gauge and adjust the number of hours he or she requires for complete recuperation. It will be found as the sleeping hours are shortened that the sleep becomes more and more sound and sweet, and the waking up more and more alert and bright. People who are to prosper in their work must not give way to ignoble ease and over indulgence in sleep. Fruitful labour, and not ease, is the true end of life, and ease is only good in so far as it sub-serves the ends of work. Sloth and prosperity can never be companions can never even approach each other. The sluggard will never overtake success, but failure will speedily catch up with him, and leave him defeated. Rest is to fit us for greater labour, and not to pamper us in indolence. When the bodily vigour is restored, the end of rest is accomplished. A perfect balance between labour and rest contributes considerably to health, happiness, and prosperity.

Time is that which we all possess in equal measure. The day is not lengthened for any man. We should therefore see to it that we do not squander its precious minutes in unprofitable waste. He, who spends his time in self indulgence and the pursuit of pleasure, presently finds himself old, and nothing has been accomplished. He, who fills full with useful pursuits the minutes as they come and go, grows old in honour and wisdom, and prosperity abides with him. Money wasted can be restored; health wasted can be restored; but time wasted can never be restored.

It is an old saying that "time is money". It is, in the same way, health, and strength, and talent, and genius, and wisdom, in accordance with the manner in which it is used; and to properly use it, the minutes must be seized upon as they come, for once they are past they can never be recalled. The day should be divided into portions, and everything - work, leisure, meals, recreation - should be attend to in its proper time; and the time of preparation should not be overlooked or ignored. Whatever a man does, he will do it better and more successfully by utilizing some small portion of the day in preparing his mind for his work. The man who gets up early in order to think and plan, that he may weigh and consider and forecast, will always manifest greater skill and success in his particular pursuit, than the man who lives in bed till the last moment, and only gets up just in time to begin breakfast. An hour spent in this way before breakfast will prove of the greatest value in making one's efforts fruitful. It is a means of calming and clarifying the mind and of focusing one's energies so as to render them more powerful and effective. The best and most abiding success is that which is made before eight o'clock in the morning. He who is at his business at six o'clock, will always other conditions being equal be a long way ahead of the man who is in bed at eight. The lie a bed heavily handicaps himself in the race of life. He gives his early-rising competitor two or three hours start every day. How can he ever hope to win with such a self imposed tax upon his time? At the end of a year that two or three hours start every day is shown in a success which is the synthesis of accumulated results. What, then, must be the difference between the efforts of these two men at the end, say, of twenty years! The lie-a-bed, too, after he gets up is always in a hurry trying to regain lost time, which results in more loss of time, for hurry always defeats its own end. The early rise, who thus economies his time, has no need to hurry, for he is always ahead of the hour, is always well up with his work; he can well afford to be calm and deliberate, and to do carefully and well whatever is in hand, for his good habit shows itself at the end of the day in the form of a happy frame of mind, and in bigger results in the shape of work skillfully and successfully done.

In the economizing of time, too, there will be many things which a man will have to eliminate from his life; some of things and pursuits which he loves, and desires to retain, will have to be sacrifice to the main purpose of his life. The studied elimination of non-essentials from one's daily life is a vital factor in all great achievement. All great men are adepts in this branch of economy, and it plays an important part in the making of their greatness. It is a form of economy which also enters into the mind, the actions, and the speech, eliminating from them all that is superfluous, and that impedes, and does not sub-serve, the end aimed at. Foolish and unsuccessful people talk carelessly and aimlessly, act carelessly and aimlessly, and allow everything that comes along good, bad, and different to lodge in their mind.

The mind of the true economist is a sieve which lets everything fall through except that which is of use to him in the business of his life. He also employs only necessary words, and does only necessary actions, thus vastly minimizing friction and waste of power.

To go to bed on time and to get up on time, to fill in every working minute with purposeful thought and effective action, this is the true economy of time.

Energy is economized by the formation of good habits. All vices are a reckless expenditure of energy. Sufficient energy is thoughtlessly wasted in bad habits to enable men to accomplish the greatest success, if conserved and used in right directions. If economy be practiced in the six points already considered, much will be done in the conservation of one's energies, but a man must go still further, and carefully husband his vitality by the avoidance of all forms of physical self indulgences and impurities, but also all those mental vices such as hurry, worry, excitement, despondency, anger, complaining and envy - which deplete the mind and render it unfit for any important work or admirable achievement. They are common forms of mental dissipation which a man of character should study how to avoid and overcome. The energy wasted in frequent fits of bad temper would, if controlled and properly directed, give a man, strength of mind, force of character, and much power to achieve. The angry man is a strong man made weak by the dissipation of his mental energy. He needs self control to manifest his strength. The calm man is always his superior in any department of life, and will always take precedence of him, both in his success, and in the estimation of others. No man can afford to disperse his energies in fostering bad habits and bad tendencies of mind. Every vice, however, apparently small will tell against him in the battle of life. Every harmful self indulgence will come back to him in the form of some trouble or weakness. Every moment of riot or of pandering to his lower inclinations will make his progress more laborious, and will hold him back from scaling the high heaven of his wishes for achievement. On the other hand, he who economizes his energies, and bends them towards the main task of his life, will make rapid progress, and nothing will prevent him from reaching the golden city of success.

It will be seen that economy is something far more profound and far reaching than the mere saving of money. It touches every part of our nature and every phase of our life. The old saying, "Take care of the pence, and the pounds will take care of themselves", may be regarded as a parable, for the lower passions as native energy; it is the abuse of that energy that is bad, and if this personal energy be taken care of and stored up and transmuted, it reappears as force of character. To waste this valuable energy in the pursuit of vice is like wasting the pence, and so losing the pounds, but to take care of it for good uses is to store up the pence of passions, and so gain the golden pounds of good. Take care, therefore, of the lower energies, and the higher achievements will take care of themselves.

The Pillar of Economy, when soundly built, will be found to be composed largely of these four qualities:-

1. Moderation

2. Efficiency

3. Resourcefulness

4. Originality

Moderation is the strong core of economy. It avoids extremes, finding the middle way in all things. It also consists in abstaining from the unnecessary and the harmful. There can be no such things as moderation in that which is evil, for that would be excess. A true moderation abstains from evil. It is not a moderate use of fire to put our hands into it, but to warm them by it at a safe distance. Evil is a fire that will burn a man though, he but touch it. A harmful luxury is best left severely alone. Smoking, snuff taking, alcoholic drinking, gambling, and other such common vices, although they have dragged thousands down to ill health, misery, and failure, have never helped one towards health, happiness and success. The man who eschews them will always be head of the man that pursues them, their talents and opportunities being equal. Healthy, happy, and long lived people are always moderate and abstemious in their habits. By moderation the life forces are preserved; by excess they are destroyed. Men, also, who carry moderation into their thoughts, allaying their passions and feelings, avoiding all unwholesome extremes and morbid sensations and sentiments, add knowledge and wisdom to happiness and health, and thereby attain to the highest felicity and power. The immoderate destroy themselves by their own folly. They weaken their energies and stultify their capabilities, and instead of achieving an abiding success, reach only, at best, a fitful and precarious prosperity.

Efficiency proceeds from the right conservation of one's forces and powers. All skill is the use of concentrated energy. Superior skill, as talent and genius, is a higher degree of concentrated force. Men are always skillful in that which they love, because the mind is almost ceaselessly centered upon it. Skill is the result of that mental economy which transmutes thought into invention and action. There will be no prosperity without skill, and one's prosperity will be in the measure of one's skill. By a process of natural selection, the inefficient fall in to their right places. Among the badly paid or unemployed; for who will employ a man who cannot, or will not, do his work properly? An employer may occasionally keep such a man out of charity; but this will be exceptional; as places of business, offices, households, and all centers of organized activity, are not charitable institutions, but industrial bodies which stand or fall but the fitness and efficiency of their individual members.

Skill is gained by thoughtfulness and attention. Aimless and inattentive people are usually out of employment - to wit, the lounger at the street corner. They cannot do the simplest thing properly, because they will not rouse up the mind to thought and attention. Recently an acquaintance of mine employed a tramp to clean his windows, but the man had refrained from work and systematic thought for so long that he had become incapable of both, and could not even clean a window. Even when shown how to do it, he could not follow the simple instructions given. This is an instance, too, of the fact that the simplest thing requires a measure of skill in the doing. Efficiency largely determines a man's place among his fellows, and leads one on by steps to higher and higher positions as greater powers are developed. The good workman is skillful, with his tools, while the good man is skillful with his thoughts. Wisdom is the highest form of skill. Aptitude in incipient wisdom. There is one right way of doing everything, even the smallest, and a thousand wrong ways. Skill consists in finding the one right way, and adhering to it. The inefficient bungle confusedly about among the thousand wrong ways, and do not adopt the right even when it is pointed out to them. They do this in some cases because they think, in their ignorance, that they know best, thereby placing themselves in a position where it becomes impossible to learn, even though it be only to learn how to clean a window or sweep a floor. Thoughtlessness and inefficiency are all too common. There is plenty of room in the world for common. There is plenty of room in the world for thoughtful and efficient people. Employers of labour know how difficult it is to get the best workmanship. The good workman, whether with tools or brain, whether with speech or thought, will always find a place for the exercise of his skill.

Resourcefulness is the outcome of efficiency. It is an important element in prosperity, for the resourceful man is never confounded. He may have many falls, but he will always be equal to the occasion, and will be on his feet again immediately. Resourcefulness has its fundamental cause in the conservation of energy. It is energy transmuted. When a man cuts off certain mental or bodily vices which have been depleting him of his energy, what becomes of the energy so conserved? It is not destroyed or lost, for energy can never be destroyed or lost. It becomes productive energy. It reappears in the form of fruitful thought. The virtuous man is always more successful than the vicious man because he is teeming with resources. His entire mentality is alive and vigorous, abounding with stored up energy. What the vicious man wastes in barren indulgence, the virtuous man uses in fruitful industry. A new life and a new world, abounding with all fascinating pursuits and pure delights, open up to the man who shuts himself off from the old world of animal vice, and his place will be assured by the resources which will well up within him. Barren seed perishes in the earth; there is no place for it in the fruitful economy of nature. Barren minds sink in the struggle of life. Human society makes for good, and there is no room in it for the emptiness engendered by vice. But the barren mind will not sink forever. When it wills, it can become fruitful and regain itself. By the very nature of existence, by the eternal law of progress, the vicious man must fall; but having fallen, he can rise again. He can turn from vice to virtue, and stand, self respecting and secure, upon his own resources.

The resourceful men invent, discover, initiate. They cannot fail, for they are in the stream of progress. They are full of new schemes, new methods, new hopes, and their life is so much fuller and richer thereby. They are men of supple minds. When a man fails to improve his business, his work, his methods, he falls out of the line of progress, and has begun to fail. His mind has become stiff and inert like the body of an aged man, and so fails to keep pace with the rapidly moving ideas and plans of resourceful minds. A resourceful mind is like a river which never runs dry, and which affords refreshment, and supplies new vigour, in times of drought. Men of resources are men of new ideas, and men of new ideas flourish where others fade and decay.

Originality is resourcefulness ripened and perfected. Where there is originality there is genius, and men of genius are the lights of the world. Whatever work a man does, he should fall back upon his own resources in the doing it. While learning from others, he should not slavishly imitate them, but should put himself into his work, and so make it new and original. Original men get the ear of the world. They may be neglected at first, but they are always ultimately accepted, and become patterns for mankind. Once a man has acquired the knack of originality, he takes his place as a leader among men in his particular department of knowledge and skill. But originality cannot be forced; it can only be developed; and it is developed by proceeding from excellence to excellence, by ascending in the scale of skill by the full and right use of one's mental powers. Let a man consecrate himself to his work, let him, so consecrated, concentrate all his energies upon it, and the day will come when the world will hail him as one of its strong sons; and he, too, like Balzac who, after many years of strenuous toil, one day exclaimed, "I am about to become a genius! I am about to become a genius!" He will at least discover, to his joy, that he has joined the company of original minds, the gods who lead mankind into newer, higher, and more beneficial ways.

The composition of the Second Pillar is thus revealed. Its building awaits the ready work man who will skillfully apply his mental energies.

Chapter 4

Third pillar - Integrity

There is no striking a cheap bargain with prosperity. It must be purchased, not only with intelligent labor, but with moral force. as the bubble cannot endure, so the fraud cannot prosper. He makes a feverish spurt in the acquirement of money, and then collapses. Nothing is ever gained, ever can be gained, by fraud. It is but wrested for a time, to be again returned with heavy interest. But fraud is not confined to the unscrupulous swindler. All who are getting, or trying to get, money without giving an equivalent are practicing fraud, whether they know it or not. Men who are anxiously scheming how to get money without working for it, are frauds, and mentally they are closely allied to the thief and swindler under whose influence they come, sooner or later, and who deprives them of their capital. What is a thief but a man who carries to its logical conclusion, or later who deprives them of their capital? What is a thief but a man who carries to its logical extreme the desire to possess without giving a just return - that is, unlawfully? The man that courts prosperity must, in all his transactions, whether material or mental, study how to give a just return for that which he receives. This is the great fundamental principle in all sound commerce, while in spiritual things it becomes the doing to others that which we would have them do to us, and applied to the forces of the universe, it is scientifically stated in the formula, "Action and Reaction are equal."

Human life is reciprocal, not rapacious, and the man who regards all others as his legitimate prey will soon find himself stranded in the desert of ruin, far away from the path of prosperity. He is too far behind in the process of evolution to cope successfully with honest man. The fittest, the best, always survive, and he being the worst, cannot therefore continue. His end, unless the change in time, is sure it is the goal, the filthy hovel, or the place of the deserted outcast. His efforts are destructive, and not constructive, and he thereby destroys himself.

It was Carlyle who, referring to Mohammed being then universally regarded by Christians as an impostor, exclaimed, "An impostor founded a religion! An impostor couldn't build a brick house." An impostor, a liar, a cheat, the man of dishonesty cannot build, as he has neither tools or material with which to build. He can no more build up a business, a character, a career, a success, than he can found a religion or build a brick house. He not only does not build, but all his energies are bent on undermining what others have built, but his being impossible, he undermines himself.

Without integrity, energy and economy will at last fail, but aided by integrity, their strength will be greatly augmented. There is not an occasion in life in which the moral factor does not play an important part. Sterling integrity tells wherever it is, and stamps its hallmark on all transactions; and it does this because of its wonderful coherence and consistency, and its invincible strength. For the man of integrity is in line with the fixed laws of things - not only with the fundamental principles on which human society rests, but with the laws which hold the vast universe together. Who shall set these at naught? Who, then, shall undermine the man of unblemished integrity? He is like a strong tree whose roots are fed by perennial springs, and which no tempest can lay low.

To be complete and strong, integrity must embrace the whole man, and extend to all the details of his life; and it must be so through and permanent, as to withstand all temptations to swerve into compromise. To fail in one point is to fail in all, and to admit, under stress, a compromise with falsehood, howsoever necessary and insignificant it may appear, is to throw down the shield of integrity, and to stand exposed to the onslaughts of evil.

The man who works as carefully and conscientiously when his employer is away as when his eye is upon him will not long remain in an inferior position. Such integrity in duty, in performing the details of his work, will quickly lead him into the fertile regions of prosperity.

The shirker, on the other hand - he who does not scruple to neglect his work when his employer is not about, thereby robbing his employer of the time and labour for which he is paid - will quickly come to the barren region of unemployment, and will look in vain for needful labour.

There will come a time, too, to the man who is not deeply rooted in integrity, when it will seem necessary to his prospects and prosperity that he should tell a lie or do a dishonest thing - I say, to the man who is not deeply rooted in this principle, for a man of fixed and enlightened integrity knows that lying and dishonesty can never under any circumstance be necessary, and therefore he neither needs to be tempted in this particular, nor can he possibly be tempted but the one so tempted must be able to cast aside the subtle insinuation of falsehood which, in a time of indecision and perplexity, arises within him, and he must stand firmly by the principle, being willing to lose and suffer rather than sink into obliquity. In this way only can he become enlightened concerning this moral principle, and discover the glad truth that integrity does not lead to loss and suffering, but to gain and joy; that honesty and deprivation are not, and cannot be, related as cause and effect.

It is this willingness to sacrifice rather than be untrue that leads to enlightenment in all spheres of life; and the man who, rather than sacrifice some selfish aim, will lie or deceive, has forfeited his right to moral enlightenment, and takes his place lower down among the devotees of deceit, among the doers of shady transactions, than men of no character and no reputation.

A man is not truly armoured with integrity until he has become incapable of lying or deceiving either by gesture, word, or act; until he sees, clearly, openly, and freed from all doubt, the deadly effects of such moral turpitude. The man so enlightened is protected from all quarters, and can no more be undermined by dishonest men than the sun can be pulled down from heaven by madmen, and the arrows of selfishness and treachery that may be poured upon him will rebound from the strong armour of his integrity and the bright shield of his righteousness, leaving him unharmed and untouched.

A lying tradesman will tell you that no man can thrive and be honest in these days of keen competition. How can such a man know this, seeing that he has never tried honest? Moreover, such a man has no knowledge of honesty, and his statement is therefore, a statement of ignorance, and ignorance and falsehood so blind a man that he foolishly imagines all are as ignorant and false as himself. I have known such tradesmen, and have seen them come to ruin. I once heard a businessman make the following statement in a public meeting:-"No man can be entirely honest in business; he can only be approximately honest." He imagined that his statement revealed the condition of the business world; it did not, it revealed his own condition. He was merely telling his audience that he was a dishonest man, but his ignorance, moral ignorance, prevented him from seeing this. Approximate honesty is only another term for dishonesty. The man, who deviated a little from the straight path, will deviate more. He has no fixed principle of right and is only thinking of his own advantage. That he persuades himself that his particular dishonesty is of a white and harmless kind, and that he is not so bad as his neighbour, is only of the many forms of self delusion which ignorance of moral principles creates.

Right doing between man and main in the varied relations and transactions of life is the very soul of integrity. It includes, but is more than, honesty. It is the backbone of human society, and the support of human institutions. Without it there would be no trust, no confidence between men, and the business world would topple to its fall.

As the liar thinks all men are liars, and treats them as such, so the man of integrity treats all men with confidence. He trusts them, and they trust him. His clear eye and open hand shame the creeping fraud so that he cannot practice his fraud on him. As Emerson has so finely put it - "Trust men and they will be true to you, even though they make an exception in your favor to all their rules of trade."

The upright man by his very presence commands the morality of those about him making them better than they were. Men are powerfully influenced by one another and as good as more powerful than evil, the strong and good man both shames and elevates, by his contact, the weak and bad.

The man of integrity carries about with him an unconscious grandeur which both awes and inspires. Having lifted himself above the petty, the mean, and the false, those coward vices slink from his presence in confusion. The highest intellectual gift cannot compare with this lofty moral grandeur. In the memory of men and the estimation of the world the man of integrity occupies a higher place than the man of genius. Buckminster says, "The moral grandeur of an independent integrity is the sublimest thing in nature." It is the quality in man which produces heroes. The man of unswerving rectitude is, intrinsically, always a hero. It only needs the occasion to bring out the heroic element. He is always, too, possessed a permanent happiness. The man of genius may be very unhappy, but not to the man of integrity. Nothing nor sickness, nor calamity, nor death - can deprive him of that permanent satisfaction which inheres in uprightness.

Rectitude leads straight to prosperity by four successive steps. First, the upright man wins the confidence of others. Second, having gained their confidence, they put trust in him. Third, this trust, never being violated, produces a good reputation; and Fourth a good reputation spreads further and further, and so bring about success.

Dishonesty has the reverse effect. By destroying the confidence of others, it produces in them suspicion and mistrust, and these bring about a bad reputation, which culminates in failure.

The Pillar of Integrity is held together by these four virile elements:

1. Honesty
2. Fearlessness
3. Purposefulness
4. Invincibility

Honesty is the surest way to success. The day at last comes when the dishonest man repents in sorrow and suffering: but not man ever needs to repent of having been honest. Even when the honest man fails - as he does sometimes, through lacking other of these pillars, such as energy, economy, or system his failure is not the grievous thing it is to the dishonest man, for he can always rejoice in the fact that he has never defrauded a fellow being. Even in his darkest hour he finds repose in a clear conscience.

Ignorant men imagine that dishonesty is a short cut to prosperity. This is why they practice it. The dishonest man is morally short sighted. Like the drunkard who sees the immediate pleasure of his habit, but not the ultimate degradation, he sees the immediate effect of a dishonest act - a larger profit but not its ultimate outcome; he does not see that an accumulated number of such acts must inevitably undermine his character, and bring his business toppling about his ears in ruin. While pocketing his gains, and thinking how cleverly and successfully he is imposing on others, he is all the time imposing on himself, and every coin thus gained must be paid back with added interest, and from this just retribution there is no possible loophole of escape. This moral gravitation is a sure and unvarying as the physical gravitation of a stone to the earth.

The tradesman, who demands of his assistants that they shall be, and misrepresents his goods to customers, is surrounding himself on all hands with suspicion, mistrust, and hatred. Even the moral weaklings, who carry out his instructions, despise him while defiling themselves with his unclean work. How can success thrive in such a poisonous atmosphere? The spirit of ruin is already in such a business, and the day of his fall is ordained.

An honest man may fail, but not because he is honest, and his failure will be honourable, and will not injure his character and reputation. His failure, too, resulting doubtless from his incapacity in the particular direction of his failure, will be a means of leading him into something more suited to his talents, and thus to ultimate success.

Fearlessness accompanies honesty. The honest man has a clear eye and an unflinching gaze. He looks his fellowmen in the face, and his speech is direct and convincing. The liar and cheat hang his head; his eye is muddy and his gaze oblique. He cannot look another man in the eye, and his speech arouses mistrust, for it is ambiguous and unconvincing.

When a man has fulfilled his obligations, he has nothing to fear. All his business relations are safe and secure. His methods and actions will endure the light of day. Should he pass through a difficult time, and, get into debt, everybody will trust him and be willing to wait for payment, and all his debts will be paid. Dishonest people try to avoid paying their debts, and they live in fear; but the honest man tries to avoid getting into debt, but when debt overtakes him, he does not fear, but, redoubling his exertions, his debts are paid.

The dishonest are always in fear. They do not fear debt, but fear that they will have to pay their debts. They fear their fellow-men, fear the established authorities, fear the results of all that they do, and they are in constant fear of their misdeeds being revealed, and of the consequences which may at any moment overtake them.

The honest man is rid of all this burden of fear. He is light hearted, and walks erect among his fellows; not assuming a part, and skulking and cringing, but being himself, and meeting eye to eye. Not deceiving or injuring any, there are none to fear, and anything and against him can only rebound to his advantage.

And this fearlessness is, in itself, a tower to strength in a man's life, supporting him through all emergencies, enabling him to battle manfully with difficulties, and in the end securing for him that success of which he cannot be dispossessed.

Purposefulness is the direct outcome of that strength of character which integrity fosters. The man of integrity is the man of direct aims and strong and intelligent purposes. He does not guess, and work in the dark. All his plans have in them some of that moral fiber of which his character is wrought. A man's work will always in some way reflect himself, and the man of sound integrity is the man of sound plan. He weights and considers and looks ahead, and so is less likely to make serious mistakes, or to bungle into a dilemma from which it is difficult to escape. Taking a moral view of all things, and always considering moral consequences, he stands on a firmer and more exalted ground than the man of mere policy and expedience; and while commanding a more extended view of any situation, he wields the greater power which a more comprehensive grasp of details with the principles involved, confers upon him. Morality always has the advantage of expediency. Its purposes always reach down far below the surface, and are therefore more firm and secure, more strong and lasting. There is a native directness, too, about integrity, which enables the man to get straight to the mark in whatever he does, and which makes failure almost impossible.

Strong men have strong purposes, and strong purposes lead to strong achievements. The man of integrity is above all men strong, and his strength is manifested in that thoroughness with which he does the business of his life; thoroughness which commands respect, admiration, and success.

Invincibility is a glorious protector, but it only envelopes the man whose integrity is perfectly pure and unassailable. Never to violate, even in the most insignificant particular, the principle of integrity, is to be invincible against all the assaults of innuendo, slander, and misrepresentation. The man who has failed in one point is vulnerable, and the shaft of evil, entering that point, will lay him low, like the arrow in the heel of Achilles. Pure and perfect integrity is proof against all attack and injury, enabling its possessor to meet all opposition and persecution with dauntless courage and sublime equanimity. No amount of talent, intellect, or business acumen can give a man that power of mind and peace of heart which come from an enlightened acceptance and observance of lofty moral principles. Moral force is the greatest power. Let the seeker for a true prosperity discover this force, let him foster and develop it in his mind and in his deeds, and as he succeeds he will take his place among the strong leaders of the earth.

Such is the strong and adamantine Pillar of integrity. Blessed and prosperous above all men will be he who builds its incorruptible masonry into the temple of his life.

Chapter 5

Fourth pillar - System

System is that principle of order by which confusion is rendered impossible. In the natural and universal order everything is in its place, so that the vast universe runs more perfectly than the most perfect machine. Disorder in space would mean the destruction of the universe; and disorder in a man's affairs destroys his work and his prosperity.

All complex organizations are built up by system. No business or society can develop into large dimensions apart from system, and this principle is preeminently the instrument of the merchant, the business man, and the organizer of institutions.

There are many departments in which a disorderly man may succeed - although attention to order would increase his success but he will not succeed in business unless he can place the business entirely in the hands of a systematic manager, who will thereby remedy his own defect.

All large business concerns have been evolved along definitely drawn systematic lines, any violation of which would be disastrous to the efficiency and welfare of the business. Complex business or other organizations are built up like complex bodies in nature, by scrupulous attention to details. The disorderly man thinks he can be careless about everything but the main end, but by ignoring the means he frustrates the end. By the disarrangement of details, organisms perish, and by the careless neglect of details, the growth of any work or concern is prevented.

Disorderly people waste an enormous amount of time and energy. The time frittered away in hunting for things is sufficient, were if conserved by order, to enable them to achieve any success, for slovenly people never have a place for anything, and have to hunt, frequently for a long time, for any article which they require. In the irritation, bad humour, and chagrin which this daily hunting for things brings about, as much energy is dissipated as would be required to build up a big business, or scale the highest heights of achievement in any direction.

Orderly people conserve both their time and energy. They never lose anything, and therefore never have to find anything. Everything is in its place, and the hand can be at once placed upon it, though it be in the dark. They can well afford to be cool and deliberate and so use their mental energies in something more profitable than irritation, bad temper and accusing others for their own lack of order.

There is a kind of genius in system which can perform apparent wonders with ease. A systematic man can get through so great a quantity of work in such a short time, and with such freedom from such exhaustion, as to appear almost miraculous. He scales the heights of success while his slovenly competitor is wallowing hopelessly in the bogs of confusion. His strict observance of the law of order enables him to reach his ends, swiftly and smoothly, without friction or loss of time.

The demands of system, in all departments of the business world, are as rigid and exacting as the holy vows of a saint, and cannot be violated in the smallest particular but at the risk of one's financial prospects. In the financial world, the law of order is an iron necessity, and he who faultlessly observes it, saves time, temper, and money.

Every enduring achievement in human society rests upon a basis of system; so true is this, that were system withdrawn, progress would cease. Think, for instance, of the vast achievements of literature the works of classic authors and of great geniuses; the great poems, the innumerable prose works, the monumental histories, the soul - stirring orations; think also the social intercourse of human society, of it religions, its legal statutes, and its vast fund of book knowledge think of all these wonderful resources and achievements of language, and then reflect that they all depend for their origin, growth, and continuance on the systematic arrangements of twenty six letters, an arrangement having inexhaustible and illimitable results by the fact of its rigid limitation within certain fixed rules.

Again; all the wonderful achievements of mathematics have come from the systematic arrangement of ten figures; while the most complex piece of machinery, with its thousands of parts working together smoothly and almost noiselessly to the achievement of the end for which it was designed, was brought forth by the systematic observance of a few mechanical laws.

Herein we see how a system simplifies that which is complex: how it makes easy that which was difficult; how it relates an infinite variety of details of the one central law or order, and so enables them to be dealt with and accounted for with perfect regularity, and with an entire absence of confusion.

The scientist names and classifies the myriad details of the universe, from the microscopic rotifer to the telescopic star, by his observance of the principle of system, so that out of many millions of objects, reference can be made to any one object in, at most, a few minutes. It is this faculty of speedy references and swift dispatch which is of such overwhelming importance in every department of knowledge and industry, and the amount of time and labour thus saved to humanity is so vast as to be incompatible. We speak of religious, political, and business systems; and so on, indicating that all things in human society are welded together by the adhesive qualities of order.

System is, indeed, one of the great fundamental principles in progress, and in the binding together, in one complete whole, of the world's millions of human beings while they are at the same time each striving for a place and are competing with one another in opposing aims and interest.

We see here how system is allied with greatness, for the many separate units whose minds are untrained to the discipline of system, are kept in their places by the organizing power of the comparatively few who perceive the urgent, the inescapable, necessity for the establishment of fixed and inviolable rules, whether in business, law, religion, science, or politics in fact, in every sphere of human activity for immediately two human beings meet together, they need some common ground of understanding for the avoidance of confusion; in a word, some system to regulate their actions.

Life is too short for confusion; and knowledge grows and progress proceeds along avenues of system which prevent retardation and retrogression, so that he who systematizes his knowledge or business, simplifies and enhances it for his successor, enabling him to begin, with a free mind, where he left off.

Every large business has its system which renders its vast machinery workable, enabling it to run like a well balanced and well oiled machine. A remarkable business man, a friend of mine, once told me that he could leave his huge business for twelve months, and it would run on without hitch till his return; and he does occasionally leave it for several months, while travelling, and on his return, every man, boy and girl; every tool, book, and machine; every detail down to the smallest, is in its place doing its work as when he left; and no trouble, no difficulty, no confusion has arisen.

There can be no marked success apart from a love of regularity and discipline, and the avoidance of friction, along with the restfulness and efficiency of mind which spring from such regularity. People who abhor discipline, whose minds are ungoverned and anarchic, and who are careless and irregular in their thinking, their habits and the management of their affairs, cannot be highly successful and prosperous and they fill their lives with numerous worries, troubles, difficulties, and petty annoyances, all of which would disappear under a proper regulation of their lives.

An unsystematic mind is an untrained mind and it can no more cope with well disciplined minds in the race of life than an untrained athlete can successfully compete with a carefully trained competitor in athletic competition in athletic races. The ill disciplined mind, that thinks anything will do, rapidly falls behind the well disciplined minds who are convinced that only the best will do in the strenuous race for the prizes of life, whether they be material, mental, or moral prizes. The man who, when he comes to do his work, is unable to find his tools, or to balance his figures, or to find the key of his desk, or the key to his thoughtless, will be struggling in his self made toils while his methodical neighbor will be freely and joyfully scaling the invigorating heights of successful achievement. The business man whose method is slovenly, or cumbersome, or behind the most recent developments of skilled minds, should only blame himself as his prospects are decadent, and should wake up to the necessity for more highly specialized and effective methods in his concern. He should seize upon everything - every invention and idea - that will enable him to economize time and labour, and aid him in thoroughness, deliberation and dispatch.

System is the law by which everything - every organism, business, character, nation, empire - is built. By adding cell to cell, department to department, thought to thought, law to law, and colony to colony in orderly sequence and classification, all things, concerns and institutions grow in magnitude, and evolve to completeness. The man, who is continually improving his methods, is gaining in building power; it therefore behoves the business man to be resourceful and inventive in the improvement of his methods, for the builders - whether of cathedrals or characters, business or religions - are the strong ones of the earth, and the protectors and pioneers of humanity. The systematic builder is a creator and preserver, while the man of disorder demolishes and destroys, and no limit can be set to the growth of a man's powers, the completeness of his character, the influence of his organization, or the extent of his business, if he but preserve intact the discipline of order, and have every detail in its place, keep every department to its special task, and tabulate and classify with such efficiency and perfection as to enable him at any moment to bring under examination or into requisition to the remotest detail in connection with his special work.

In system is contained these four ingredients:

1. Readiness
2. Reccuracy
3. Utility
4. Comprehensiveness

Readiness is aliveness. It is that spirit of alertness by which a situation is immediately grasped and dealt with. The observance of system fosters and develops this spirit. The successful General must have the power of readily meeting any new and unlooked for move on the part of the enemy; so every business man must have the readiness to deal with any unexpected development affecting his line of trade; and so also must the man of thought be able to deal with the details of any new problems which may arise. Dilatoriness is a vice that is fatal to prosperity, for it leads to incapability and stupidity. The men of ready hands, ready hearts, and ready brains, who know what they are doing, and do it methodically, skillfully, and with smooth yet consummate dispatch are the men who need to think little of prosperity as an end, for it comes to them whether they seek it or not; success runs after them, and knocks at their door; and they unconsciously command it by the superb excellence of their faculties and methods.

Accuracy is of supreme importance in all commercial concerns and enterprises, but there can be no accuracy apart from system, and a system which is more or less imperfect will involve its originator in mistakes more or less disastrous until he improves it.

Inaccuracy is one of the commonest failings, because accuracy is closely allied to self-discipline, and self-discipline, along with that glad subjection to external discipline which it involves, is an indication of high moral culture to which the majority, have not yet attained. If the inaccurate man will not willingly subject himself to the discipline of his employer or instructor, but thinks he knows better, his failing can never be remedied, and he will thereby bind himself down to an inferior position, if in the business world; or to imperfect knowledge, if in the world of thought.

The prevalence of the vice of inaccuracy (and in view of its disastrous effect it must be regarded as a vice, though perhaps one of the lesser vices) is patent to every observation in the way in which the majority of people relate a circumstance or repeat a simple statement of fact. It is nearly always made untrue by more or less marked inaccuracies. Few people, perhaps (not reckoning those who deliberately lie), have trained themselves to be accurate in what they say, or are so careful as to admit and state their liability to error, and from this common form of inaccuracy many untruths and misunderstandings arise.

More people take pains to be accurate in what they do than in what they say, but even here inaccuracy is very common, rendering many inefficient and incompetent, and unfitting them for any strenuous and well sustained endeavour. The man who habitually uses up a portion of his own or his employer's time in trying to correct his errors, or for the correction of whose mistakes another has to be employed, is not the man to maintain any position in the work a day world; much less to reach a place among the ranks of the prosperous.

There never yet lived a man who did not make some mistakes on his way to his particular success, but he is the capable and right minded man who perceives his mistakes and quickly remedies them, and who is glad when they are pointed out to him. It is habitual and persistent inaccuracy which is a vice; and he is the incapable and wrong minded man who will not see or admit his mistakes, and who takes offence when they are pointed out to him.

The progressive man learns by his own mistakes as well as by the mistakes of others. He is always ready to test good advice by practice, and aims at greater and ever greater accuracy in his methods, which means higher and higher perfection, for accuracy is perfect, and the measure of a man's accuracy will be the measure of his uniqueness and perfection.

Utility, or usefulness, is the direct result of method in one's work. Labour arrives at fruitful and profitable ends when it is systematically pursued. If the gardener is to gather in the best produce, he must not only sow and plant, but he must sow and plant at the right time; and if any work is to be fruitful in results, it must be done seasonably, and the time for doing a thing must not be allowed to pass by.

Utility considers the practical end; and employs the best means to reach that end. It avoids side issues, dispenses with theories, and retains its hold only on those things which can be appropriated to good uses in the economy of life.

Unpractical people burden their minds with useless and unverifiable theories, and court failure by entertaining speculations which, by their very nature, cannot be applied in practice. The man whose powers are shown in what he does, and not in mere talking or arguing, avoids metaphysical quibbling and quandaries, and applies himself to the accomplishment of some good and useful end.

That which cannot be reduced to practice should not be allowed to hamper the mind. It should be thrown aside, abandoned, and ignored. A man recently told me that if his theory should be proved to have no useful end, he should still retain his hold upon it as a beautiful theory. If a man chooses to cling to so-called "beautiful" theories which are proved to have no use in life, and no substantial basis of reality, he must not be surprised if he fails in his wordy undertakings, for he is an unpractical man.

When the powers of the mind are diverted from speculative theorizing to practical doing whether in material or moral directions, skill, power, knowledge, and prosperity increase. A man's prosperity is measured by his usefulness to the community, and a man is useful in accordance with that he does, and not because of the theories which he entertains.

The carpenter fashions a chair; the builder erects a house; the mechanic produces a machine; and the wise man moulds a perfect character. Not the schismatic, the theorists and the controversialists, but the workers, the makers, and the doers are the salt of the earth.

Let a man turn away from the mirages of intellectual speculation, and begin to do something and to do it with all his might, and he will thereby gain a special knowledge, wield a special power, and reach his own unique position and prosperity among his fellows.

Comprehensiveness is that quality of mind which enables a man to deal with a large number of related details, to grasp them in their entirety, along with the single principle which governs them and binds them together. It is a masterly quality, giving organizing and governing power, and is developed by systematic attention to details. The successful merchant holds in his mind, as it were, all the details of his business, and regulates them by a system adapted to his particular form of trade. The inventor has in his mind all the details of his machine, along with their relation to a central mechanical principle, and so perfects his invention. The author of a great poem or story relates all his characters and incidents to a central plot, and so produces a composite and enduring literary work. Comprehensiveness is analytic and synthetic capacity combined in the same individual. A capacious and well ordered mind, which holds within its silent depths an army of details in their proper arrangement and true working order, is the mind that is near to genius, even if it has not already arrived. Every man cannot be a genius nor does he need to be, but he can be gradually evolving his mental capacity by careful attention to system in his thoughts and business, and as his intellect depends and broadens his powers will be intensified and his prosperity accentuated.

Such, then, are four corner pillars in the Temple of Prosperity, and of themselves they are sufficient to permanently sustain it without the addition of the remaining four. The man who perfects himself in Energy, Economy, Integrity, and System will achieve an enduring success in the work of his life, no matter what the nature of that work may be. It is impossible for one to fail who is full of energy, who carefully economizes his time and money and virtuously husbands his vitality, who practices unswerving integrity, and who systematizes his work by first systematizing his mind.

Such a man's efforts will be rightly directed, and that, too, with concentrated power, so that they will be effective and fruitful. In addition he will reach a manliness and an independent dignity which will unconsciously command respect and success, and will strengthen weaker ones by its very presence in their midst. "Seest thou a man diligent in business; he shall stand before kings, he shall not stand before mean men," says Scripture of such a one.

He will not beg, or whimper, or complain, or cynically blame others, but will be too strong and pure and upright a man to sink himself so low. And so standing high in the nobility and integrity of his character, he will fill a high place in the world and in the estimation of men. His success will be certain and his prosperity will endure. "He will stand and not fall in the battle of life."

Chapter 6

Fifth Pillar - Sympathy

The remaining pillars are the four central pillars in the Temple of Prosperity. They gave it greater strength and stability, and add both to its beauty and utility. They contribute greatly to its attractiveness, for they belong to the highest moral sphere, and therefore to great beauty and nobility of character. They, indeed, make a man great, and place him among the comparatively few whose minds are rare, and that shine apart in sparkling purity and bright intelligence.

Sympathy should not be confounded with that maudlin and superficial sentiment which, like a pretty flower without root, presently perishes and leaves behind neither seed nor fruit. To fall into hysterical some suffering abroad, is not sympathy. Neither are bursts of violent indignation against the cruelties and injustices of others nor any indication of a sympathetic mind. If one is cruel at home - if he badgers his wife, or beats his children, or abuses his servants, or stabs his neighbors with shafts of bitter sarcasm what hypocrisy is in his profession of love for suffering people who are outside the immediate range of his influence! What shallow sentiment informs his bursts of indignation against the injustice and hard heartedness in the world around him?

Says Emerson of such - "Go, love they infant; love thy wood chopper; be good natured and modest; have that grace; and never varnish your hard uncharitable ambition with this incredible tenderness for black folk a thousand miles off. They love afar is spite at home". The test of a man is in his immediate acts, and not in ultra sentiments; and if those acts are consistently informed with selfishness and bitterness, if those at home hear his steps with dread, and feel a joyful relief on his departure, how empty are his expressions of sympathy for the suffering or down trodden how futile his membership of a philanthropic society.

Though the well of sympathy may feed the spring of tears, that spring more often draws its supply from the dark pool of selfishness, for when selfishness is thwarted it spends itself in tears.

Sympathy is a deep, silent, inexpressible tenderness which is shown in a consistently self forgetful gentle character. Sympathetic people are not gushing and spasmodic, but are permanently self restrained, firm, quiet, unassuming and gracious. Their undisturbed demeanour, where the suffering of others is concerned, is frequently mistaken for indifference by shallow minds, but the sympathetic and discerning eye recognizes, in their quiet strength and their swiftness to aid while others are weeping, and wringing their hands, the deepest, soundest sympathy.

Lack of sympathy is shown in cynicism, ill-natured sarcasm, bitter ridicule, taunting and mockery, and anger and condemnation, as well as in that morbid and false sentiment which is a theoretical and assumed sympathy, having no basis in practice.

Lack of sympathy arises in egotism; sympathy arises in love. Egotism is involved in ignorance; love is allied to knowledge. It is common with men to imagine themselves as separate from their fellows, with separate aims and interests; and to regard themselves as right and others wrong in their respective ways. Sympathy lifts a man above this separate and self-centered life and enables him to live in the hearts of his fellows, and to think and feel with them. He puts himself in their place, and becomes, for the time being, as they are. As Whitman, the hospital hero, expresses it - "I do not ask the wounded person." It is a kind of impertinence to question a suffering creature. Suffering calls for aid and tenderness, and not for curiosity; and the sympathetic man or woman feels the suffering, and ministers to its alleviation.

Nor can sympathy boast, and wherever self praise enters in, sympathy passes out. If one speaks of his many deeds of kindness, and complains of the ill treatment he has received in return, he has not done kindly deeds, but has yet to reach that self forgetful modesty, which is the sweetness of sympathy.

Sympathy, in its real and profound sense, is oneness with others in their strivings and sufferings, so that the man of sympathy is a composite being; he is, as it were, a number of men, and he views a thing from a number of different sides, and not from one side only, and that his own particular side. He sees with the others men's eyes, hears with their ears, thinks with their minds, and feels with their hearts. He is thus able to understand men who are vastly different from himself; the meaning of their lives is revealed to him, and he is united to them in the spirit of goodwill. Said Balzac - "The poor fascinate me; their hunger is my hunger; I am with them in their homes; their privations I suffer; I feel the beggar's rags upon my back; I for the time being become the poor and despised man." It reminds us of the 'saying' of One greater than Balzac, that a deed done for a suffering little one was done for him.

And so it is; sympathy leads us to the hearts of all men, so that we become spiritually united to them, and when they suffer we feel the pain; when they are glad we rejoice with them; when they are despised and persecuted, we spiritually descend with them into the depths, and take into our hearts their humiliation and distress; and he who has this binding, uniting spirit of sympathy, can never be cynical and condemnatory can never pass thoughtless and cruel judgments upon his fellows; because in his tenderness of heart he is ever with them in their pain.

But to have reached this ripened sympathy, it must needs be that one has loved much, suffered much and sounded the dark depths of sorrow. It springs from acquaintance with the profoundest experiences, so that a man has conceit, thoughtlessness, and selfishness burnt out of his heart. No man can have true sympathy who has not been, in some measure at least, "a man of sorrows, and acquainted with grief," but the sorrow and grief must have passed, must have ripened into a fixed kindness and habitual calm.

To have suffered so much in a certain direction that the suffering is finished, and only its particular wisdom remains, enables one, wherever that suffering presents itself, to understand and deal with it by pure sympathy; and when one has been "perfected by suffering" in many directions, he becomes a centre of rest and healing for the sorrowing and broken hearted who are afflicted with the affections which he has experienced and conquered. As a mother feels the anguish of her suffering child, so the man of sympathy feels the anguish of suffering men.

Such is the highest and holiest sympathy, but a sympathy much less perfect is a great power for good in human life and a measure of it is everywhere and every day needed. While rejoicing in the fact that in every walk in life there are truly sympathetic people, one also perceives that harshness, resentment, and cruelty are all too common. These hard qualities bring their own sufferings, and there are those who fail in their business, or particular work, entirely because of the harshness of their disposition. A man who is fiery and resentful, or who is hard, cold and calculating, with the springs of sympathy dried up within him, even though he be otherwise an able man, will, in the end scarcely avoid disaster in his affairs. His heated folly in the one case, or cold cruelty in the other, will gradually isolate him from his fellows and from those who are immediately related to him in his particular avocation, so that the elements of prosperity will be eliminated from his life, leaving him with a lonely failure, and perhaps a hopeless despair.

Even in ordinary business transactions, sympathy is an important factor, for people will always be attracted to those who are of a kindly and genial nature, preferring to deal with them rather than with those who are hard and forbidding. In all spheres where direct personal contact plays an important part, the sympathetic man with average ability will always take precedence of the man of greater ability but who is unsympathetic.

If a man be a minister or a clergyman, a cruel laugh or an unkind sentence from him will seriously injure his reputation and influence, but particularly his influence, for even they who admire his good qualities will, through his unkindness, unconsciously have a lower regard for him in their personal esteem.

If a business man professes religion people will expect to see the good influence of that religion on his business transactions. To profess to be a worshipper of the gentle Jesus on Sunday, and all the rest of the week be a hard, grasping worshipper of mammon, will injure his trade, and detract considerably from his prosperity.

Sympathy is a universal spiritual language which all, even the animals, instinctively understand and appreciate, for all beings and creatures are subject to suffering, and this sameness of painful experience leads to that unity of feeling which we call sympathy.

Selfishness impels men to protect themselves at the expense of others; but sympathy impels them to protect others by the sacrifice of self; and in this sacrifice of self there is no real and ultimate loss, for while the pleasure of selfishness are small and few, the blessings of sympathy are great and manifold.

It may be asked, "How can a business man; whose object is to develop his own trade, practice self-sacrifice?" Even man can practice self sacrifice just where he is, and in the measure that he is capable of, understand it. If one contends that he cannot practice a virtue, for were his circumstances different, he would still have the same excuse. Diligence in business is not incompatible with self sacrifice, for devotion to duty, even though that duty be trade, is not selfishness, but may be an unselfish devotion. I know a business man who, when a competitor who had tried to 'cut him out' in business, cut himself out and failed, set that same competitor up in business again. Truly a beautiful act of self sacrifice; and the man that did it is, today, one of the most successful and prosperous of business men.

The most prosperous commercial traveler I have ever known was overflowing with exuberant kindness and geniality. He was as innocent of all "tricks of trade" as a new born infant, but his great heart and manly uprightness won for him fast friends wherever he went. Men were glad to see him come into their office or shop or mill, and not alone for the good and bracing influence he brought with him, but also because his business was sound and trustworthy. This man was successful through sheer sympathy, but sympathy so pure and free from policy, that he himself would probably have denied that his success could be attributed to it. Sympathy can never hinder success. It is selfishness that blights and destroys. As goodwill increases, man's prosperity will increase. All interests are mutual, and stand or fall together, and as sympathy expand the heart, it extends the circle of influence, making blessings, both spiritual and material, to more greatly abound.

Fourfold are the qualities which make up the great virtue of sympathy, namely:-

1. Kindness

2. Generosity

3. Gentleness

4. Insight

Kindness, when fully developed, is not a passing impulse but a permanent quality. An intermittent and unreliable impulse is not kindness, though it often goes under that name. There is no kindness in praise if it be followed by abuse. The love which seems to prompt the spontaneous kiss will be of little account if it be associated with a spontaneous spite. The gift which seemed so gracious will lose its value should the giver afterwards wish its value in return. To have one's feelings aroused to do a kind action towards another by some external stimulus pleasing to one's self, and

shortly afterwards to be swayed to the other extreme towards the
same person by an external event unpleasing to one's self, should
be regarded as weakness of character; and it is also a selfish condition, and when he pleases us, to be thinking of one's self only. A
true kindness is unchangeable, and needs no external stimulus to
force it into action. It is a well from which thirsty souls can always
drink, and it never runs dry. Kindness, when it is a strong virtue,
is bestowed not only on those who please us, but also upon those
whose actions go contrary to our wish and will, and it is a constant
and never - varying glow of genial warmth.

There are some actions of which men repent; such are all unkind actions. There are other actions of which men do not repent,
and such are all kind actions. The day comes when men are sorry
for the cruel things they said and did; but the day of gladness is
always with them for the kindly things they have said and done.

Unkindness mars a man's character, it mars his face as time
goes on, and it mars that perfection of success which he would
otherwise reach.

Kindness beautifies the character, it beautifies the face with the
growth of the years, and it enables a man to reach that perfection
of success to which his intellectual abilities entitle him. A man's
prosperity is mellowed and enriched by the kindness of his disposition.

Generosity goes with a larger hearted kindness. If kindness be
the gentle sister, Generosity is the strong brother. A free, open
handed and magnanimous character is always attractive and influential. Stringiness and meanness always repel; they are dark,
cramped, narrow, and cold. Kindness and generosity always attack; they are sunny, genial, open, and warm. That which repels
makes for isolation and failure; that which attracts makes for
union and success.

Giving is as important a duty as getting; and he who gets all he
can and refuses to give, will at last be unable to get; for it is as
much a spiritual law that we cannot get unless we give, as that we
cannot give unless we get.

Giving has always been taught as a great and important duty
by all the religious teachers. This is because giving is one of the
highways of personal growth and progress. It is a means by which
we attain to greater and greater unselfishness, and by which we
prevent the falling back into selfishness. It implies that we rec-

ognize our spiritual and social kinship with our fellow-men, and are willing to part with a portion of that we have earned or possess, for man who, the more he gets, hungers for more still, and refuses to loosen his grasp upon his accumulating store, like a wild beast with its prey, is retrogressing; he is shutting himself out from all the higher and joy giving qualities, and from free and life giving communion with unselfish, happy human hearts. Dickens's Scrooge in "A Christmas Carol" represents the condition of such a man with graphic vividness and dramatic force.

Our public men in England to-day (probably also in America) are nearly all (I think I might say all, for I have not yet met an exception) great givers. These men - Lord Mayors, Mayors, Magistrates, Town and City Councilors, and all men filling responsible public offices - being men who have been singularly successful in the management of their own private affairs, are considered the best men for the management of public affairs, and numerous noble institutions throughout the land are perpetual witnesses to the munificence of their gifts. Nor have I been able to find any substantial truth in the accusation, so often hurled against such men by the envious and unsuccessful, that their riches are made unjustly. Without being perfect men, they are an honourable class of manly, vigorous, generous, and successful men, who have acquired riches and honour by sheer industry, ability and uprightness.

Let a man beware of greed, of meanness, of envy, of jealousy, of suspicion, for these things, if harboured, will rob him of all that is best in life, aye, even all that is best in material things, as well as all that is best in character and happiness. Let him be liberal of heart and generous of hand, magnanimous and trusting, not only giving cheerfully and often of his substance, but allowing his friends and fellow-men freedom of thought and action - let him be thus, and honour, plenty, and prosperity will come knocking at the door for admittance as his friends and guests.

Gentleness is akin to divinity. Perhaps no quality is so far removed from all that is coarse, brutal and selfish as gentleness, so that when one is becoming gentle, he is becoming divine. It can only be acquired after much experience and through great self-discipline. It only becomes established in a man's heart when he has controlled and brought into subjection his animal voice, a distinct, firm, but quiet enunciation, and freedom from excitement, vehemence, or resentment in peculiarly aggravating circumstances.

If there is one quality which, above all others, should distinguish the religious man, it is the quality of gentleness, for it is the hall mark of spiritual culture. The rudely aggressive man is an affront to cultivated minds and unselfish hearts. Our word 'gentlemen' has not altogether departed from its original meaning. It is still applied to one who is modest and self-restrained, and is considerate for the feelings and welfare of others. A gentle man one whose good behavior is prompted by thoughtfulness and kindliness is always loved, whatever may be his origin. Quarrelsome people make a display in their bickering and recriminations - of their ignorance and lack of culture. The man who has perfected himself in gentleness never quarrels. He never returns the hard word; he leaves it alone, or meets it with a gentle word which is far more powerful than wrath. Gentleness is wedded to wisdom and the wise man has overcome all anger in himself, and so understands how to overcome it in others. The gentleman is saved from most of the disturbances and turmoil's with which uncontrolled men afflict themselves. While they are wearing themselves out with wasteful and needless strain, he is quiet and composed, and such quietness and composure are strong to win in the battle of life.

Insight is the gift of sympathy. The sympathetic mind is the profoundly perceiving mind. We understand by experience, and not by argument. Before we can know a thing or being, our life must touch its or his life. Argument analyzes the outer skin, but sympathy reaches to the heart. The cynic sees the hat and coat, and thinks he sees the man. The sympathetic seer sees the man, and is not concerned with the hat and coat. In all kinds of hatred there is a separation by which each misjudges the other. In all kinds of love there is a mystic union by which each knows the other. Sympathy, being the purest form of this the greatest poet because he has the largest heart. No other figure in all literature has shown such a profound knowledge of the human heart and of nature both animate and inanimate. The personal Shakespeare is not to be found in his works; he is merged, by sympathy, into his characters. The wise man and the philosopher; the madman and the fool; the drunkard and the harlot - these he, for the time into their particular experiences and knew them better than they knew themselves. Shakespeare has no partiality, no prejudice; his sympathy embraces all, from the lowest to the highest.

Prejudice is the great barrier to sympathy and knowledge. It is impossible to understand those against whom one harbours a prejudice. We only see men and things as they are when we divest our minds of partial judgments. We become seers as we become sympathizers. Sympathy has knowledge for her companion.

Inseparable are the feeling heart and the seeing eye. The man of pity is the man of prophecy. He whose heart beats in tune with all hearts, to him the contents of all hearts are revealed. Nor are past and future any longer insoluble mysteries to the man of sympathy. His moral insight apprehends the perfect round of human life.

Sympathetic insight lifts a man into the consciousness of freedom, gladness and power. His spirit inhales joy as his lungs inhale air. There are no longer any fears of his fellow-men of competition, hard times, enemies, and the like. These groveling illusion have disappeared, and there has opened up before his awakened vision a realm of greatness and grandeur.

Chapter 7

Sixth Pillar - Sincerity

Human society is held together by its sincerity. A universal false-ness would beget a universal mistrust which would bring about a universal separation, if not destruction. Life is made sane, whole-some, and happy, by our deep rooted belief in one another. If we did not trust men, we could not transact business with them, could not even associate with them. Shakespeare's "Timon" shows us the wretched condition of a man who, through his own folly, has lost all faith in the sincerity of human nature. He cuts him-self off from the company of all men, and finally commits suicide. Emerson has something to the effect that if the trust system were withdrawn from commerce, society would fall to pieces; that sys-tem being an indication of the universal confidence men place in each other. Business, commonly supposed by the shortsighted and foolish to be all fraud and deception is based on a great trust - a trust that men will meet and fulfill their obligations. Payment is not asked until the goods are delivered; and the fact of the con-tinuance of this system for ages, proves that most men do pay their debts, and have no wish to avoid such payment.

Back of all its shortcomings, human society rests on a strong basis of truth. Its fundamental note in sincerity. Its great leaders are all men of superlative sincerity; and their names and achieve-ments are not allowed to perish - a proof that the virtue of sincer-ity is admired by all the race.

It is easy for the insincere to imagine that everybody is like them-selves, and to speak of the "rottenness of society", - though a rot-ten thing could endure age after age, for is not everything yellow to the jaundiced eye? People, who cannot see anything good in the constitution of human society, should overhaul themselves. Their trouble is near home. They call good, evil. They have dwelt cynical-ly and peevishly on evil till they cannot see good, and everything and everybody appears evil. "Society is rotten from top to bottom", I heard a man say recently; and he asked me if I did not think so. I replied that I should be sorry to think so; that while society had many blemishes, it was sound at the core, and contained within itself the seeds of perfection.

Society indeed, is so sound that the man who is playing a part for the accomplishment of entirely selfish ends cannot long prosper, and cannot fill any place as an influence. He is soon unmasked and disagreed; and the fact that such a man can, for even a brief period, batten on human credulity, speaks well for the trustfulness of men, if it reveals their lack of wisdom.

An accomplished actor on the stage is admired, but the designing actor on the stage of life brings himself down to ignominy and contempt. In striving to appear what he is not, he becomes as one having no individuality, no character, and he is deprived of all influence, all power, all success.

A man of profound sincerity is a great moral force, and there is no force - not even the highest intellectual force - that can compare with it. Men are powerful in influence according to the soundness and perfection of their sincerity. Morality and sincerity are so closely bound up together, that where sincerity is lacking, morality, as a power, is lacking also, for insincerity undermines all the other virtues, so that they crumble away and become of no account. Even a little insincerity robs a character of all its nobility, and makes it common and contemptible. Falseness is so despicable a vice and no man of moral weight can afford to dally with pretty complements, or play the fool with trivial and howsoever light, in order to please, and he is no longer strong and admirable, but is become a shallow weakling whose mind has no deep well of power from which men can draw, and no satisfying richness to stir in them a worshipful regard.

Even they, who are for the moment flattered with the painted lie, or pleased with the deftly woven deception, will not escape those permanent under currents of influence which move the heart and shape the judgment to fixed and final issues, while these designed delusions create but momentary ripples on the surface of the mind.

"I am very pleased with his attentions," said a woman of an acquaintance, "but I would not marry him". "Why not?" she was asked. "He doesn't ring true", was the reply.

Ring true, a term full of meaning. It has reference to the coin which, when tested by its ring, emits a sound which reveals the sterling metal throughout, without the admixture of any base material. It comes up to the standard, and will pass anywhere and everywhere for its full value.

So with men. Their words and actions emit their own peculiar influence. There is in them an inaudible sound which all other men inwardly hear and instinctively detect. They know the false ring from the true, yet know not how they know. As the outer ear can make the most delicate distinctions in sounds, so the inner ear can make equally subtle distinctions between souls. None are ultimately deceived but the deceiver. It is the blind folly of the insincere that, while flattering themselves upon their successful simulations, they are deceiving none but themselves. Their actions are laid bare before all hearts. There is at the heart of man a tribunal whose judgments do not miscarry. If the senses faultlessly detect, shall not the soul infallibly know! This inner infallibility is shown in the collective judgment of the race. This judgment is perfect; so perfect than in literature, art, science, invention, religion - in every department of knowledge - it divides the good from the bad, the worthy from the unworthy, the true from the false, zealously guarding and preserving the former, and allowing the latter to perish. The works, words, and deeds of great men are the heirlooms of the race, and the race is not careless of their value. A thousand men write a book, and one only is a work of original genius, yet the race singles out that one, elevates and preserves it, while it consigns the nine hundred and ninety nine copyists to oblivion. Ten thousand men utter a sentence under a similar circumstance, and one only is a sentence of divine wisdom, yet the race singles out that saying for the guidance of posterity, while the other sentences are heard no more. It is true that the race slays its prophets, but even that slaying becomes a test which reveals the true ring, and men detect its tureens. The slain one has come up to the standard, and the deed of his slaying is preserved as furnishing infallible proof of his greatness.

As the counterfeit coin is detected, and cast back into the melting pot, while the sterling coin circulates among all men, and is valued for its worth, so the counterfeit word, deed, or character is perceived, and is left to fall back into the nothingness from which it emerged, a thing unreal, powerless, dead.

Spurious things have no value, whether they be bric-a-brac or men. We are ashamed of imitations that try to pass for the genuine article. Falseness is cheap. The masquerader becomes a by-word; he is less than a man; he is a shadow, a spook, a mere mask. Trueness is valuable. The sound hearted man becomes an exemplar; he is more than a man; he is a reality; a force, a moulding principle, by falseness all is lost - even individuality dissolves for falseness is nonentity, nothingness. By trueness everything is gained, for trueness is fixed, permanent, real.

It is all important that we be real; that we harbour no wish to appear other than what we are; that we simulate no virtue, assume no excellency, adopt no disguise. The hypocrite thinks he can hood wink the world and the eternal law of the world. There is but one person that he hoodwinks, and that is himself, and for that the law of the world inflicts its righteous penalty. There is an old theory that the excessively wicked are annihilated. I think to be a pretender is to come as near to annihilation as a man can get, for there is a sense in which the man is gone, and in his place there is but a mirage of shams. The hell of annihilation which so many dread, he has descended into; and to think that such a man can prosper is to think that shadows can do the work of entities, and displace real men.

If any man thinks he can build up a successful career on pretences and appearances, let him pause before sinking into the abyss of shadows; for in insincerity there is no solid ground, no substance, no reality; there is nothing on which anything can stand, and no material with which to build; but there are loneliness, poverty, shame, confusion, fears, suspicions, weeping, groaning, and lamentations; for if there is one hell lower, darker, fouler than all others, it is the hell of insincerity.

Four beautiful traits adorn the mind of the sincere man; they are:-

1. Simplicity
2. Attractiveness
3. Penetration
4. Power

Simplicity is naturalness. It is simple being, without fake or foreign adornment. Why are all things in nature so beautiful? Because they are natural. We see them as they are, no task they might wish to appear, for in sooth they have no wish to appear, for in sooth they have no wish to appear otherwise. There is no hypocrisy in the world of nature outside of human nature. The flower which is so beautiful in all eyes would lose its beautify in all eyes would nature we look upon reality, and its beauty and perfection gladden and amaze us. We cannot find anywhere a flaw, and are conscious of our incapacity to improve upon anything, even to the most insignificant. Everything has its own peculiar perfection, and shines in the beauty of unconscious simplicity.

One of the modern social cries is, "Back to nature". It is generally understood to mean a cottage in the country, and a piece of land to cultivate. It will be of little use to go into the country if we take our shams with us; and any veneer which may cling to us can as well be washed off just where we are. It is good that they who feel burdened with the conventions of society should fly to the country, and court the quiet of nature, but it will fail if it by anything but a means to that inward redemption which will restore us to the simple and the true.

But though humanity has wandered from the natural simplicity of the animal world, it is moving towards a higher, a divine simplicity. Men of great genius are such because of their spontaneous simplicity. They do not feign; they are. Lesser minds study style and effect. They wish to cut a striking figure on the stage of the world, and by that unholy wish they are doomed to mediocrity. Said a man to me recently, "I would give twenty years of my life to be able to write an immortal hymn." With such an ambition a man cannot write a hymn. He wants to pose. He is thinking of himself, of his own glory. Before a man can write an immortal hymn, or create any immortal work he must give, not twenty years of his life to ambition but his can-do anything great, and must sing, paint, write, out of ten thousand bitter experiences, ten thousand failures, ten thousand conquests, ten thousand joys. He must know Gethsemane; he must work with blood and tears.

Retaining his intellect and moral powers, and returning to simplicity, a man becomes great. He forfeits nothing real. Only the shams are cast aside, revealing the standard gold of character. Where there is sincerity there will always be simplicity --- simplicity of the kind that we see in nature, the beautiful simplicity of truth.

Attractiveness is the direct outcome of simplicity. This is seen in the attractiveness of all natural objects; to which we have referred, but in human nature it is manifested as personal influence. Of recent years certain pseudomystics have been advertising to sell the secret of "personal magnetism" for so many dollars, by which they

purport to show vain people how they can make themselves attractive to others by certain "occult" means as though attractiveness
can be bought and sold, and put on and off like powder and paint.
Nor are people who are anxious to be thought attractive, likely to
become so, for their vanity is a barrier to it. The very desire to be
thought attractive is, in itself, a deception, and it leads to the practice of numerous deceptions. It infers, too, that such people are
conscious of lacking the genuine attractions and graces of character, and are on the lookout for a substitute; but there is no substitute for beauty of mind and strength of character. Attractiveness,
like genius, is lost by being coveted, and possessed by those who
are too solid and sincere of character to desire it. There is nothing in human nature, nor talent, nor intellect, nor affection, nor
beauty of features that can compare in attractive power with that
soundness of mind and wholeness of heart which we call sincerity.
There is a perennial charm about a sincere man or woman, and
they draw about themselves the best specimens of human nature.
There can be no personal charm apart from sincerity. Infatuation
there may be, and is, but this is a kind of disease, and is vastly
different from the indissoluble bond by which sincere people are
attached. Infatuation ends in painful disillusion, but as there is
nothing hidden between sincere souls, and they stand upon that
solid ground of reality, there is no illusion to be displayed.

Leaders among men attract by the power of their sincerity. The
measures of their sincerity is the measure **of** their sincerity. The
greatest talent may be a man's intellect; he can never be a permanent leader and guide of men unless he be sincere. For a time
he may sail jauntily upon the stream of popularity and believe
himself secure, but it is only that he may shortly fall the lower in
popular odium. He cannot long deceive the people with his painted
front. They will soon look behind, and find of what spurious stuff
he is made. He is like a woman with a painted face. She thinks
she is admired for her complexion, but all know it is paint, and
despise her for it. She has one admirer - herself, and the hell of
limitation to which all the insincere commit themselves, is the hell
of self admiration.

Sincere people do not think of themselves, of their talent, their
genius, their virtue, their beauty and because they are so unconscious of themselves, they attract all, and win their confidence,
affection, and esteem.

Penetration belongs to the sincere. All shams are unveiled in their presence. All simulators are transparent to the searching eye of the sincere man. With one clear glance he sees through all their flimsy pretences. Tricksters wither under his strong gaze, and want to get away from it. He who has rid his heart of all false-ness and entertains only that which is true, has gained the power to distinguish the false from the true in others. He is not deceived who is not self deceived.

As men, looking around on the objects of nature, infallibly dis-tinguish them such as a snake, a bird, a horse, a tree, a rose, and so on – so the sincere man distinguishes between the variety of characters. He perceives in a movement, a look, a word, an act, the nature of the man, and acts accordingly. He is on his guard without being suspicious. He is prepared for the pretender without being mistrustful. He acts from positive knowledge, and not from negative suspicion. Men are open to him, and he reads their con-tents. His penetrative judgment pierces to the centre of actions. His direct and unequivocal conduct strengthens in others the good, and shames the bad, and he is a staff of strength to those who have not yet attained to his soundness of heart and head.

Power goes with penetration. An understanding of the nature of actions is accompanied with the power to meet and deal with all actions in the right and best way. Knowledge is always power, but knowledge of the nature of actions is superlative power, and he who possesses it becomes a Presence to all hearts, and modifies their actions for good. Long after his bodily presence has passed away, he is still a moulding force in the world and is a spiritual reality working subtly in the minds of men, and shaping them towards sublime ends. At first his power local and limited, but the circle of righteousness which he has set moving, continues to extend and extended till it embraces the whole world, and all men are influenced by it.

The sincere man stamps his character upon all that he does, and also upon all people with whom he comes in contact. He speaks a word in season, and someone is impressed; the influence is com-municated to another, and another, and presently some despair-ing soul ten thousand miles away hears it and is restored. Such a power is prosperity in itself, and its worth is not to be valued in coin. Money cannot purchase the priceless jewels of character, but labour in right doing can, and he who makes himself sincere, who acquires a robust soundness throughout his entire being, will become a man of singular success and rare power.

Such is the strong pillar of sincerity. Its supporting power is too great that once it is completely erected, the Temple of Prosperity is secure. Its walls will not crumble; its rafters will not decay; its roof will not fall in. It will stand while the man lives, and when has passed away it will continue to afford a shelter and a home for others through many generation.

Chapter 8

Seventh Pillar - Impartiality

To get rid of prejudice is a great achievement. Prejudice piles obstacles in a man's way - obstacles to health, success, happiness, and prosperity, so that he is continually running up against imaginary enemies, who, when prejudice is removed, are seen to be friend. Life, indeed, a sort of obstacle race to the man of prejudice, a race wherein the obstacles cannot be negotiated and the goal is not reached; whereas to the impartial man life is a day's walk in a pleasant country, with refreshment and rest at the end of the day.

To acquire impartiality, a man must remove that innate egotism which prevents him from seeing anything from any point of view other than this own. A great task truly; but a notable, and one that can be well begun now, even if it cannot be finished. Truth can "remove mountains", and prejudice is a range of mental mountains beyond which the partisan does not see, and of which he does not believe there is any beyond. These mountains removed, however, there opens to the view the unending vista of mental variety blended in one glorious picture of light and shade, of colour and tone, gladdening beholding eyes.

By clinging to stubborn prejudice what joys are missed, what friends are sacrificed, what happiness is destroyed, and what prospects are blighted! And yet freedom from prejudice is a rare thing. There are few men who are not prejudiced partisans upon the subjects which are of interest to them. One rarely meets a man that will dispassionately discuss his subject from both sides, considering all the facts and weighing all the evidence so as to arrive at truth on the matter. Each partisan has his own case to make out. He is not searching for truth, for he is already convinced that his own conclusion is the truth, and that all else is error; but he is defending his own case, and striving for victory. Neither does he attempt to prove that he has the truth by a calm array of facts and evidence, but defends his position with more or less heat and agitation.

Prejudice causes a man to form a conclusion, sometimes without any basis of fact or knowledge, and then to refuse to consider anything which does not support that conclusion; and in this way prejudice is a complete barrier to the attainment of knowledge. It binds a man down to darkness and ignorance, and prevents the development of his mind in the highest and noblest directions. More than this, it also shuts him out from communion with the best minds, and confines him to the dark and solitary cell of his own egotism.

Prejudice is a shutting up of the mind against the entrance of new light, against the perception of more beauty, against the hearing of diviner music. The partisan clings to his little, fleeting, flimsy opinion, and thinks it the greatest thing in the world. He is so in love with his own conclusion (which is only a form of self love), that he thinks all men ought to agree with him, and he regards men as more or less stupid who do not see as he sees, while he praises the good judgment of those who are one with him in his view. Such a man cannot have knowledge, cannot have truth. He is confined to the sphere of opinion (to his own self created illusions) which is outside the realm of reality. He moves in a kind of self infatuation which prevents him from seeing the commonest facts of life, while his own theories - usually more or less groundless - assume, in his mind, overpowering proportions. He fondly imagines that there is but one side to everything, and that side is his own. There are at least two sides to everything, and he it is who finds the truth in a matter who carefully examines both sides with all freedom from excitement, and without any desire for the predominance of one side over another.

In its divisions and controversies the world at large is like two lawyers defending a case. The counsel for the prosecution presents all the facts which prove his side, while counsel for the defense presents all the facts which support his contention, and each belittles or ignores, or tries to reason away, the facts of the other. The Judge in the case, however, is like the impartial thinker among men: having listened to all the evidence on both sides, he compares and sifts it so as to form an impartial summing up in the cause of justice.

Not that this universal partiality is a bad thing, nor as in all other extremes, nature here reduces the oppositions of conflicting parties to a perfect balance; moreover, it is a factor in evolution; it stimulates men to think who have not yet developed the power to rouse up vigorous thought at will, and it is a phase through which all men have to pass. But it is only byway - and a tangled, confused and painful one - towards the great highway of Truth. It is the area of which impartiality is the perfect round. The partisan sees a portion of the truth, and thinks it the whole, but the impartial thinker sees the whole truth which includes all sides. It is necessary that we see truth in sections, as it were, until, having gathered up all the parts, we may piece them together and form the perfect circle, and the forming of such circle is the attainment of impartiality.

The impartial man examines, weighs, and considers, with freedom from prejudice and from likes and dislikes. His one wish is to discover the truth. He abolishes preconceived opinions and lets facts and evidence speak for themselves. He has no case to make out for himself, for he knows that truth is unalterable, that his opinions can make no difference to it, and that it can be investigated and discovered. He thereby escapes a vast amount of friction and nervous wear and tear to which the feverish partisan is subject; and in addition, he looks directly upon the face of Reality, and so becomes tranquil and peaceful.

So rare is freedom from prejudice that wherever the impartial thinker may be, he is sure, sooner or later, to occupy a very high position in the estimation of the world, and in the guidance of its destiny. Not necessarily an office in worldly affairs, for that is improbable, but an exalted position in the sphere of influence. There may be such a one now, and he may be a carpenter, a weaver, a clerk; he may be in poverty or in the home of a millionaire; he may be short or tall, or of any complexion, but whatever and wherever he may be, he has, though unknown, already begun to move the world, and will one day be universally recognized at a new force and creative centre in evolution.

There was one such some nineteen hundred years ago. He was only a poor, unlettered carpenter; He was regarded as a madman by His own relatives, and he came to an ignominious end in the eyes of His countrymen, but He sowed the seeds of an influence which has altered the whole world.

There was another such in India some twenty five centuries ago. He was accomplished, highly educated, and was the son of a capitalist and landed proprietor a petty king. He became a penniless, homeless mendicant, and to day one third of the human race worship at his shrine, and are restrained and elevated by his influence.

"Beware when the great God lets loose a thinker on this plane," says Emerson; and a man is not a thinker who is bound by prejudice; he is merely the strenuous upholder of an opinion. Every idea must pass through the medium of his particular prejudice, and receive its colour, so that dispassionate thinking and impartial judgment are rendered impossible. Such a man sees everything only in its relation, or imagined relation, to his opinion, whereas the thinker sees things as they are. The man who has so purified his mind of prejudice and of all the imperfections of egotism as to be able to look directly upon reality, has reached the acme of power; he holds in his hands, as it were, the vastest influence, and he will wield this power whether he knows it or not; it will be inseparable from his life, and will go from him as perfume from the flower. It will be in his words, his deeds, in his bodily postures and the motions of his mind, even in his silence and the stillness of his frame. Wherever he goes, even though he should fly to the desert, he will not escape this lofty destiny, for a great thinker is the centre of the world; by him all men are held in their orbits and all thought gravitates towards him.

The true thinker lives above and beyond the seething whirlpool of passion in which mankind is engulfed. He is not swayed by personal consideration, for he has grasped the importance of impersonal principles, and being thus a noncombatant in the clashing warfare of egotistic desires, he can, from the vantage ground of an impartial but not indifferent watcher, see both sides equally, and grasp the cause and meaning of the fray.

Not only the Great Teachers, but the greatest figures in literature, are those who are free from prejudice, who, like true mirrors, effect things impartially. Such are Whitman, Shakespeare, Balzac, Emerson, Homer. These minds are not local, but universal. Their attitude is cosmic and not personal.

They contain within themselves all things and beings all worlds and laws. They are the gods who guide the race, and who will bring it at last out of its fever of passion into their own serene land.

The true thinker is the greatest of men, and his destiny is the most exalted. The altogether impartial mind has reached the divine, and it basks in the full daylight of Reality.

The four great elements of impartiality are

1. Justice

2. Patience

3. Calmness

4. Wisdom

Justice is the giving and receiving of equal values. What is called "striking a hard bargain" is a kind of theft. It means that the purchaser gives value for only a portion of his purchase, the remainder being appropriated as clear gain. The seller also encourages it by closing the bargain.

The just man does not try to gain an advantage; he considers the true values of things, and moulds his transactions in accordance therewith. He does not let "what will pay" come before "what is right", for he knows that the right pays best in the end. He does not seek his own benefit to the disadvantage of another, for he knows that a just action benefits, equally and fully, both parties to a transaction. If "one man's loss is another man's gain," it is only that the balance may be adjusted later on. Unjust gains cannot lead to prosperity, but are sure to bring failure. A just man could no more take from another an unjust gain by what is called a "smart transaction" that he could take it by picking his pocket. He would regard the one as dishonest as the other.

The bargaining spirit in business is not the true spirit of commerce. It is the selfish and thieving spirit which wants to get something for nothing. The upright man purges his business of all bargaining, and builds it one the more dignified basis of justice. He supplies "a good article" at its right price, and does not alter. He does not soil his hands with any business which is tainted with fraud. His goods are genuine and they are properly priced.

Customers who try to "beat down" a tradesman in their purchases are degrading themselves. Their practice assumes one or both of two things, namely, that either the tradesman is dishonest and is overcharging (a low, suspicious attitude of mind), or that they are eager to cajole him out of his profit (an equally base attitude), and so benefit by his loss. The practice of "bearing down" is altogether a dishonest one, and the people who pursue it most assiduously are those who complain most of being "imposed on" and this is not surprising, seeing that they themselves are all the time trying to impose upon others.

On the other hand, the tradesman who is anxious to get all he can out of his customers, irrespective of justice and the right values of things, is a kind of robber, and is slowly poisoning his success, for his deeds will assuredly come home to him in the form of financial ruin.

Said a man of fifty to me other day, "I have just discovered that all my life I have been paying fifty percent, more for everything than I ought to." A just man cannot feel that he has ever paid too much for anything, for he does not close with any transaction which he considers unjust; but if a man is eager to get everything at half price, them he will be always meanly and miserably mourning that he is paying double for everything. The just man is glad to pay full value for everything, whether in giving or receiving and his mind is untroubled and his days are full of peace.

Let a man above all avoid meanness, and strive to be ever more and more perfectly just, for if not just, he can be neither honest, nor generous, nor manly, but is a kind of disguised thief trying to get all he can, and give back as little as possible. Let him eschew all bargaining, and teach bargainers a better way by conducting his business with that exalted dignity which commands a large and meritorious success.

Patience is the brightest jewel in the character of the impartial man. Not a particular patience with a particular thing - like a girl with her needlework, or a boy building his toy engine but on unswerving considerateness, a sweetness of disposition at all times and under the most trying circumstances, an unchangeable and gentle strength which no trial can mar and no persecution can break. A rare possession, it is true, and one not to be expected for a long time yet from the bulk of mankind, but a virtue that can be reached by degree, and even a partial patience will work wonders in a man's life and affairs, as a confirmed impatience all work devastation. The irascible man is courting speedy disaster, for who will care to deal with a man who continually going off like ground powder when some small spark of complaint or criticism falls upon him! Even his friends will one by one desert him, for who would court the company of a man who rudely assaults him with an impatient and fiery tongue over every little difference or misunderstanding.

A man must begin to wisely control himself, and to learn the beautiful lessons of patience, if he is to be highly prosperous, if he is to be a man of use and power. He must learn to think of others, to act for their good, and not alone for himself; to be considerate, for bearing, and long suffering. He must study how to have a heart at peace with men who differ from him on those things which he regards as most vital. He must avoid quarrelling as he would avoid drinking a deadly poison. Discords from without will be continually overtaking him, but he must fortify himself against them; he must study how to bring harmonies out of them by the exercise of patience.

Strife is common: it pains the heart and distorts the mind. Patience is rare; it enriches the heart and beautifies the mind. Every cat can spit and fume; it requires no effort, but only a looseness of behavior. It takes a man to keep his mornings through all events, and to be painstaking and patient with the shortcomings of humanity. But patience wins. As soft water wears away the hardest rock, so patience overcomes all opposition. It gains the hearts of men. It conquers and controls.

Calmness accompanies patience. It is a great and glorious quality. It is the peaceful haven of emancipated souls after their long wanderings on the tempest-riven ocean of passion. It makes the man who has suffered much, endured much, experienced much, and has finally conquered.

A man cannot be impartial who is not calm. Excitement, prejudice, and partiality spring from disturbed passions. When personal feeling is thwarted, it rises and seethes like a stream of water that is dammed. The calm man avoids this disturbance by directing his feeling from the personal to the impersonal channel. He thinks and feels for others as well as for himself. He sets the same value on other men's opinions as on his own. If he regards his own work as important, he sees also that the work of other men is equally important. He does not content for the merit of his own against the demerit of that of others. He is not overthrown, like Humpty Dumpty, with a sense of self importance. He has put aside egotism for truth, and he perceives the right relations of things. He has conquered irritability, and has come to see that there is nothing in itself that should cause irritation. As well, be irritable with a pansy because it is not a rose, as with a man because he does not see as you see. Minds differ, and the calm man recognizes the differences as facts in human nature.

The calm, impartial man, is not only the happiest man, he also has all his powers at his command. He is sure, deliberate, executive, and swiftly and easily accomplishes in silence what the irritable men slowly and laboriously toil through with much effort. His mind is purified, poised, concentrated, and is ready at any moment to be directed upon a given work with unerring power. In the calm mind all contradictions are reconciled, and there is radiant gladness and perpetual peace. As Emerson puts it: "Calmness is joy fixed and habitual".

One should not confound indifference with calmness, for it is at the opposite extreme. Indifference is lifelines, while calmness is glowing life and full orbed power. The calm man has partly or entirely conquered self, and having successfully battled with the selfishness within, he knows how to meet and overcome it successfully in others. In any moral content the calm man is always the victor. So long as he remains calm, defeat is impossible.

Self control is better than riches and calmness is a perpetual benediction.

Wisdom abides with the impartial man. Her counsels guide him; her wings shield him; she leads him along pleasant ways to happy destinations.

Wisdom is many sided. The wise man adapts himself to others. He acts for their good, yet never violates the moral virtues or the principles of right conduct. The foolish man cannot adapt himself to others; he acts for himself only, and continually violates the moral virtues and the principles of right conduct. There is a degree of wisdom in every act of impartiality, and once a man has touched and experience the impartial zone, he can recover it again and again until he finally establishes himself in it.

Every thought, word, and act of wisdom tells on the world at large, for it is fraught with greatness. Wisdom is a well of knowledge and a spring of power. It is profound and comprehensive, and is so exact and all inclusive as to embrace the smallest details. In its spacious greatness it does not overlook the small. The wise mind is like the world; it contains all things in their proper place and order, and is not burdened thereby. Like the world also, it is free, and unconscious of any restrictions; yet it is never loose, never erring, never sinful and repentant. Wisdom is the steady, grown up being of whom folly was the crying infant. It has outgrown the weakness and dependence, the errors and punishments of infantile ignorance, and is erect, poised, strong, and serene.

The understanding mind needs no external support. It stands of itself on the firm ground of knowledge; not book-knowledge, but ripened experience. It has passed through all minds, and therefore knows them. It has traveled with all hearts, and knows their journeying in joy and sorrow.

When wisdom touches a man, he is lifted up and transfigured. He becomes a new being with new aims and powers, and he inhabits a new universe in which to accomplish a new and glorious destiny.

Such is the Pillar of impartiality which adds its massive strength and incomparable grace to support and beautify the Temple of Prosperity.

Chapter 9

Eighth Pillar - Self-reliance

Every young man ought to read Emerson's essay on 'Self Reliance'. It is the manliest, most virile essay that was ever penned. It is calculated to cure alike those two mental maladies common to youth, namely, self depreciation and self conceit. It is almost as sure to reveal to the prig the smallness and emptiness of his vanity as it is to show the bashful man the weakness and ineffectuality of his dividence. It is a new revelation of manly dignity; as much a revelation as any that was vouchsafed to ancient seer and prophet, and perhaps a more practical, eminently suited to his mechanic age, coming, as it does from a modern prophet of a new type and called in a new race, and its chief merit is its powerfully tonic quality.

Let not self-reliance be confounded with self conceit, for as high and excellent as is the one, just so low and worthless is other. There cannot be anything mean in self reliance, while in self conceit there cannot be anything great.

The man that never says "no" when questioned on subjects of which he is entirely ignorant, to avoid, as he imagines, being thought ignorant, but confidently puts forward guesses and assumptions as knowledge, will be known for his ignorance, and ill esteemed for his added conceit. An honest confession of ignorance will command respect where a conceited assumption of knowledge will elicit contempt.

The timid, apologetic man who seems almost afraid to live, who fears that he will do something not in the approved way, and will subject himself to ridicule, is not a full man. He must needs imitate others, and have no independent action. He needs that self reliance which will compel him to fall back on his own initiative, and so become a new example instead of the slavish follower of an old one. As for ridicule he who is hurt by it is no man. The shafts or mockery and sarcasm cannot pierce the strong armour of the self reliant man. They cannot reach the invincible citadel of his honest heart to sting or wound it. The sharp arrows of irony may rain upon him, but he laughs as they are deflected by the strong breast plate of his confidence, and fall harmless about him.

"Trust thyself", says Emerson, 'every heart vibrates to that iron string". Throughout the ages men have so far leaned, and do still lean, upon external makeshifts instead of standing upon their own native simplicity and original dignity. The few who have had the courage to so stand, have been singled out and elevated as heroes; and he is indeed the true hero who has the hardihood to let his nature speak for itself, who has that strong metal which enables him to stand upon his own intrinsic worth.

It is true that the candidate for such heroism must endure the test of strength. He must not be shamed from his ground by the bugbears of an initiate conventionalist. He must not fear for his reputation or position, or for his standing in the church or his prestige in local society. He must learn to act and live as independently of these considerations as he does of the current fashions in the antipodes. Yet when he has endured this test, and stander and odium have failed to move or afflict him, he has become a man indeed, one that society will have to reckon with, and finally accept on his own terms.

Sooner or later all men will turn for guidance to the self reliant man, and while the best minds do not make a prop of him they respect and value his work and worth, and recognize his place among the goods that have gone before.

It must not be thought an indication of self reliance to scorn to learn. Such an attitude is born of a stubborn superciliousness which has the elements of weakness, and is prophetic of a fall, rather than the elements of strength and the promise of high achievement which are characteristic of self - reliance. Pride and vanity must not be associated with self rests upon incidentals and appurtenances - on money, clothing, property, prestige, position and these lost, all is lost. Self reliance rests upon essentials and principles on worth, probity, purity, sincerity, character, truth and whatever may be lost is of little account, for these are never lost. Pride tries to hide its ignorance by ostentation and assumption, and is unwilling to be thought a learner in any direction. It stands, during its little fleeting day, on ignorance and appearance, and the higher it is lifted up today the lower it will be cast down tomorrow. Self reliance has nothing to hide, and is willing to learn; and while there can be no humility where pride is, self reliance and humility are compatible, nay more, they are complementary, and the sublimes form of self reliance is only found associated with the profoundest humility. "Extremes meet" says Emerson "and there is no better example than the haughtiness of humility. No aristocrat, no prince born to the purple, can begin to compare with the self respect of the saint. Why is he so lowly, but that he knows that he can well afford it, resting on the largeness of God in him?" It was Buddha who, in this particular, said; "Those who, either now or after I am dead, shall be a lamp unto themselves, relying upon themselves only and not relying upon any external help, but holding fast to the truth as their lamp, and seeking their salvation in the truth alone, shall not look for assistance to any one beside themselves, it is they, among my disciples, who shall reach the very top most height. But they must be willing to learn". In this saying, the repeated insistence on the necessity for relying upon one's self alone, coupled with the final exhortation to be eager to learn, is the wisest utterance on self reliance that I know. In it, the Great Teacher comprehends that perfect balance between self trust and humility which the man of truth must acquire.

"Self - trust is the essence of heroism". All great men are self reliant, and we should use them as teachers and exemplars and not as props and perambulators. A great man comes who leans upon no one, but stands alone in the solitary dignity of truth, and straightway the world begins to lean upon him, begins to make him an excuse for spiritual indolence and a destructive self-abasement. Better than cradling our vices in the strength of the great would it be to newly light our virtues at their luminous lamp. If we rely upon the light of another, darkness will over take us, but if we rely upon our own light we have but to keep it burning. We may both draw light from another and communicate it, but to think it sufficient while our own lamp is rusting in neglect, is shortly to find ourselves abandoned in darkness. Our own inner light is the light which never fails us.

What is the "inner light" of the Quakers but another name for self reliance? We should stand upon what we are, not upon what another is. "But I am so small and poor", you say: well, stand upon that smallness, and presently it will become great. A babe must needs suckle and cling, but not so man. Henceforth he goes upon his own limbs. Men pray to God to put into their hands that which they are framed to reach out for; to put into their mouth the food

for which they should strenuously labour. But men will outgrow
this spiritual infancy. The time will come when men will no more
pay a priest to pray for them and preach to them.

Man's chief trouble is a mistrust of himself, so that the self trusting man becomes a rare and singular spectacle. If a man look
upon himself as a "worm", what can come out of him but an ineffectual wriggling? Truly, "He that humbleth shall be exalted," but
not he that degradeth himself. A man should see himself as he
is, and if there is any unworthiness in him, he should get rid of
it, and retain and rely upon that which is of worth. A man is only
debased when he debases himself; he is exalted when he lives an
exalted life.

Why should a man, with ceaseless iterations, draw attention to
his fallen nature? There is a false humility which takes a sort of
pride in vice. If one has fallen, it is that he may rise and be the
wiser for it. If a man falls into a ditch, he does not lie there and call
upon every passer-by to mark his fallen state, he gets up and goes
on his way with greater care. So if one has fallen into the ditch of
vice, let him rise and be cleansed, and go on his way rejoicing.

There is not a sphere in life wherein a man's influence and prosperity will not be considerably increased by even a measure of self
reliance, and to the teacher - whether secular or religious to or-
ganizers, managers, overseers, and in all positions of control and
command, it is indispensable equipment.

The four grand qualities of self reliance are:-

1. Decision

2. Steadfastness

3. Dignity

4. Independence

Decision makes a man strong. The wearer is the weakling. A man
who is to play a speaking part, however small, in the drama of life
must be decisive and know what he is about. Whatever he doubts,
he must not doubt his power to act. He must know his part in life,
and put all his energy into it. He must have some solid ground
of knowledge from which to work, and stand securely on that. It
may be only the price and quality of stock, but he must know his
work thoroughly, and know that he knows it. he must be ready
at any time to answer for himself when his duty is impugned. He

should be so well grounded upon his particular practice as not to be affected with hesitation on any point or in any emergence. It is a true saying that "the man that hesitates is lost". No one believes in him who does not believe in himself, who doubts, halts, and wavers, and cannot extricate himself from the tangled threads of two courses. Who would deal with a tradesman who did not know the price of his own goods, or was not sure where to find them? A man must know his business. If he does not know his own, who shall instruct him? He must be able to give a good report of the truth that is in him, must have that deceive touch which skill and knowledge only can impart.

Certainty is a great element in self reliance. To have weight, a man must have some truth to impart, and all skill is a communication of truth. He must "speak with authority and not as the scribes". He must master something, and know that he has mastered it, so as to deal with it lucidly and understandingly, in the way of a master, and not to remain always an apprentice.

Indecision is a disintegrating factor. A minute's faltering may turn back the current of success. Men who are afraid to decide quickly for fear of making a mistake, nearly always makes a mistake when they do act. The quickest, in thought and action, are less liable to blunder, and it is better to act with decision and make a mistake than to act with indecision and make a mistake than to act with indecision and make a mistake, for in the former case there is but error, but in the latter, weakness is added to error.

A man should be decided always, both where he knows and where he does not know. He should be as ready to say "no" as "yes", as quick to acknowledge his ignorance as to impart his knowledge. If, he stands upon fact, and acts from the simple truth he will find no room for halting between two opinions.

Make up your mind quickly, and act decisively. Better still, have a mind that is already made up and then decision will be instinctive and spontaneous.

Steadfastness arises in the mind that is quick to decide. It is indeed a final decision upon the best course of conduct and the best path in life. It is the vow of the soul to stand firmly by its principles whatever betide. It is neither necessary nor unnecessary that there by any written or spoken vow, for unswerving loyalty to a fixed principle is the spirit of all vows.

The man without fixed principles will not accomplish much. Expediency is a quagmire and a thorny waste, in which a man is continually sticking in the shifting mud of his own moral looseness, and is pricked and scratched with the thorns of his self created disappointments.

One must have some solid ground on which to stand among one's fellows. He cannot stand on the bog of concession. Shiftiness is a vice of weakness, and the vices of weakness do more to undermine character and influence than the vices of strength. The man that is vicious through excess of animal strength takes a shorter cut to truth - when his mind is made up that he who is vicious through lack of virility, and whose chief vice consists in not having a mind of his own upon anything. When one understands that power is adaptable to both good and bad ends, it will not surprise him that the drunkards and harlots should reach the kingdom of heaven before the diplomatic religionists. They are at least through in the course which they have adopted, vile though it be, and thoroughness is strength. It only needs that strength to be turned from bad to good, and lo! The loathed sinner has become the lofty saint!

A man should have a firm, fixed, determined mind. He should decide upon those principles which are best to stand by in all issues, and which will most safely guide him through the maze of conflicting opinions, and inspire him with unflinching courage in the battle of life. Having adopted his principles, they should be more to him than gain or happiness, more even than life itself, and if he never deserts them he will find that they will never desert him; they will defend him from all enemies, deliver him safely from all dangers, light up his pathway through all darkness and difficulties. They will be to him a light in darkness, a resting place from sorrow, and a refuge from the conflicts of the world.

Dignity clothes, as with a majestic garment, the steadfast mind. He who is as unyielding as a bar of steel when he is expected to compromise with evil, and as supple as a willow wand in adapting himself to that which is good, carries about with him a dignity that calms and uplifts others by its presence.

The unsteady mind, the mind that is not anchored to any fixed principles, that is stubborn where its own desires are threatened, and yielding where its own moral welfare is at stake, has no gravity, no balance, no calm composure.

The man of dignity cannot be down-trodden and enslaved, because he has ceased to tread upon and enslave himself. He at once disarms, with a look, a word, a wise and suggestive silence, any attempt to demean him. His mere presence is a wholesome reproof to the flippant and the unseemly, while it is a rock of strength to the lover of the good.

But the chief reason why the dignified man commands respect is, not only that he is supremely self respecting, but that he graciously treats all others with a due esteem. Pride loves itself, and treats those beneath it with supercilious contempt, for love of self and contempt for others are always found together in equal degrees, so that the greater the self love, the greater the arrogance. True dignity arises, not from self love, but from self sacrifice that is, from unbiased adherence to a fixed central principle. The dignity of the Judge arises from the fact that in the performance of his duty he sets aside all personal consideration, and stands solely upon the law; his little personality, impermanent and fleeting' becomes nothing, while the law, enduring and majestic, becomes all. Should a Judge, in deciding a case, forget the law, and fall into personal feeling and prejudice, his dignity would be gone. So with the man of stately purity of character, he stands upon the divine law, and not upon personal feeling, for immediately a man gives way to passion he has sacrificed dignity, and takes his place as one of the multitude of the unwise and uncontrolled.

Every man will have composure and dignity in the measure that he acts from a fixed principle. It only needs that the principle be right, and therefore unassailable. So long as man abides by such a principle, and does not waver or descend into the personal element, attacking passions, prejudices and interests, however powerful, will be weak and ineffectual before the unconquerable strength of an incorruptible principle, and will at last yield their combined and unseemly confusion to his single and majestic right.

Independence is the birthright of the strong and well controlled man. All men love and strive for liberty. All men aspire to some sort of freedom.

A man should labour for himself or for the community. Unless he is a cripple, a chronic invalid, or is mentally irresponsible, he should be ashamed to depend upon others for all he has, giving nothing in return. If one imagines that such a condition is freedom, let him know that it is one of the lowest forms of slavery. The time will come when, to be a drone in the human hive, even (as matters are now) a respectable drone and not a poor tramp, will be a public disgrace, and will be no longer respectable.

Independence, freedom, glorious liberty, come through labour and not from idleness, and the self reliant man is too strong, too honourable, too upright to depend upon others, like a sucking babe, for his support. He earns with hand or brain, the right to live as becomes a man and a citizen; and this he does whether born rich or poor for riches are no excuse for idleness; rather are they an opportunity to labour, with the rare facilities which they afford, for the good of the community.

Only he who is self supporting is free, self reliant, independent.

Thus, is the nature of the Eight Pillars explained. On what foundation they rest, the manner of their building, their ingredients, the fourfold nature of the material of which each is composed, what positions they occupy, and how they support the Temple, all may now build; and he who knew but imperfectly may know more perfectly; and he who knew perfectly may rejoice in this systematization and simplification of the moral order in Prosperity. Let us now consider the Temple itself, that we may know the might of its Pillars, the strength of its walls, the endurance of its roof, and the architectural beauty and perfection of the whole.

Chapter 10

The Temple of Prosperity

The reader who has followed the course of this book with a view to obtaining information on the details of money making, business transactions, profit and loss in various undertakings, prices, markets, agreements, contracts, and other matters connected with the achievement of prosperity, will have noted an entire absence of any instruction on these matters of detail. The reason for this is fourfold, namely:-

First: Details cannot stand alone, but are powerless to build up anything unless intelligently related to principles.

Second: Details are infinite, and are ceaselessly changing, while principles are few, and are eternal and unchangeable.

Third: Principles are the coherent factors in all details, regulating and harmonizing them, so that to have right principles is to be right in all the subsidiary details.

Fourth: A teacher of truth in any direction must adhere rigidly to principles, and must not allow himself to be drawn away from them into the ever-changing maze of private particulars and personal details, because such particulars and details have only a local right, and are only necessary for certain individuals, while principles are universally right and are necessary for all men.

He, who grasps the principles of this book so as to be able to intelligently practice them, will be able to reach the heart of this fourfold reason. The details of a man's affairs are important, but they are his details or the details of his particular branch of industry, and all outside that branch are not concerned with them, but moral principles are the same for all men; they are applicable to all conditions, and govern all particulars.

The man who works from fixed principles does not need to harass himself over the complications of numerous details. He will grasp, as it were, the entire details in one single thought, and will see them through and through, illumined by the light of the principle to which they stand related, and this without friction, and with freedom from anxiety and strain.

Until principles are grasped, details are regarded, and dealt with, as primary matters, and so viewed they lead to innumerable complications and confused issues. In the light of principles, they are seen to be secondary facts, and so seen, all difficulties connected with them are at once overcome and annulled by a reference to principles.

He who is involved in numerous details without the regulating and synthesizing element of principles is like one lost in a forest, with no direct path along which to walk amid the mass of objects. He is swelled up by the details, while the man of principles contains all details within himself; he stands outside them, as it were, and grasps them in their entirety, while the other man can only see the few that are nearest to him at the time.

All things are contained in principles. They are the laws of things, and all things observe their own law. It is an error to view things apart from their nature. Details are the letter of which principles are the spirit. It is as true in art, science, literature, commerce, as in religion, that "the letter killeth, the spirit of giveth life." The body of a man, with its wonderful combination of parts, is important, but only in its relation to the spirit. The spirit being withdrawn, the body is useless and is put away. The body of a business, with all its complicated details is important, but only in its relation to the vivifying principles by which it is controlled. These withdrawn, the business will perish.

To have the body of prosperity - its material presentation - we must first have the spirit of prosperity, and the spirit of prosperity is the quick spirit of moral virtue. Moral blindness prevails. Men see money, property, pleasure, leisure, etc., and, mistaking them for prosperity, strive to get them for their own enjoyment, but, when obtained, they find no enjoyment in them.

Prosperity is at first a spirit, an attitude of mind, a moral power, a life, which manifests outwardly in the form of plenty, happiness, joy. Just as a man cannot become a genius by writing poems, essay as plays, but must develop and acquire the soul of genius - when the writing will follow as effect to cause-so one cannot become prosperous by hoarding up money, and by gaining property and possessions, but must develop and acquire the soul of virtue, when the material accessories will follow as effect to cause, for the spirit of virtue is the spirit of joy, and it contains within itself all abundance, all satisfaction, all fullness of life.

There is no joy in money, there is no joy in property, there is no joy in material accumulations or in any material things of itself. These things are dead and lifeless. The spirit of joy must be in the man or it is nowhere. He must have within him the capacity for happiness. He must have the wisdom to know how to use these things, and not merely hoard them. He must possess them, and not be possessed by them. They must be dependent upon him, and not he upon them. They must follow him, and not be forever running after them; and they will inevitably follow him, if he has the moral elements within to which they are related.

Nothing is absent from the Kingdom of heaven; it contains all good, true, and necessary things, and "the Kingdom of God is within you." I know rich people who are supremely happy, because they are generous, magnanimous, pure and joyful; but I also know rich people who are very miserable, and these are they who looked to money and possessions for their happiness, and have not developed the spirit of good and of joy within themselves.

How can it be said of a wretched man that he is "prosperous", even if his income be ten thousand pounds a year? There must be fitness, and harmony, and satisfaction in a true prosperity. When a rich man is happy, it is that he brought the spirit of happiness to his riches, and not that the riches brought happiness to him. He is a full man with full material advantages and responsibilities, while the miserable rich man is an empty man looking to riches for that fullness of life which can only be evolved from within.

Thus prosperity resolves itself into a moral capacity, and in the wisdom to rightfully use and lawfully enjoy the material things which are inseparable from our earthly life. If one would be free without, let him first be free within, for if he be bound in a spirit by weakness, selfishness, or vice, how can the possession of money liberate him? Will it not rather become, in his hands, a ready instrument by which to further enslave himself?

The visible effects of prosperity, then, must not be considered alone, but in their relation to the mental and moral cause. There is a hidden foundation to every building; the fact that it continues to stand is proof of that. There is a hidden foundation to every form of established success; its permanence proves that it is so. Prosperity stands on the foundation of character, and there is not in all the wide universe, any other foundation. True wealth is weal, welfare, well being, soundness, wholeness, and happiness. The wretched rich are not truly wealthy. They are merely encumbered with money, luxury, and leisure, as instruments of self torture. By their possessions they are self cursed.

The moral man is ever blessed, ever happy, and his life, viewed as a whole, is always a success. To these there is no exception, for whatever failures he may have in detail, the finished work of his life will be sound, whole, complete; and through all he will have a quiet conscience, an honorable name, and all manifold blessings which are inseparable from richness of character, and without this moral richness, financial riches will not avail or satisfy.

Let us briefly recapitulate, and again view the Eight Pillars in their strength and splendour.

Energy - Rousing one's self up to strenuous and unremitting exertion in the accomplishment of one's task.

Economy - Concentration of power, the conservation of both capital and character, the latter being mental capital, and therefore of the utmost importance.

Integrity - Unswerving honesty; keeping inviolate all promises, agreements, and contracts, apart from all considerations of loss or gain.

System - Making all details, subservient to order, and thereby relieving the memory and the mind of superfluous work and strain by reducing many to one.

Sympathy - Magnanimity, generosity, gentleness, and tenderness; being open handed, free, and kind.

Sincerity - Being sound and whole, robust and true; and therefore not being one person in public and another in private, and not assuming good actions openly while doing bad actions in secret.

Impartiality - Justice; not striving for self, but weighing both sides, and acting in accordance with equity.

Self - Reliance - Looking to one's self only for strength and support by standing on principles which are fixed and invincible, and not relying upon outward things which at any moment may be snatched away.

How can any life be other than successful which is built on these Eight Pillars? Their strength is such that no physical or intellectual strength can compare with it; and to have built all the eight perfectly would render a man invincible. It will be found, however, that men are often strong in one or several of these qualities, and weak in others, and it is this weak element that invites failure. It is foolish, for instance, to attribute a man's failure in business to his honesty. It is impossible for honesty to produce failure. The cause of failure must be looked for in some other direction - in the lack, and not the possession, of some good necessary quality. Moreover, such attribution of failure to honesty is a slur on the integrity of commerce; and a false indictment of those men, numerous enough, who are honourably engaged in trade. A man may be strong in Energy, Economy, and System, but comparatively weak in the other five. Such a man will just fail of complete success by lacking one of the four corner pillars, namely, Integrity. His temple will give way at that weak corner, for the first four Pillars must be well built before the Temple of Prosperity can stand secure. They are the first qualities to be acquired in a man's moral evolution, and without them the second four cannot be possessed. Again, if a man be strong in the first three, and lack the fourth, the absence of order will invite confusion and disaster into his affairs; and so on with any partial combination of these qualities, especially of the first four, for the second four are of so lofty a character that at present men can but possess them, with rare exceptions, in a more or less imperfect form. The man of the world, then, who wishes to secure an abiding success in any branch of commerce, or in one of the many lines of industry in which men are commonly engaged, must build into his character, by practice, the first four moral Pillars. By these fixed principles he must regulate his thought, his conduct, and his affairs; consulting them in every difficulty, making every detail serve them, and above all, never deserting them under any circumstance to gain some personal advantage or to save some personal trouble, for to so desert them is to make one's self vulnerable to the disintegrating elements of evil, and to become assailable to accusations from others. He who so abides by these four principles will achieve a full measure of success in his own particular work, whatever it may be; his Temple of Prosperity will be well built and well supported, and it will stand secure. The perfect practice of these four principles is within the scope of all men who are willing to study them with that object in view, for they are so simple and plain that a child could grasp their meaning, and their perfection in conduct does not call for an unusual degree of self sacrifice, though it demands some self denial and personal discipline without which there can be no success in this world of action. The second four pillars, however, are principles of a more profound nature, are more difficult to understand and practice, and call from the highest degree of self sacrifice and self effacement. Few, at present, can reach that detachment from the personal element which their perfect practice demands, but the few who accomplish this in any marked degree will vastly enlarge their powers and enrich their life, and will adorn their Temple of Prosperity with a singular and attractive beauty which will gladden and elevate all beholders long after they have passed away.

But those who are beginning to build their Temple of Prosperity in accordance with the teaching of this book, must bear in mind that a building requires time to erect, and it must be patiently raised up, brick upon brick and stone upon stone, and the Pillars must be firmly fixed and cemented, and labour and care will be needed to make the whole complete. And the building of this inner mental Temple is none the less real and substantial because invisible and noiseless, for in the raising up of his, as of Solomon's Temple which was "seven years in building" - it can be said, "there was neither hammer nor axe nor any tool of iron heard in the house, while it was in the building".

Even so oh, reader, construct thy character... raise up the house of thy life, build up thy Temple of Prosperity. Be not as the foolish who rise and fall upon the uncertain flux of selfish desires: but be at peace in thy labour, crown thy career with completeness, and so be numbered among the wise who, without uncertainty, build upon a fixed and secure foundation - even upon the Principles of Truth which endure forever.

CPSIA information can be obtained
at www.ICGtesting.com
Printed in the USA
BVHW041744060220
571647BV00011B/411